# SALVO!

By the same author

*Masters Next to God*
*They Sank the Red Dragon*
*The Fighting Tramps*
*The Grey Widow Maker*
*Blood and Bushido*

# SALVO!

## EPIC NAVAL GUN ACTIONS

### BERNARD EDWARDS

CASSELL

Cassell Military Classics

*For Edward Victor Edwards RN,*
*who was once a part of all this*

Cassell
Wellington House, 125 Strand
London WC2R 0BB

First published by Arms and Armour 1995
This Cassell Military Classics edition 1999

British Library Cataloguing in Publication Data
A catalogue record for this book is available from
the British Library

ISBN 0-304-35171-7

Edited and designed by
Roger Chesneau/DAG Publications Ltd
Cartography by Peter Burton

Printed and bound in Great Britain by
Cox & Wyman Ltd , Reading, Berks

359
EDW

ADU-6603

# Contents

# Introduction

In eighteenth-century sea warfare, fought with muzzle-loading cannon at the unmissable range of 100 yards, the broadside was all important. The guns were fixed, and the only means of taking aim was through positioning the ship herself. In battle, it was usual for two ponderous ships-of-the-line to spend hours manoeuvring into position to discharge the maximum amount of shot simultaneously in order to inflict maximum damage on the enemy. The commander who succeeded in positioning his ship to fire the first broadside was invariably the victor.

The demise of sail and the introduction of steam power, with all its huge advantages in ship handling, signalled a revolution in naval gunnery And then came the explosive shot, a French invention of the 1820s consisting of a hollow cannon ball containing a 4lb charge of gunpowder. Within fifteen years the breech-loading, shell-firing gun had appeared on the gundeck The effect of the new gun on the 'wooden walls' of the day was devastating, one well-aimed shell often being enough to burn a ship down to the waterline A clear demonstration of the shape of things to come was given on the eve of the Crimean War On 30 November 1853 a Russian squadron under Admiral Nakhimov, which included five steam-powered warships and mounted 76 shell-firing guns, cornered Osman Pasha's Turkish fleet in the Black Sea port of Sinope. Although the Turkish ships were under the protection of shore batteries, in four hours Nakhimov's guns set on fire and sank every ship in the harbour – seven frigates, two corvettes, two transports and two paddle steamers, all built of wood Casualties in the Turkish ships alone were put at nearly 3,000 dead; how many died in the town of Sinope, engulfed by flames spreading from the burning ships and completely destroyed, is not recorded.

There was now an urgent need for some form of protection for the vulnerable hulls of wooden ships, and it was the French who again came up with the answer In 1859 they launched the 5,600-ton frigate *Gloire*, built of oak, but with a 12-centimetre thick belt of iron armour around her hull. Her guns were a new design of 66-pounders, breech-loading with rifled barrels and firing shells. In her day the *Gloire* was a formidable man-of-war, the first of the 'ironclads' The British followed a year later with HMS *Warrior*, the Royal Navy's first ironclad. She was a steam frigate of 9,210 tons, having 4½-inch iron armour on a teak hull and armed with twenty-six 68-pounder muzzle-loaders and ten 110-pounder and four 70-pounder breech-loaders. The days of 'wooden ships and iron men' were clearly drawing to a close, but it would be some years before the maritime traditionalists would accept the iron-built warship. They based their argument on, of all things, the fact that shot holes in iron plates could not be successfully plugged with wooden stoppers, as was the case with a timber ship.

Despite the opposition of the die-hards, developments in naval gunnery continued unchecked, the most radical change being the mounting of guns in revolving turrets, as opposed to fixed batteries, allowing them to fire ahead, astern or on either side of the ship. One of the first vessels so equipped was HMS *Captain*, launched in 1869. She was a 6,900-ton steamer, carrying a full set of sails and mounting four 25-ton guns in revolving turrets However, the *Captain*'s builders failed to take sufficient account of adding the heavy turrets to an already considerable topweight of masts, rigging and sails. The ship capsized in a gale in the Bay of Biscay

Sails and gun turrets obviously did not go well together, and the sails, being by then an increasingly unnecessary encumbrance, had to go. By the beginning of the twentieth century, fast, highly manoeuvrable battleships, mounting 12-inch guns in hydraulically powered turrets controlled from a central point, were hurling shells at one another from a range of 20,000 yards with devastating accuracy. Naval gunnery had come a long way since the crude, gunwale-to-gunwale slogging matches of Horatio Nelson's day

The surface warship, with ever-increasing firepower, ruled the waves until well into the Second World War, surmounting even the deadly menace of the submarine-launched torpedo. Then, as the year 1941 drew to a close, came the first real indication that the end of many centuries of broadsides and salvos was at hand. On 10 December the 36,700-ton British battleship *Prince of Wales*, said to be the finest of her kind afloat, and her consort, the 32,000-ton battlecruiser *Repulse*, mounting between them six 15-inch, ten 14-inch, sixteen 5.25-inch and twenty 4-inch guns, were both sunk in less than an hour by Japanese aircraft. Their big guns were powerless against attack from the air.

The point of no return was reached at the Battle of Midway, in June 1942, when Japanese and American fleets fought a prolonged and bloody battle without the ships' coming within 100 miles of each other. On both sides the big guns swung helpless in their turrets while carrier-borne aircraft swooped and dived around them, sowing death and destruction with bomb, torpedo and machine gun. At the end of the action the Japanese had lost four aircraft carriers, a heavy cruiser and 3,500 men and the Americans one carrier, a destroyer and 307 men – all this without one broadside or one salvo being fired

Today, sea warfare has taken on a totally different form. Ships now hide below the horizon, firing guided missiles at each other, and never meet. The close-quarters naval action has disappeared into history. This book records some of the best.

# 1

# Yalu River

*20 September 1894*

The year 1862 was a momentous one. Civil war raged in America, Britain was in the full flush of her Industrial Revolution, and continental Europe, as ever, hovered on the brink of internal conflict. Meanwhile, on the other side of the world, a gauntlet was thrown down at the feet of Western interference. On the Japanese island of Kyushu, a British merchant, Charles Richardson, when about his lawful business in the port of Kagoshima, was murdered by the locals The British Government demanded recompense, but none was forthcoming – the insular Japanese did not even offer an apology for Richardson's murder. The inevitable retribution came early in the following year, when a British fleet commanded by Admiral Kuper sailed into Kagoshima Sound and reduced the port to a smoking ruin.

At that time Japan had no fighting ships to defend the realm, but the forts of Kagoshima, equipped only with primitive stone-shotted guns, hit back defiantly at Admiral Kuper's warships. Amongst those manning the guns of Kagoshima on that infamous day was 16-year-old Heihachiro Togo, a young Samurai of the Satsuma clan When the battle was over – and lost – Togo swore on the graves of his ancestors that Japan would never again suffer the humiliation of being unable to meet an aggressor at sea, ship for ship, gun for gun There were many in Japan who shared Togo's determination.

A few years after Kagoshima, Japan slipped into civil war as the Shogun Princes fought to subdue the emerging forces for change. The Princes failed, and the nation that for centuries had been content to stagnate in genteel isolation threw off the feudal yoke and began to industrialize along European lines. With industrialization came a swelling population and a desperate search for export markets. This led to a desire – again, following the European example – to reach out and colonize. As a means to this end, the new Japan first required a powerful navy.

Since Nelson's crushing defeat of France and Spain at Trafalgar more than half a century earlier, Britain had dominated the seas around Europe and beyond No other nation had such expertise in the building of warships and the training of crew to man them, and so it was to her that Japan turned to for help in setting up her own navy. She ordered the best ships British yards could build and sent her officers to be taught the arts of seafaring and sea-fighting by the Royal Navy. With them went Heihachiro Togo.

Togo took command of his first ship in Japan's Imperial Navy in 1879, at the beginning of a period of great turbulence in the affairs of the Far East. Much of the trouble could be laid at the doors of the big European trading powers,

Britain, France, Germany and Russia, all of whom were intent on securing new markets in the East. As the end of the century drew near, the focus of attention became the Korean peninsula, long dominated by China but now showing an increasing tendency to lean towards its next nearest neighbour, Japan. Under the pretence of establishing peace and stability in Korea, Japan had been quietly working to take over her weaker neighbour by stealth. China, fearing the loss of her erstwhile satellite, was making threatening noises. While the two Eastern rivals were thus preoccupied, Britain had moved into Burma, the French had moved into Indo-China and Russia was working on a take-over of Manchuria. All the ingredients for war were in the mixing pot, waiting for the catalyst to be added

In the morning of 20 July 1894 a Japanese Flying Squadron of three ironclad cruisers was on patrol in the Gulf of Asan on the west coast of Korea. The ships were an impressive trio, led by the 4,150-ton *Naniwa Kan*, which was under the command of Captain Heihachiro Togo. The *Naniwa Kan*, British-built and said to be one of the most powerful ironclad cruisers in the world, was almost 300 feet long and carried two 10.2-inch and six 5.9-inch guns, four torpedo tubes and fourteen machine guns. She had a top speed of 18.7 knots. Her consorts were the 4,180-ton *Yoshino*, armed with four 6-inch and eight 4 7-inch guns and also British-built, and the Japanese-built *Akitsushima*, a third-rate cruiser of 3,150 tons mounting four 6-inch and six 4.7-inch guns. The latter had a speed of 19 knots; the *Yoshino* was reputedly capable of 23

Togo's orders were to sweep the Gulf of Asan for Chinese transports rumoured to be landing troops on the Korean coast. However, as, to the best of his knowledge, China and Japan were not yet at war, the captain was somewhat unsure what to do should he come upon such vessels But the sea was calm and the day promised to be pleasantly warm, and he decided to meet that challenge when he came to it He did not have long to wait.

Just before 9 o'clock the Japanese squadron was nearing the head of the gulf when two unidentified ships were seen emerging from the entrance to the port of Asan As they drew nearer, it became clear that the approaching ships were Chinese men-of-war, and, purely as a precautionary measure, Togo ordered his men to stand by their guns. The Chinese ships were the 2,355-ton ironclad cruiser *Tsi Yuen*, carrying two 8 2-inch and one 5.9-inch guns, and the 1,300-ton *Kwang Yi*, a lightly armed sloop. Both ships were steaming at full speed for the open sea, and they had no transports with them. In the circumstances, Togo decided to let them pass unchallenged.

It was at this point that an uneasy peace changed to war, for the leading Chinese ship, the *Tsi Yuen*, suddenly altered course and headed straight for the Japanese squadron, her bow-wave foaming and her funnels belching black smoke. Her actions caused Togo to assume that she was about to attack with torpedoes, and he gave the order to open fire The *Naniwa Kan* heeled under the blast as her great 10 2-inch Krupp guns thundered out in unison. The *Yoshino* and *Akitsushima* joined in with their lighter guns, the *Tsi Yuen* and *Kwang Yi* replied, and within minutes a full-scale battle was in progress – the first action ever to be fought by Chinese and Japanese ironclads.

The British-trained Japanese gunners were soon bracketing the Chinese ships, and then scoring hits. The *Tsi Yuen* sustained heavy damage and the

*Kwang Yi* was unscathed, but neither of the ships' captains had any stomach for the fight: before long they had turned tail and were fleeing back towards the shelter of Asan harbour, with the *Yoshino* and *Akitsushima* in pursuit

The *Naniwa* did not join in the chase, for Togo had seen two more ships entering the gulf from seaward. These proved to be a merchant ship flying the British flag, escorted by another Chinese warship. This raised serious problems for Togo, for, although, following the attack on his ships by the *Tsi Yuen*, he assumed that his country must be at war with China, he thought it unlikely that the British would be involved Yet, through his telescope, he could see that the merchantman was crowded with troops, almost certainly Chinese, and on their way in to Asan. They must be prevented from landing.

Togo opened fire on the Chinese warship, which turned out to be the sloop *Tsao Kiang*. Without more ado, the latter ran away at full speed, leaving her charge to fend for herself. Togo was reluctant to interfere with a ship flying the Red Ensign, but he patently could not ignore her military passengers. Holding her under his guns, Togo sent away a boarding party, which returned with the news that the trooper was the 2,134-ton *Kow Shing*, owned by the Indo-China Steam Navigation Company of London and commanded by Captain T. R. Galsworthy. She was under charter to the Chinese Government and had on board 1,500 Chinese soldiers, fourteen field guns and their ammunition and a German artillery officer, Captain C. von Hanneken. Galsworthy protested loudly against his detention, declaring that he was on a lawful voyage, Britain and Japan not being at war, and that Togo had no right to hold his ship. Galsworthy was technically correct, but Togo was not about to allow 1,500 fully armed Chinese troops to land on Korean soil. He demanded surrender.

The situation on board the *Kow Shing* was chaotic. Galsworthy was in favour of surrendering, but he and his officers were surrounded by Chinese with loaded guns, who made no secret of what would happen to them it they refused to take the ship into Asan. The Chinese general argued that the Japanese would not dare sink a ship under the British flag, but Galsworthy was not convinced. Much as he feared the Chinese guns, he feared the wrath of his owners more. He declined to continue the voyage. It was stalemate.

This dangerous confrontation went on for nearly four hours, with the Japanese threatening, the Chinese obstinately refusing to surrender and Galsworthy and the *Kow Shing*'s British officers caught in the middle. Then Togo did something of which his Royal Navy mentors would not have approved. He torpedoed the helpless merchantman, pounded her with his big guns and, when she sank, machine-gunned the troops struggling in the water Only Captain Galsworthy, his chief officer, his boatswain, Captain von Hanneken and 41 Chinese survived

Togo's ill-judged and brutal action elicited a howl of protest from Admiral Fremantle, commanding the British Far Eastern Fleet, and, later, rumbles of disapproval from the Foreign Office, but as far as Britain was concerned the incident was soon closed. For the Chinese, however, the attack on the *Tsi Yuen* and *Kwang Yi*, followed by the slaughter of more than a thousand of their troops in the *Kow Shing*, could mean only one thing: China and Japan were at war

The cruel irony of the Asan Gulf incident was that it all came about as the result of an unfortunate accident. The *Tsi Yuen* did not intentionally charge

Togo's Flying Squadron, as it had appeared to the Japanese. The ships would have passed each other with no more than the exchange of hostile stares if the *Tsi Yuen*'s steering gear had not jammed at the crucial moment, causing her to take an involuntary run at the *Naniwa Kan* and her consorts. The Sino-Japanese War, although brewing for a long time, was, like so many wars, sparked off by an unfortunate misunderstanding – and the callous actions of Heihachiro Togo following the confrontation destroyed any hope of negotiation

Togo's masters in Tokyo were certainly not pleased with his heavy-handed diplomacy. They feared that Russia might come to China's aid, in which case the Imperial Japanese Navy would have to face not only the Chinese Fleet in the Yellow Sea but also the Russian Asiatic Fleet operating out of Vladivostok, both of which were believed to have superior ships. But, for the time being, Russia stayed uncommitted, and the build-up to the war on land went ahead. At the northern end of the Yellow Sea, in Korea Bay, the Chinese Fleet, under Admiral Ting, occupied itself with covering the landing of troops near the Yalu River, while further south Admiral Yuko Ito's Japanese ships did the same on the Taidong river. For six weeks after the declaration of war the rival fleets had no contact with each other.

On 16 September the Japanese Navy, having carried out a landing operation at Chinnampo, was returning to sea. Admiral Ito had with him a powerful force comprising ten cruisers, a gunboat, an armed merchantman and a flotilla of torpedo boats. Ito's flagship, the 4,277-ton *Matsushima*, mounted one 12.5-inch and eleven 4 7-inch guns, as did her sister ships *Itsukushima* and *Hasidate* The *Fuse* and *Takachico* carried two 10 2-inch and six 5.9-inch, the 2,200-ton *Hiyei* one 10.2-inch and two 5.9-inch and the 2,450-ton *Chiyoda* ten 4.7-inch guns. Togo's Flying Squadron, the *Naniwa Kan*, *Yoshino* and *Akitsu-shima*, were also in company.

Having completed his mission, Admiral Ito, tired of playing nursemaid to a flock of troop transports, took his ships north into Korea Bay looking for action He had an unconfirmed report that the Chinese were landing troops at the mouth on the Yalu River, about 100 miles to the north  Steaming in line abreast, their immaculate paintwork gleaming and their funnels trailing black smoke, the Japanese ships stretched from horizon to horizon, an impressive sight. Unfortunately, they were constrained by the speed of the slowest ship, the 1,650-ton armed merchantman *Saikio Maru*, and progress was made at little more than 10 knots. Ito fumed, for he was anxious to demonstrate the prowess of his fleet.

The report received of Japanese landings at the head of Korea Bay was correct  Six Chinese transports, carrying 4,500 troops and 80 pieces of artillery, had entered the Yalu River and were discharging their cargo as Ito steamed north  Offshore, at the mouth of the river, the escorting force of two battleships, nine cruisers, four gunboats and six torpedo boats had anchored, forming a shield to prevent any interference with the landings from seaward  Admiral Ying, in command of the expedition, flew his flag in the battleship *Ting Yuen*, a German-built ship of 7,430 tons. She had a top speed of 14 knots and carried four 12-inch and four 6-inch guns in barbettes, armour-protected raised platforms on deck; her sister ship, the *Chen Yuen*, anchored close by, was identical  The larger cruisers, the *King Yuen*, *Lai Yuen* and *Ping Yuen*, each of

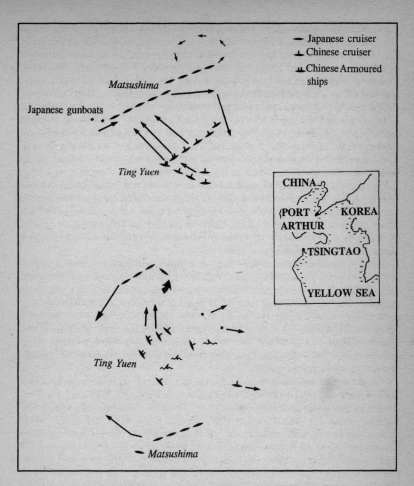

**Battle of the Yalu River, 20 September 1894**

2,850 tons, were 16-knot ships armed with 8-inch and 6-inch guns, while the 2,300-ton *Tsi Yuen* and *Chi Yuen* were similarly armed  The smaller Chinese cruisers, the *Kwang Chia*, *Kwang Ping*, *Yang Wei* and *Chao Yung*, the latter pair British built, were, at 1,300 tons, little more than sloops but carried an assortment of 10-inch and 4.7-inch guns. It was a large and formidable fleet, but the presence on board the ships of a number of British, American and German advisers, including Captain von Hanneken, late of the *Kow Shing*, indicated some weakness in the calibre of the Chinese officers  That may have been so, but the fact that Admiral Ting had chosen to anchor his ships rather than stand off the river entrance with full steam up did not say much for the advice his foreign experts were presumably giving him

At daybreak on the 17th the Japanese fleet was in sight of Hai-yang Island, 35 miles off the coast at the northern end of Korea Bay and 100 miles east of Port Arthur, China's main naval base. As the grey light of the dawn paled and the first rays of the rising sun touched the tall peaks of Hai-yang, Admiral Ito's lookouts were on full alert, but they could see no sign of the Chinese fleet. The gunboat *Akagi* was sent to check the deep-water anchorage on the western side of the island, but here again there was no trace of the enemy. Ito decided to continue on towards the mouth of the Yalu River, some 70 miles to the north-east. It was the typhoon season, but as the sun climbed in a flawless blue sky it showed the promise of a fine autumn day unmarred by strong winds. With the *Matsushima* impatiently in the van, the great fleet swept on majestically, eager for confrontation

Hai-yang dropped astern, and for the next three and a half hours the fleet steamed at full speed, working up to 18 knots and leaving the hard-pressed gunboat *Akagi* and the *Saikio Maru* straggling in its wake. The enthusiasm of the Japanese stokers sent tall columns of smoke drifting skywards, where, trapped by a temperature inversion, the smoke merged to form an extensive black cloud in an otherwise unmarred sky

Ito's unintentional warning beacon was sighted by Admiral Ting's lookouts at around 10.30 that morning, by which time the disembarkation of the troops and their equipment was nearing completion. Ting recognized that the smoke signalled the imminent arrival of a large enemy fleet, which left him in something of a dilemma. He could not leave the transports unprotected, but, on the other hand, if his fleet remained at anchor it would be at a distinct disadvantage. After some deliberation he gave the order for all ships to weigh anchor and steam out to sea. Forty minutes later the Chinese warships, in some disarray, had formed a ragged line of battle across the entrance to the Yalu River. Behind them, with the landing operation suspended, the transports had also weighed anchor and were seeking refuge in the shallows.

The opposing fleets came in sight of each other at 11 40, ten ironclads on each side and probably the greatest concentration of guns seen afloat since Trafalgar. The Japanese mounted in all three 12.5-inch, seven 10.2-inch, eight 6-inch, twenty 5.9-inch and fifty-seven 4.7-inch, while the Chinese mustered eight 12-inch, five 10-inch, thirteen 8-inch, eighteen 6-inch, one 5.9-inch and sixteen 4.7-inch  In weight of firepower it was a fairly even match, but it was the men behind the guns who would decide the outcome of the day, and Admiral Ito, leading his ships in his flagship *Matsushima*, harboured no doubts as to who would see victory.

Heihachiro Togo, whose Flying Squadron formed the rearguard of the battle fleet, supported the Admiral's view. He had the advantage of having inspected the Chinese ships when they were on a courtesy visit to Yokohama before the war. He had been amazed by the casual attitude of the Chinese officers, the lack of discipline of the men and the generally slipshod state of the ships. Furthermore, the experience of the Gulf of Asan, when he had easily put to flight three Chinese warships, was proof enough of their reluctance to fight. From the neat, orderly bridge of the *Naniwa Kan* Togo could see nothing to frighten him.

Admiral Ting, the quality of his ships and men apart, was already at a great disadvantage. If he kept his ships close inshore he would be unable to manoeuvre freely for fear of running aground on the numerous shoals off the river entrance. On the other hand, if he steamed out to meet the Japanese fleet there was the risk of some of the enemy's smaller ships slipping through his line to get at the transports  He compromised, advancing a few miles out to sea, then formed his cruisers into line abreast, with the two battleships at the centre of the line. The smaller cruisers *Kwang Chia* and *Kwang Ping*, with four torpedo boats, he sent back to guard the transports against attack.

As he approached the enemy, Admiral Ito manoeuvred his ships into two parallel lines ahead, the heavier cruisers, with the *Chiyoda*, *Hiyei* and the torpedo boats, bringing up the rear. In every ship men stood to their guns, loaded and ready to fire on the command. At the *Matsushima*'s yardarm a huge Japanese Imperial Standard, which carried a gold chrysanthemum on a deep red background, whipped defiantly in the breeze. The flag provided the only frivolous splash of colour in the well-drilled formation of sombre-painted ships. The Chinese ships, on the other hand, with their gaily painted, ornate woodwork on deck and multi-coloured displays of bunting at the halyards, might well have been taking part in a carnival. But even carnivals must be organized: Ting's undulating line of battle appeared to lack all coherence, and its advance was now noticeably lacking in enthusiasm.

Ito had eased back the speed of his ships and the opposing fleets moved towards each other at a closing speed of 17 knots. The sun was nearing its zenith and, without a single cloud to veil its brilliance, reflected back from the mirror-like sea with a dazzling glare. This put the south-facing Chinese ships at a double disadvantage, which might have accounted for some of their lack of co-ordination. There was, however, a great deal of apprehension on both sides, for, with the exception of Togo's Flying Squadron and the foreign advisers in the Chinese ships, most were yet to hear a gun fired in battle.

For the next 45 minutes the two fleets stood slowly on towards each other, the distance between them closing yard by yard, but, so it seemed, each resolving not to be the first to fire  It was a silent game of poker, played out on a silver sea  The stakes were high, the penalty for the loser certain death and destruction.

Ting was the first to crack  At 12.45, unable to bear the tension any longer, he gave the order for a ranging shot to be fired. Instantaneously – the *Chen Yuen*'s gunners had been nervously fingering their lanyards for some time – one of the battleship's 37-ton, 12-inch guns thundered out and slammed back in recoil, scattering its unwary crew to the four corners of the barbette  The heavy shell screeched through the still air, reached the top of its trajectory, curved downwards and fell half a mile short of the leading Japanese ships  At 6,000 yards, the range was far too great for the 12-inch, but, the flagship having fired, and in the absence of orders to the contrary, the rest of Admiral Ting's ships now opened up with every gun they could bring to bear. It was a noisy exhibition of indiscipline that served only to provide rich pickings for the fishermen of Korea Bay when they came sailing out to cast their nets.

The Japanese ships made no response to the provocation but continued to bear down on the Chinese in their impeccable line-ahead formation. Then, when Ito judged the range to be right, a string of flags was broken out at the *Matsushima*'s yardarm and the two lines of Japanese ships wheeled to port and formed one line ahead, exposing their full broadsides to the enemy. Speed was increased to 14 knots and, on another signal from the flagship, the guns of the fleet roared out in unison, adding a disciplined voice to the ragged cannonade begun by the Chinese. The battle had commenced.

Much of the Japanese fire was directed at the two battleships *Ting Yuen* and *Chen Yuen*, and both were hit repeatedly. As Ito's ships were now steaming across the bows of the Chinese vessels they were at a temporary disadvantage; their line might easily have been pierced, with disastrous results, if Ting had increased speed, but he made no attempt to do so The Chinese fleet in fact appeared to be in state of paralysis, plodding doggedly on at 6 knots and throwing out a wall of shot and flame they hoped would clear a path for their advance The truth was that, since the outbreak of the war six weeks earlier, the Chinese had not thought it necessary to exercise their ships, and, face to face with the enemy for the first time, they had no clear plan of action. The cruiser *Tsi Yuen*, survivor of the brush with Togo's Flying Squadron at Asan, was the first ship to be hit, and, true to form, she broke away from the line and ran for the sanctuary of Port Arthur. She was closely followed by the *Kwang Chia*.

The gap in the Chinese ranks left by the fleeing ships offered the Japanese an unexpected opportunity to break through and attack from behind. Ito was quick to act, and he sent in the cruisers *Yoshino* and *Akitsushima* with three torpedo boats in support. Panic broke out in the Chinese fleet The *Chi Yuen* and *Chao Yung* went full astern, and all ships in the immediate vicinity turned their guns on the Japanese infiltrators, who were beaten back by the sheer weight of fire directed at them. In the mêlée the *Chao Yung*, twisting and turning to avoid the Japanese torpedo boats, ran ashore, and all efforts to refloat her failed. She was soon reduced to a blazing hulk by the accurate fire of Ito's gunners. The battleship *Chen Yuen* was hit several times above and below the waterline, and her 12-inch guns were put out of action, but she fought on, using her smaller guns to some effect Her determined fight was in no way due to her commander, Commodore Lin, who had deserted the battleship's bridge in a blind panic when the shells began to fall. Lin's American adviser, Commander Philo N. McGiffin, had taken over, and would fight the ship to the end.

In the midst of their nightmare, the Chinese found another weakness in their ships exposed. The profusion of carved and painted woodwork on their decks showed itself to be a serious hazard, any shell-burst almost certainly leading to a fire In the *Chao Yung* and *Yang Wei*, fires on deck prevented ammunition reaching the 10-inch guns, thereby rendering these ships all but useless as fighting units. The *Yang Wei*, engulfed in flames, followed the *Chao Yung* ashore.

The cruiser *Chi Yuen*, commanded by Captain Tang, and with Chief Engineer Purvis, a Scot, in the engine-room, had taken a severe battering from the Japanese guns and was making so much water that Purvis feared she would sink. He conveyed his fears to Captain Tang, who then foolishly decided to inflict some damage on the enemy while he was still able to do so. Ringing for full speed, Tang charged at the nearest Japanese ship with the intention of ramming. Unfortunately for the Chinese captain, he had chosen as his target the 23-knot *Yoshino*, the fastest ship in Ito's fleet. The Japanese cruiser had no difficulty in avoiding the *Chi Yuen* and opened fire on her with all guns at close range  Other Japanese ships joined in, and the *Chi Yuen* was quickly reduced to a burning hulk  She sank, taking most of her crew with her.

And so the battle raged on throughout the afternoon, with the Chinese, having recovered some of their nerve, giving as good as they received  The cruiser *Lai Yuen* was ablaze from end to end but her guns fired on; her sister ship, the *King Yuen*, took a plunging shell through her decks, caught fire and capsized. The two battleships *Ting Yuen* and *Chen Yuen* each received between three and four hundred direct hits. On the Japanese side, the flagship *Matsushima* was hit by a 12-inch shell which exploded among some ready-use ammunition and caused terrible carnage  Otherwise, only the *Yoshino* and the armed merchant ship *Saikio Maru* sustained heavy damage  By nightfall the opposing sides had fought each other to a standstill, many of the ships being out of ammunition  The battle ended with Admiral Ito withdrawing his ships to the south, leaving the remains of the Chinese fleet to limp back to its base at Port Arthur.

One who was later to express his puzzlement over Ito's decision to discontinue the action when darkness fell was Commander McGiffin, adviser to the faint-hearted Commodore Lin of the *Chen Yuen*. The American reported that by then the *Chen Yuen* was down to her last twenty rounds of ammunition for her big guns, while her smaller guns were without a shell among them  This was, in fact, the situation in many of the Chinese ships. Additionally, they had suffered heavily, losing the 10-inch gun cruisers *Chao Yung* and *Yang Wei*, the *Chi Yuen*, Admiral Ting's fastest ship, and the 2,850-ton cruiser *King Yuen*  Most of the remaining ships had sustained major damage, and Ting had lost nearly 1,000 men, with another 500 wounded, including himself. The Japanese fleet was relatively intact, having only three ships damaged, 90 men killed and 204 wounded. If Ito had chosen to press home his advantage that night he might well have destroyed the Chinese fleet altogether and thus shortened the war considerably. As it was, Ting's surviving ships were repaired within a few weeks, and although they were reluctant to put to sea again they remained a real threat to Japanese troop movements around the coast.

Interested observers, especially the Europeans, considered the Battle of Yalu River to have been a victory for the Chinese, for although the Japanese appeared to have won the day they failed to prevent the landing of Chinese troops, which was the primary object of their attack. For those same Europeans, certainly the British and Germans, having built many of the ships and guns involved, Yalu River, regardless of its final outcome, was of great significance. It was the first major encounter involving ironclad ships using heavy breech-loading guns. The battle had, in other words, been a test run for much of the new maritime technology coming out of Europe at the time. The lessons learned would be of considerable value in the future.

# 2

# Heligoland Bight

*28 August 1914*

O n 24 June 1914, twenty years after the Battle of Yalu River, a 21-year-old Serbian student, Gavrilo Princip, shot and killed Archduke Franz Ferdinand in Sarajevo, the capital of the former Turkish province of Bosnia. This clumsy assassination of the heir to the Austrian throne, whose wife also died in the hail of bullets, was sufficient to reactivate the rumbling volcano that was Central European politics at the beginning of the twentieth century. Austria declared war on Serbia, thereby providing an excuse for Germany, Russia, France and, belatedly, Great Britain to order General Mobilization. Five weeks later Europe went up in flames, and the conflagration would spread to much of the world and take four years and 20 million lives to quench. The fighting on land quickly sucked in the armies of half a dozen nations, but at sea the Great War was to be, in general, a duel fought between the navies of Britain and Germany. The seeds had been sown seventeen years earlier.

In 1897 Queen Victoria had been on the British throne for 50 years and in June of that year the nation acknowledged the old monarch's unmatched reign with an orgy of pageantry. One of the most spectacular events was a triumphal review of the Fleet at Spithead by Her Majesty aboard the Royal Yacht. On that day, anchored in The Solent in immaculate formation, were 21 battleships, 53 cruisers, 30 destroyers, 24 torpedo boats and a host of smaller craft. It was a sight to inspire supreme confidence in the hearts of Victoria's loyal subjects and strike fear into the hearts of her enemies. And these ships were drawn only from Home Waters. In the Mediterranean, the Indian Ocean, the Pacific and the furthest corners of the globe, other ships of the Royal Navy guarded Britain's far flung empire. In 1897 Britannia truly ruled the waves.

Among the heads of state present at the first Spithead Review was Kaiser Wilhelm of Germany, the grandson of Queen Victoria. Wilhelm was deeply impressed by this magnificent array of sea power assembled off Portsmouth – probably the greatest the world had ever seen – and he was aware that this was not just an ostentatious display of toy ships. For all its highly polished brass and white-leaded rigging, this was a fighting navy, its ships built in the world's finest shipyards and manned by men inspired by Nelson's glorious victory at Trafalgar. It might be that Germany possessed the largest and most efficient army in the world, but after Spithead Kaiser Wilhelm's dearest wish was for a navy to match that of his illustrious grandmother.

While Wilhelm was away in England, 48-year-old Alfred von Tirpitz was appointed State Secretary of Germany's Imperial Naval Office, the equivalent of Britain's First Lord of the Admiralty Grand-Admiral von Tirpitz, a torpedo expert who had commanded the German Far East Squadron, was a Prussian of high intellect and imagination, with grandiose dreams of naval supremacy for his country. When the Kaiser returned home inspired by the wonders of Spithead, Tirpitz eagerly seized the opportunity to promote his plans for the new Imperial Navy. Under pressure from Kaiser Wilhelm the German Treasury opened its purse, and by 1900 construction was under way to bring the German Fleet up to nineteen battleships, 42 cruisers and twelve divisions of torpedo boats. These ships were scheduled to be in service no later than 1905, and would cost 408 million marks. With regard to the role of his new navy, Tirpitz said: 'Our fleet is to be so constructed that it can unfold its highest battle function between Heligoland and the Thames.' By that time there was no doubt in the German mind as to who the main enemy would be.

Britain's answer to the threat of an enlarged German navy was the 'dreadnought' type battleship, the first being launched in February 1906. HMS *Dreadnought* displaced 17,900 tons, was powered by steam turbines, giving her a maximum speed of 21 knots, and carried ten 12-inch guns. On her first gun trials she showed herself capable of firing full broadsides at 30-second intervals, spewing out a total of 10 tons of shell every eight minutes. With a guaranteed 75 per cent accuracy at a range of over 20,000 yards, nothing could stand up to the guns of HMS *Dreadnought* and those of her type who came after her

In July 1914, at the last Spithead Review before war brought a halt to all pageantry, the Home Fleet, under the command of Admiral Sir George Callaghan, put on an unprecedented display of twenty dreadnought battleships, 36 pre-dreadnoughts, four battlecruisers and flotillas of cruisers, destroyers and submarines stretching as far as the eye could see. But this time the review was more than just a show of strength: it was a test mobilization for the war that was then only weeks away When the war came, Britain was hoping for another Trafalgar that would destroy at one fell swoop the threat of Germany's growing sea power But Admiral Tirpitz's High Seas Fleet had no intention of being drawn out into the open. Against the might of the Royal Navy Tirpitz could field only thirteen dreadnoughts, sixteen pre-dreadnoughts, five battlecruisers and around 80 cruisers, destroyers and submarines. The guns of his big ships were all inferior to their British equivalents, so direct confrontation was out of the question When, just before midnight on 4 August 1914, the Admiralty signalled all ships, 'Commence hostilities against Germany', the High Seas Fleet had retired behind the defensive minefields laid across the approaches to Germany's North Sea ports. The big ships lay snug and safe in their bases at Wilhelmshaven, Cuxhaven and Bremerhaven, while the cruisers, destroyers and submarines kept watch off the fortified island of Heligoland

Heligoland, a 180-foot high rocky island of 150 acres, lies fifteen miles off the mouths of the Rivers Elbe, Jade, Weser and Eider, the gateways to Germany's North Sea ports. During the Napoleonic War of 1803–15 the island was taken from the Danes by the British and served as a base to break Napoleon's attempted blockade of Britain In 1890 Germany, realizing the key strategic importance of Heligoland, handed over to Britain her African colonies of

Uganda and Zanzibar in exchange for sovereignty over the island. During the next fifteen years the island's fortifications were strengthened, so that it became an offshore shield for the German ports, especially for the Elbe and the Kiel Canal, Germany's 'back door' to the Baltic. The sea to the south and west of Heligoland is well guarded by shoals and sandbanks, but there is deep water in the Bight, the channel to the north-east. In order to deny easy access to this channel, two days before the outbreak of war German minelayers sowed extensive minefields, behind which a force of cruisers, destroyers and U-boats patrolled, guarding the lairs of the High Seas Fleet. The persistent foul weather in the area – mist, fog, gales and short, punishing seas – combined with the guns and minefields to make an attack on the Bight a most unattractive proposition. It was clear that if the Royal Navy wished to bring the High Seas Fleet to battle it must first breach the defences of Heligoland.

It fell to the destroyer HMS *Lance* to fire the first British shots of the war when at 11.00 in the morning of 5 August 1914, in company with other ships of the Second Flotilla, she caught a German vessel laying mines in the Thames Estuary. Three days earlier the 2,163-ton *Königin Luise* had been fulfilling a peaceable role with the Hamburg-Amerika Linie; then she had been commandeered by the German Navy and sent to sea at short notice, with a cargo of mines but without guns to defend herself When the British surprised the minelayer at work, her commander, Fregattenkapitän Biermann, took the only possible course and made off at his full speed of 22 knots. The destroyers *Lance* and *Landrail* gave chase. Less than an hour later, the *Königin Luise* was on fire and sinking, with half her complement of 130 dead or wounded. She went down soon after noon, taking 85 men with her.

Later that day the *Lance* sighted another steamer acting suspiciously and, thinking that this was a second German minelayer at work, went in to attack without hesitation The stranger turned out to be a British cross-channel steamer, carrying, of all people, the German Ambassador to London, who was being given safe conduct home. A potentially disastrous diplomatic blunder was avoided only by the quick intervention of *Lance*'s flotilla leader, the light cruiser *Amphion*, who put herself between the steamer and the overenthusiastic destroyer Ironically, when returning to Harwich next day, HMS *Amphion* struck one of the mines laid by the *Königin Luise* and sank, taking with her 169 men, including eighteen survivors from the German minelayer. The loss of a light cruiser just sixteen months old and 151 highly trained seamen in exchange for the sinking of a small, unarmed ex-passenger ship could hardly be regarded as a victory for the Royal Navy.

Right from the declaration of war, the consensus of opinion, both in the Admiralty and in Britain at large, had been that there would be an early clash in the North Sea between the British Grand Fleet and Germany's Hochseeflotte (High Seas Fleet). It was confidently envisaged that in a great broadside-for-broadside battle the two fleets would re-enact Trafalgar, with victory of course going to the descendants of Drake and Nelson. Later events would prove this to be a fond pipedream, but for the time being very little in the way of shot and shell was exchanged between the two fleets. The Royal Navy patrolled the North Sea, the English Channel and the Western Approaches, diligently scouring the sea lanes for a worthy opponent, but, apart from the odd skulking

U-boat, little was to be seen of the Germans. Tirpitz was holding his ships behind the shield of Heligoland, and as the long, hot summer days of August 1914 drifted past and the first shadows of approaching autumn appeared, the seas around the British Isles were deceptively quiet

There were many at the Admiralty, and in the Royal Navy, who were prepared to let sleeping dogs lie, but two serving officers, 41-year-old Commodore Roger Keyes, commanding the 8th Submarine Flotilla, and 44-year-old Commodore Reginald Tyrwhitt, commander of the Harwich Force, were impatient to come to grips with the enemy. Towards the end of August submarines of the 8th Flotilla, on watch off Heligoland, reported increased activity by German warships to the east of the island; it had become routine for a strong force of cruisers and destroyers to venture out into the Bight each night, presumably to meet the perceived threat of an incursion by British ships. On hearing of this, Keyes and Tyrwhitt drew up an audacious plan. It was suggested that light cruisers and destroyers of the Harwich Force penetrate Heligoland Bight, with the intention of luring the German patrols – and perhaps bigger fish – out into the open sea, where they would be set upon by Keyes' submarines and a squadron of light cruisers lying in wait

The persistent badgering by Keyes and Tyrwhitt in favour of their plan, combined with the pressing need to show the British public that their hugely expensive navy was not entirely impotent, persuaded the Admiralty to act It was decided that the light cruisers *Arethusa* and *Fearless*, with 31 destroyers of the 1st and 3rd Flotillas of the Harwich Force, all under the command of Commodore Tyrwhitt and accompanied by three submarines of the 8th Flotilla, would make a sortie into Heligoland Bight in the early hours of 29 August Cover was to be provided to the west of Heligoland by the 1st Light Cruiser Squadron, under the command of Commodore William Goodenough and comprising the 6-inch gun cruisers *Southampton*, *Lowestoft*, *Nottingham*, *Liverpool* and *Birmingham*.

The naval correspondent of *The Times* wrote enthusiastically on 29 August:

> The British cruiser squadrons from Sir John Jellicoe's Fleet, with some destroyer flotillas, have had a quite brilliant little scrap with the enemy Their operations have been crowned with complete success, and that without very much loss to our side

The reality of the Battle of Heligoland Bight was rather different

The Harwich Force – two light cruisers and 31 destroyers – sailed from Harwich in the small hours of 27 August, with Commodore Tyrwhitt leading in HMS *Arethusa* The plan was to cross the North Sea during the daylight hours and arrive to the west of Heligoland after dark that night. Goodenough's 1st Light Cruiser Squadron, based at Rosyth, was already at sea and steaming at full speed for the rendezvous For Commodore Tyrwhitt, leading the long procession of darkened ships through the network of treacherous shoals that foul the approaches to Harwich, the first three hours at sea were a long drawn out nightmare For obvious reasons, most of the buoys marking the shallow patches had been removed and navigation was largely by dead reckoning – a highly risky operation in these waters It did not help that the 3,500-ton *Arethusa* was a newly commissioned ship, her officers and men being strangers not only to one another but to the ship and her equipment. But it was an ordeal for which Reginald Tyrwhitt's thirty years of service with the Royal Navy had prepared him well.

The first streaks of the new dawn were showing in the east when the *Arethusa* at last cleared the Gabbard Shoals and broke out into open water. One by one the other ships followed her and spread out into a loose line abreast. Tyrwhitt ordered an increase in speed and set a north-easterly course to pick up the Dutch coast at Texel Island It was only now that he had time to give thought to the dangerous operation on which he and his men were embarked The submarines of the 8th Flotilla, already on station off Heligoland, had reported sightings of German destroyers and torpedo boats, and Tyrwhitt feared that the element of surprise might be lost. But there was no going back, and he intended before dawn the next day to cut the enemy ships off from their bases and drive them out to sea on to the guns of Goodenough's cruisers. The composition of Tyrwhitt's force, two 6-inch gun cruisers and 31 destroyers, was ample for the job in hand, but the Commodore was acutely conscious that neither he nor any of his men had seen serious action before. Touring the Empire and showing the flag in His Majesty's peacetime Navy was one thing; facing the enemy's guns was different altogether. It was not only the chill in the early morning air that caused Tyrwhitt to turn up the collar of his thick bridge coat

At the best of times, without the benefit of modern electronic aids, navigation near the western shores of the southern North Sea is fraught with difficulties. The coasts of Holland and Belgium consist largely of low sand dunes, visible from seaward at a maximum of ten miles or so in clear weather. The coasts are fringed by numerous long sandbanks running parallel to the shore, and the tidal streams are strong and unpredictable. In the poor visibility prevalent in the area, the mariner who approaches too close to the coast is sorely tempting Providence.

The Dutch island of Texel, one of the outer defences of the Zuider Zee (Ijsselmeer), is, in keeping with the rest of the coast, low and featureless Undulating sand dunes hold back the sea, but much of the interior of the thirteen-mile long island is below sea level. In 1914 the only prominent landmarks on the island were the tall church spires of the villages of De Burg and Oude Schild. On the seaward side an extensive line of horseshoe-shaped shoals, known as the Haaks Grounds, extends $5\frac{1}{2}$ miles offshore Even in clear weather Texel should be given a wide berth.

When the Harwich Force neared Dutch coast the weather was hazy, but Commodore Tyrwhitt was obliged to close the land to establish his position It was much to the credit of *Arethusa*'s navigator that, a little after 9 a m., first the church spires of Texel and then the hazy line of the shore came into sight. When a favourable comparison had been made with the chart, Tyrwhitt veered away from the land and signalled his ships to form line astern. The islands of Vlieland, Terschelling and Ameland slipped by to starboard, and then the land curved back to the east and Holland gave way to Germany They were entering enemy waters. Now Tyrwhitt blessed the mist that closed in around them as they steamed north-eastwards, hidden from any German patrols that might cross their path.

The leading ships of the squadron were to the west of Heligoland by midnight and made contact with the three British submarines keeping station off the island. The weather had deteriorated to a mixture of drizzle and fog, adding to the misery of those who stood watch on the open bridges, on lookout and at the guns of the British ships. At times the damp curtain drew aside to reveal the dark, brooding hump of Heligoland, barely distinguishable were it not for a few careless lights showing low down on the foreshore Of the enemy ships there was no sign, and it now only remained to wait for the dawn. Coming on top of a harrowing day, and with the anticipation of battle ahead, it was a time for cool heads and strong nerves

Unknown to Tyrwhitt, or to Commodore Goodenough, whose ships were now approaching from the west, decisions had been made in London which would have a major effect on their operation. Coincident with the planned sortie into the Heligoland Bight, Royal Marine reinforcements would be ferried into Ostend to meet an expected attack on the port by German troops The Admiralty had therefore decided to enlarge the scale of the raid in order to keep the German Navy occupied and away from the Belgian coast. Soon after Goodenough's cruisers cleared the Firth of Forth, they were followed out by the 1st Battle Cruiser Squadron, comprising the 13.5-inch gun HMS *Lion*, *Queen Mary* and *Princess Royal* and the 12-inch *New Zealand*. In command was Rear-Admiral Sir David Beatty, flying his flag in the *Lion*. It is not clear whether it was intended that Beatty's squadron should join in the Heligoland raid or simply provide cover for the smaller ships Complete radio silence was being kept, and, with Tyrwhitt and Goodenough unaware of Beatty's approach, the Admiralty was inviting chaos to attend the operation.

It was also unknown to the two commodores – and, for that matter, to Beatty – that the Germans had got wind of the raid and were setting up a trap for the British ships. In addition to the destroyers and torpedo boats on patrol in Heligoland Bight, the German light cruisers *Mainz*, *Köln*, *Stettin*, *Danzig*, *Stralsund*, *Frauenlob* and *Ariadne* were lying in Wilhelmshaven under full steam, ready to dash out into the Bight when the British arrived Konteradmiral Leberecht Maas flew his flag in the *Köln*, while the *Mainz*, commanded by Kapitän zur See Paschen, had among her complement Kapitänleutnant von Tirpitz, the son of the Grand-Admiral

The *Arethusa* passed north of Heligoland at dawn on the 28th and swept down into the Bight at full speed, leading the thirteen destroyers of the 3rd Flotilla, closely followed by HMS *Fearless* and the 1st Flotilla. In the half-light the sleek, grey-painted ships, their sharp bows cleaving the waves and their battle ensigns streaming in the wind, made a brave sight. Visibility was about two miles, and not improved by the clouds of black smoke pouring from the blistering funnels of the ships. At 6.53 the first enemy ship, the destroyer *G194*, was sighted and the *Arethusa* and her destroyers altered course to attack A swarm of German destroyers and torpedo boats then appeared out of the mist and a fierce battle ensued, the Germans running for the shelter of Heligoland and Tyrwhitt's ships giving chase. The German destroyer *V187* and a torpedo boat were sunk in the engagement, and more would have followed them to the bottom had not Tyrwhitt been forced to break off when he came within range of the guns of Heligoland's forts

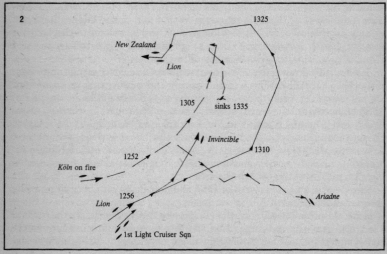

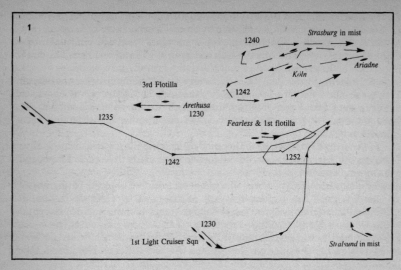

*Heligoland Bight, 28 August 1914*

Tyrwhitt led his flotilla back into the mist-shrouded Bight in search of more vulnerable targets and immediately ran into trouble in the form of the German cruisers *Stettin* and *Frauenlob* The enemy ships, displacing 3,480 and 2,706 tons respectively, were formidable opponents, armed with twelve 4 1-inch guns, four 5-pounders and two 18-inch torpedo tubes. *Arethusa* confronted them and engaged with her 6-inch guns at 3,000 yards *Fearless* joined her, and for the next 35 minutes the four ships fought it out with no quarter given on either side As they twisted and turned, crossing each other's wakes as they manoeuvred to gain the advantage, the sea around them was churned into a foaming battleground pockmarked by bursting shells and blackened by trailing clouds of funnel smoke.

At 8.25 *Arethusa* scored a hit on the bridge of one enemy cruiser, whereupon both broke off the action and escaped into the mist. The British ships were once again nearing the menace of the guns of Heligoland and the *Arethusa* had been hard hit, many of her guns being knocked out and her speed having been reduced to 10 knots There could be no thought of pursuit Lieutenant Reginald Godsell, serving in a destroyer of the 3rd Flotilla, said, 'How we got out of it alive I don't know By right we should have been sunk by the Heligoland forts and the German cruisers.'

While Commodore Tyrwhitt was debating whether to take his damaged cruiser out of the action altogether, the *Mainz* burst through the curtain of mist, coming from the east in response to a call for help from the *Stettin* and *Frauenlob*. The 4,362-ton *Mainz* had a top speed of 27 knots, and she was glad of every one when *Arethusa*, *Fearless* and all the destroyers within range opened fire on her Kapitän zur See Paschen retired back into the mist without delay, followed by a hail of shells

Hard on the heels of the *Mainz* went the destroyers HMS *Laertes*, *Laurel*, *Lysander* and *Liberty*, all eager to use their torpedoes. Unfortunately for them, the *Mainz*'s gunners were first rate and at 4,000 yards their salvos began to hit home. The *Laurel*, having launched all her torpedoes to no good effect, received a German broadside square amidships, blasting her centre gun and its crew into oblivion She dropped out of the fight with dense clouds of smoke and steam pouring from her The *Liberty* was the next to be hit, again as she raced forward in an attempt to torpedo the *Mainz* A salvo of 4.1-inch shells destroyed her bridge, killing everyone on it, including her commander, Lieutenant-Commander Nigel Barttelot. The *Lysander* escaped untouched, but the *Laertes*, following in her wake, caught the full blast of the German's guns Four direct hits, one in her boiler room, brought the destroyer to a standstill and in flames. Commander Goldsmith, captain of the *Laertes*, claimed that at least one of his torpedoes hit the German cruiser, but this was not substantiated In all, the destroyer attack was a disaster for the British, resulting in three ships badly damaged and 49 men killed and wounded.

The *Mainz* suffered only minor shell damage, and it seemed that she would be left free to cause more havoc when she ran headlong into Commodore Goodenough's 1st Light Cruiser Squadron, which had moved in to assist Tyrwhitt All five British cruisers, HMS *Southampton*, *Birmingham*, *Nottingham*, *Lowestoft* and *Liverpool*, opened up at 6,000 yards, scoring hit after hit on the *Mainz* with their 6-inch guns. Within fifteen minutes the German cruiser was a blazing shambles, an easy target for the torpedoes of the destroyer *Lydiard* Her hull ripped open, the *Mainz* capsized and sank, taking 89 men with her.

German ships were now coming in from all sides, and the low clouds pressing down on the Heligoland Bight echoed back the thunder of guns and the piercing whistle of shells. Konteradmiral Maas's flagship, the light cruiser *Köln*, sighted the crippled *Arethusa* and began to set about her. It was a fight the British cruiser was certain to lose, but then, to the amazement of Commodore Tyrwhitt and the consternation of Admiral Maas, Beatty's flagship, the battlecruiser *Lion*, suddenly burst onto the scene at 27 knots, her 13 5s spitting flame and smoke. Admiral Maas wisely abandoned his onslaught on the *Arethusa* and made a dash for the open sea. Beatty followed, and although the *Köln*'s 30,000 shaft horsepower turbines were built for 26 knots, the German cruiser was not fast enough. For the next twenty minutes the big guns of the *Lion* hammered away at her, causing fearful damage and casualties. Then came a diversion that saved the *Köln* – for the time being.

Out of the mist came the 2,659-ton German cruiser *Ariadne*, her 4.1-inch guns swinging from side to side in search of a target. It is unlikely that her commander, Kapitän zur See Seebohm, intended to challenge the *Lion*, but the British battlecruiser, given a choice of targets, postponed her annihilation of the *Köln* and turned her guns on the *Ariadne*. Faced with such unequal odds, Seebohm swiftly reversed course, but Beatty came after him. For the first ten minutes of the chase the *Ariadne* was unscathed, then the *Lion* got home two salvos that reduced the German cruiser's speed to 15 knots Other ships of Beatty's squadron joined in, and the unfortunate *Ariadne* was soon on fire and sinking, with 76 of her complement dead and another 76 wounded. The British battlecruisers withdrew before she sank, leaving the way clear for the *Danzig* and *Stralsund* to slip in and take off Seebohm and the surviving members of his crew.

It was just sheer bad luck for the *Köln* that she chose this moment to make a dash for Wilhelmshaven She was making all possible speed to the east when she ran straight into the path of the *Lion* as the battlecruiser was returning to seaward after finishing off the *Ariadne*. It was all over in ten minutes, the German flagship destroyed piecemeal by the *Lion*'s 13.5-inch guns. Of the *Köln*'s total complement of 507, only one man survived.

The Battle of Heligoland Bight, the first major naval engagement of the 1914–18 war, lasted for five hours and was notable for a total lack of coherent communication and co-ordination among the many British ships involved – this in spite of the fact that they engaged in so much wireless traffic that the listening Germans could not fail to grasp that something big was on. There appears to have been no clear plan of action passed to the various units involved, and at times the operation developed into a farce that might easily have become a major tragedy for the Royal Navy. The British light cruisers chased their own destroyers, believing them to be the enemy; the destroyers likewise chased the cruisers. Beatty's battlecruisers were at one stage attacked by British submarines, one of which also tried to torpedo Goodenough's flagship, the *Southampton* – fortunately in both cases with negative results. The poor visibility prevailing, the threat of hidden mines and shoals, the sheer mass of ships involved and the need to make haste all made for confusion. But, in a supposedly highly trained force like the Royal Navy, there was no excuse for the lack of clear communications between ships and for the poor identification procedures. However, for all its apparent chaos, the Battle of Heligoland Bight showed that British initiative and audacity was capable for making up for an appalling absence of overall direction. The German Imperial Navy was badly shaken by this attack on their supposedly impregnable stronghold, and was thereafter always reluctant to meet the Royal Navy on equal terms

Heligoland also showed up a noticeable difference in the British and German attitudes towards rescuing survivors  The British destroyers, in a properly humane manner, put themselves at considerable risk to save lives from sinking German ships but in so doing frequently found themselves under attack from other German ships  A typical example was the case of the destroyer HMS *Defender*, engaged in picking up survivors from the German destroyer *V187*  While engaged on her errand of mercy, the *Defender* was so heavily shelled by a German cruiser that she was forced to abandon her boats, leaving an officer and nine men adrift  Luckily the British submarine *E4* appeared on the scene and picked up the rescuers, leaving the German survivors to row for Heligoland.

When the smoke of battle finally cleared, Heligoland emerged as a clear victory for the Royal Navy  The Germans lost the light cruisers *Mainz*, *Köln* and *Ariadne* and the destroyer *V187*  At least three more of their cruisers were damaged, and total casualties amounted to 712 dead, 149 wounded and 381 taken prisoner  The British, on the other hand, sustained only one cruiser and three destroyers damaged and 32 men killed and 55 wounded. Nevertheless, Heligoland was a shambles. The engagement showed that, for all its outward show of strength, the Royal Navy had been asleep for more than a century  It would have to do better next time.

# 3

# Carmania and Cap Trafalgar

*14 September 1914*

Although best known for his victory at Agincourt, England's King Henry V was also the first monarch to build and maintain a fleet of ships exclusively for the defence of the realm. Henry's 'Royal Navy' consisted of only three ships, the godly trio *Grace de Dieu*, *Trinity* and *Holy Ghost*, but they created a precedent. When his illustrious descendant Henry VIII died 130 years later, he left behind him a fleet of 50 ships manned by 8,000 seamen. The Tudor king's daughter, Elizabeth I, on the other hand, appears not to have paid much attention to her Navy. When, on 19 July 1588, the ships of the Spanish Armada reached the Channel, they outnumbered the English warships by more than four to one. The brunt of the battle that followed was not borne by the Royal Navy but by a hastily assembled fleet of armed merchantmen under the command of Sir Martin Frobisher

Further development of the armed merchant ship was carried out by the Honourable East India Company, which was granted a charter to trade in the East by Elizabeth in 1600. The Company's first ship, the *Red Dragon*, was of 600 tons burthen and mounted only 36 guns. In later years East Indiamen tended to be around 1,200 tons and, such were the hazards of the trade, carried as many as fifty-six 18-pounders. So nearly did these ships and their crews resemble men-of-war that they were often commandeered by the Admiralty for service with the Royal Navy

Until the beginning of the nineteenth century the armament carried by merchant vessels increased so much that it was found necessary to set a limit to the number of guns a privately owned ship mounted, lest its crew be tempted into piracy After Trafalgar, with the prospect of many years of peace ahead, the mood changed and guns in merchant ships ceased to be of importance. As maritime commerce became more competitive, guns became recognized as 'dead freight' and they were dropped altogether The day of the armed merchantman was over, but its value when national security was threatened would not be forgotten

From the time the first steamship crossed the Atlantic in 1838, a battle developed between American and European interests for the domination of this lucrative trade, which would eventually involve the transfer of 60 million emigrants. In the front line of this battle was the dynamic American entrepreneur J Pierpoint Morgan, who in 1902 formed the giant International Mercantile Marine Company with a capital of $120 million One by one the United States shipping companies on the Atlantic trade dropped out, or were bought up by IMM Then Pierpoint Morgan turned his eyes to Europe IMM bought up the bulk of the shares of the Leyland Line, then acquired Ismay's White Star Line, the Dominion Line, Atlantic Transport and 51 per cent of the stock of the prestigious Holland-America Line. This left only Cunard, the French Compagnie Générale Transatlantique and the two big German operators, Hamburg-Amerika and Norddeutscher Lloyd, outside Pierpoint Morgan's alliance. With the aid of Albert Ballin, Hamburg-Amerika's chief executive, the German company was persuaded to join IMM, but the government-subsidized Compagnie Générale Transatlantique and Norddeutscher Lloyd firmly resisted all American advances. That left the unsubsidized Cunard under extreme pressure from IMM The company was eventually saved in 1903 by financial help from the British Government, given with the proviso that in the event of war the Government was entitled to commandeer any of Cunard's ships for naval service Britain was about to rediscover the armed merchant cruiser, and when the keel of the Cunard liner *Carmania* was laid down a year later the Admiralty paid close attention to her construction.

For many years German shipowners had prospered on the North Atlantic run, offering reliable passages with plain food and modest accommodation to the hordes of hopeful emigrants seeking a new life across the water At the turn of the century, as the flow of the America-bound impoverished eased, so the Germans changed policy, building faster and more luxurious ships designed to attract a better class of passenger. Cunard, long concerned with quality rather than quantity, had no alternative but to rise to the competition, particularly that being offered by the elegant new liners of Hamburg-Amerika and Norddeutscher Lloyd. And so the so-called 'pretty sisters', *Caronia* and *Carmania*, emerged.

The *Carmania*, the second of the 'sisters' to be built, was launched by John Brown of Clydebank in the winter of 1905 She was of 19,650 tons gross, 650 feet long and 72 feet in the beam, and she was one of the first liners to be powered by steam turbines, this by way of an experiment in preparation for the two 'super liners', *Lusitania* and *Mauretania*, planned for 1907 The *Carmania* recorded 20.4 knots on her trials, although in service her speed rarely exceeded 18$\frac{1}{2}$. She was specifically built for the Liverpool–New York and Fiume–Naples–New York passenger trades and carried 300 first, 326 second and 2,000 third class passengers Her fuel consumption, at 230 tons of coal a day, was excessive, but she soon gained the reputation of being a very comfortable ship in bad weather On the North Atlantic run this was a decided advantage

The *Carmania*'s early career was unexciting, but in January 1912 she tarnished her good name for stability when she ran into a North Atlantic storm of unprecedented ferocity Her lifeboats were wrecked, much of her cabin furniture was reduced to matchwood and she rolled so violently that bunks smashed through bulkheads into adjoining cabins. The run of bad luck continued into the summer, when she was badly damaged by fire when alongside in Liverpool. The following year she was to redeem herself in a spectacular manner In October 1913 the 3,602-ton Canadian cargo steamer *Volturno*, on passage from Rotterdam to United States ports with 540 steerage passengers and 93 crew, caught fire in mid-Atlantic Mountainous seas were running, and it was impossible to launch lifeboats The *Volturno* was, however, equipped with the new wireless telegraphy, and she sent out a call for help.

The *Carmania*, then bound from New York to Queenstown and commanded by Captain James Barr, was first on the scene. She arrived at noon to find the *Volturno* lying helpless in the trough of the waves and burning fiercely. The crew of the Canadian ship had panicked, and in an insane attempt to launch the lifeboats had fouled the ship's propellers with the boat falls Unable to move her engines, the *Volturno* lay beam-on to the waves, rolling her bulwarks under. On her after deck a seething mass of humanity was visible, and, as the *Carmania* drew nearer, pathetic cries for help could be heard across the heaving waters.

Captain Barr took his ship as close to the *Volturno* as safety would allow and dropped a boat manned by First Officer Gardner and a volunteer crew. The distance between the two ships was not great, but the boat was small and the intervening sea in fearful turmoil. After a valiant two-hour struggle to reach the burning ship, in which all but three of the rescue boat's oars were lost or broken, Gardner was forced to admit defeat and turn back. The return journey to the *Carmania* was an even greater test of strength and courage, Gardner's crew by this time being utterly exhausted It was only with great difficulty that they finally reached the side of their ship and were hoisted aboard.

It was clearly pointless to risk another boat, and Barr now manoeuvred his ship to within 100 feet of the *Volturno*'s stern with the intention of putting a line aboard. This was a magnificent feat of raw seamanship, for the huge, 19,000-ton Cunarder, rising and falling on the mountainous seas, completely dwarfed the little emigrant ship and was constantly in danger of crashing down on her. After several unsuccessful attempts to pass a line, Barr was forced to sheer away with the cries of anguish of the poor souls huddled on the *Volturno*'s poop ringing in his ears. Happily, the story did not end there Called in by the *Carmania*'s wireless, a fleet of ten ships was soon standing by the *Volturno* With Captain Barr directing the operation, and a tanker pouring oil on the water, ships' boats eventually rescued 520 passengers and crew from the stricken Canadian vessel.

Whilst the *Carmania* was engaged on her mission of mercy in the North Atlantic, many miles to the east, at the Bremer Vulkan Shipyard on the River Weser, Hamburg-Südamerikanische Dampschiffahrts-Gesellschaft – the Hamburg-South America Line – was taking delivery of a ship designed to be the jewel in its crown. The 18,710-ton, 18-knot *Cap Trafalgar* did not match the *Carmania* in size or speed, but her accommodation, with its palm gardens and luxury suites, was infinitely more grand. The Hamburg-South America Line was responding to a demand from German emigrants who had settled, and grown prosperous, in Brazil and Chile for a higher standard of service to and from the homeland. For the next twelve months the two ships, *Carmania* and *Cap Trafalgar*, made their separate ways back and forth across the Atlantic, their paths never crossing. But one day they were destined to meet – in a far distant place and under the most dramatic circumstances.

When Austria declared war on Serbia on 28 July 1914 and sent Europe towards an orgy of death and destruction, the *Carmania* was lying in Manhattan, taking on stores for her next Atlantic crossing. It was not thought necessary to interrupt her routine – as always, she was heavily booked with American passengers intent on spending the summer in Europe – and she sailed on schedule on the 31st of the month. Seven days later, still on schedule, she arrived in Liverpool and disembarked her passengers. It was then that the British Government stepped in to collect payment due for its support of Cunard over a decade earlier. The *Carmania* was commandeered by the Admiralty and a horde of workmen swarmed over her, ripping out the ornate and highly inflammable woodwork in her passenger rooms. Armour plate was riveted over her most vulnerable regions, and her gleaming white superstructure suffered the indignity of being painted drab wartime grey Her transformation was completed with the installation of gun emplacements on deck, into which eight old 4.7-inch guns were lowered and bolted down

A week later, almost as though she were keeping her peacetime schedule, but with not a steamer chair nor afternoon tea tray in sight, HMS *Carmania* emerged from Liverpool to take her preordained place in the ranks of the Royal Navy In command was Captain Noel Grant RN, while the liner's erstwhile master, Captain James Barr, now Commander RNR, was relegated to second in command. The Royal Navy had also supplied a number of gunnery officers and ratings, but the majority of the *Carmania*'s merchant service crew had stayed with her This was a perfectly feasible arrangement in the circumstances, and one that had worked well in Drake's day: Captain Barr and his men would continue to sail the ship while Captain Grant and his Royal Navy team would do the fighting. It was to be hoped that this fighting would not be of too serious a nature, for the *Carmania* was poorly armed and, being high out of the water as were all big passenger liners, dangerously vulnerable in battle. But at the time it was intended to use armed merchant cruisers such as her only on the Northern Patrol, sedately criss-crossing the gap between the Outer Hebrides and Iceland, on the lookout for enemy or neutral merchant ships attempting to run the blockade with cargo for German ports

HMS *Carmania*'s first assignment was not, however, on the Northern Patrol but nearer home in the St George's Channel – a short patrol to allow her mixed crew to get to know each other's strengths and weaknesses and to allow Captain Grant to put his ship through her paces as a man-of-war. She had not been more than twenty-four hours off Ireland when orders were received for her to proceed at all speed to Halifax, Nova Scotia, to take up patrol duty there Then, a day out into the Atlantic, a somewhat puzzled Captain Grant was told to head south-west for Bermuda, where he would receive further orders.

The *Carmania* arrived in Bermuda on 23 August, where Grant was told to join Admiral Cradock's squadron in the West Indies. Having been resigned to spending the winter in the cold water of the North Atlantic, this change of orders was welcomed by the *Carmania*'s crew. But first they had the unpleasant task of coaling ship, which, working at the usual pace of the Bermudians, occupied a full five filthy, back-breaking days. Then there was just time for Grant and his men to have tropical uniforms run up by local tailors before they headed south into warmer waters.

In times of peace, Rear-Admiral Christopher Cradock's West Indies Squadron served its country well, showing the flag and beating the drum in some of the more remote parts of the Empire. In 1914, with the world at war, the squadron looked less impressive, being made up of the ageing armoured cruisers *Good Hope* and *Monmouth*, the light cruiser *Glasgow* and the armed merchant cruiser *Otranto*. Cradock's flagship, the *Good Hope*, carried two ancient 9.2-inch guns, and both *Good Hope* and *Monmouth* had 6-inch guns mounted so low that they were rendered unusable with any sort of a sea running. These two ships were also manned by reservists so recently recalled to the colours that a great deal more working up was needed before they were ready to face the enemy. The *Glasgow*, fast and soundly manned with regulars, made up for the shortcomings of her heavier sisters, but the ex-passenger liner *Otranto*, armed with a few 4.7s, might prove to be a serious liability when it came to a fight. Into this illustrious company, at the end of August 1914, came HMS *Carmania* – perhaps another headache for Admiral Cradock.

Cradock's immediate task was to seek out and destroy the German light cruisers *Dresden* and *Karlsruhe*, known to be at large in West Indian waters. Intelligence reports also indicated that, further south, a number of fully loaded German colliers were lying in Brazilian ports, with the obvious intention of proceeding to sea to refuel German warships as and when required  Cradock decided that the *Carmania* was an ideal ship to keep an eye on this developing situation, so a few days after she joined the squadron she was dispatched to investigate.

As the *Carmania* hurried south on her mission, Hamburg-South America's *Cap Trafalgar* left her berth in Montevideo and slipped out of the River Plate. Some twenty-four hours later she rendezvoused off Bahía Blanca with the gunboat *Eber*, which had crossed the Atlantic from German South-West Africa. The *Eber* had on board eight 4.1-inch guns, six quick-firing pom-poms, a great deal of ammunition for these guns and trained naval crews to man them, all of which were passed across to the *Cap Trafalgar* at sea. Her identity then became *Hilfskreuzer B*, and Korvettenkapitän Wirth of the *Eber* took command, his orders to attack and sink British cargo ships, which were still trading with South American ports in large numbers. The Admiralty suspected that the German Navy had already established a number of secret supply depots for raiders in the South Atlantic, one of the most obvious being the island of Trinidade, which lies some 600 miles off the coast of Brazil. The *Carmania* was ordered to reconnoitre the island

The morning of 14 September 1914 dawned fine and calm, with blue skies and even bluer seas – 'flying fish weather', the *Carmania*'s older hands called it, and a far cry from the miseries of the North Atlantic. As soon as the sun came up, turning the high tradewind clouds from grey to a fluffy white, the lookout high in the armed merchant cruiser's crow's nest reported land ahead. With the bridge alerted, the *Carmania* pressed on at full speed and soon the vague smudge on the horizon became recognizable as the tall peak of Trinidade, with the Martin Vaz Rocks showing as three dark blue specks close eastwards.

Trinidade, having no connection with the lush West Indian island of similar name, is a barren, volcanic island 2,020 feet high, measuring three miles by one mile  At its western extremity a spectacular column of rock, aptly named The Monument, rises sheer from the sea to a height of 850 feet. Nearby is another remarkable rock, closely resembling the Rio de Janeiro's famous Sugar Loaf and inevitably so named. The south end of the island terminates in a prominent 800-foot high bluff. On shore is a petrified forest and hordes of land crabs that will attack a man if he is off his guard. Trinidade is an awesome, uninviting island, and all attempts at habitation, first by Britain (whose Astronomer Royal, Edmond Halley, annexed the island in 1700) and then by Brazil, have come to naught.

The island did once serve a useful role, in that it lies near the lower limit of the South-East Trades and in the days of the great windjammers was a convenient landmark both outward and homeward. On the south-western side there is a small, sheltered anchorage in which a ship may find temporary refuge in an emergency; otherwise the island has always been given a wide berth Legend has it that pirates of the eighteenth century used this anchorage, and there is reputed to be a fortune in gold and silver buried ashore. On that morning in September 1914, when the *Carmania* approached Trinidade, a pirate of a different age was occupying the anchorage.

The plume of black smoke drifting skywards from the far side of Trinidade alerted Captain Grant, and, deciding that any occupant of the anchorage was unlikely to be friendly, he cleared his ship for action. He shaped his course to approach from the east At 11 30, being a firm believer in the Royal Navy's philosophy that men fight best on a full stomach, he sent all those who could be spared to dinner The men who remained at their posts quietened their rumbling stomachs and moved up a notch in readiness.

Grant took his ship in towards the island cautiously, and with a certain amount of trepidation. These waters were unknown to him, or to Commander Barr The chart, such as it was, gave deep water right up to the steep cliffs, but this was an area of great instability, where subterranean volcanoes rumbled on the sea bed, erupting from time to time Trinidade itself had been born in this way, and who was to say what needle-sharp peaks lay hidden just below the surface of the water offshore, waiting to rip out the bottom of an unsuspecting ship?

At five miles off the island, and still in deep water, Grant swung the *Carmania* round to port and ran down the eastern side of the island towards the tall headland at the southern end, behind which lay the anchorage. The smoke plume still climbed into the sky, but there was no saying what ship it came from At best, Grant expected to see a German supply ship holed up in the anchorage, awaiting the call from any warship in need of fuel or provisions

The surprise was complete when the AMC slid past the headland and the anchorage opened up Not one ship was at anchor, but three, one of which was a large, twin-funnel liner, every bit as big as the *Carmania* herself The other two, obviously colliers, were alongside the big ship, their derricks swung out and hatches open Plainly, a bunkering operation was in progress

Recovering from the initial shock of the scene revealed, Grant focused his binoculars on the anchored liner. Her hull was painted grey and her two funnels black with red tops – a colour scheme used by Union Castle Line, which sailed the Southampton to South Africa run with passengers. But she was too big and too far off her course to be a Union Castle ship. Grant came to the conclusion that she must be German – most probably North German Lloyd's 17,300-ton *Berlin*, a 17-knotter known to have recently been commissioned as a commerce raider and armed with eight 4.1-inch guns Commander Barr, who knew the *Berlin* well when she was on the Genoa–New York service, confirmed Grant's identification. Both British officers were mistaken The ship they had surprised was the *Cap Trafalgar*, which had jettisoned one of her three funnels after sailing from Montevideo – hence her resemblance to the *Berlin*. The *Berlin*, was in fact still in a German port, loading mines which she would lay off Northern Ireland some weeks later

It was clear that the *Cap Trafalgar* had quickly realized her danger, for the sound of bugles echoed across the water and the smoke from her funnels began to billow as she hastily raised steam. The colliers swung their derricks in and broke away from her side  The anchorage was still out of range of Grant's 4 7s, so he was powerless to stop the German raider putting to sea. He rang for emergency full speed, and with her brawny stokers piling on the coal the British liner vibrated urgently as her turbines whined up to a high-pitched scream. The big ship's four propellers bit into the water, and for the first time since her trials on the Firth of Clyde she worked up to a speed in excess of 20 knots. Commander Barr, now conning the ship, put aside all fears of under-water obstacles and passed the southern tip of Trinidade at hailing distance.

By the time the *Carmania* had shot clear of the end of the island, her tall funnels leaving broad swathes of black smoke trailing astern, the *Cap Trafalgar* had cleared the anchorage and was steaming to the north. Korvettenkapitän Wirth, knowing full well he must stand and fight, required all the sea room he could get.

By now Grant had identified his quarry as one of Hamburg-South America's finest, a ship he believed could match his knot for knot. He had come to accept the inevitability of a long chase, and then a battle fought at the extreme range of their guns, when the unexpected happened. He saw the *Cap Trafalgar*'s wake begin to curve and her silhouette broaden. She was turning back to accept his challenge

The two ex-liners, products of an age of elegance that would never return, steamed towards each other in a show of magnificent defiance A huge, black, white and red ensign of the Imperial German Navy flew from the *Cap Trafalgar*'s gaff, while the *Carmania* had hoisted battle ensigns at the masthead and at the peak of the main gaff  The two ships made a brave sight against the backdrop of a brooding Trinidade, which in the day of the old buccaneers had perhaps been witness to many such a confrontation.

When the distance between them had closed to under five miles, the two ships began to circle each other warily, like two amateur boxers posing as experienced heavyweights. They were evenly matched, each with ancient guns that lacked punch and with paper-thin hulls that would take little piercing  Overhead, the great white-breasted albatrosses – birds, it was said, that carried on their wings the souls of seamen long departed this world – glided silently on the uplift of the trade wind and watched and waited . .

At 7,500 yards the *Carmania* put a shot across the German ship's bows, as though warning her to come no closer. The *Cap Trafalgar* ignored the warning, continued on and opened up a rapid fire with her 4.1s. Her shells were over at first, then they bracketed the *Carmania*, and then the German gunners found the range and held it  The *Carmania*'s gunners replied in kind.

For the next two hours the two ships blasted away at each other without let-up, closing the range all the time and both inflicting grievous damage  Early German shells demolished the *Carmania*'s bridge, smashed her steering gear, severed all internal communications and brought down her wireless aerials, so putting her at a severe disadvantage. In all, the *Carmania* received no fewer than 79 direct hits, many below the waterline She began to list as water poured in below decks and her speed fell to 16 knots. Several serious fires broke out on the upper deck, and when her main deck water line was cut, bucket chains were organized to quell the fires. As the distance between the two ships narrowed, the *Cap Trafalgar* opened up with her heavy machine guns, and men died as they fought the fires. And all this time the *Carmania*'s guns hit back until their barrels glowed hot and shell cases choked the scuppers.

The *Cap Trafalgar* was also on fire on deck, but Grant's gunners had been concentrating on hitting her below the waterline and at last their efforts began to bear fruit. The German ship took a list to starboard which became more and more pronounced as shells continued to punch holes in her hull. Suddenly those manning the *Carmania*'s shattered bridge saw the *Cap Trafalgar* swing out her boats and she veered away to port, heading for the shore. By this time the German AMC was sinking and Korvettenkapitän Wirth had made the decision to beach her on the steeply shelving shore.

Wirth had left his decision too late. When she was less than a mile from the shore the *Cap Trafalgar* slowed, her list increased sharply and then she suddenly fell over on her side, dipping her still smoking funnels in the sea Briefly she lay on her side like a great exhausted whale, then she heaved herself upright and, lifting her stern high in the air, plunged to her last resting place. In a few minutes all that remained of the once proud liner was a patch of broken wreckage, men struggling in the water and five lifeboats filled with survivors

The *Cap Trafalgar* had fought an honourable fight, and in the spirit of those days, when honour was all, the men who had brought about her end found time to cheer their vanquished enemy When she had gone, they returned to their efforts to control the fires threatening their own ship. When one of the German colliers moved in to pick up survivors, Grant did not intervene. Of the *Cap Trafalgar*'s total complement of 330, it was later learned that 51 had been lost, including her commander, Korvettenkapitän Wirth

The *Carmania* was also taking on a serious list, and her decks were a total shambles, with fires burning everywhere Five of her crew had been killed, four more were dying, and 27 were wounded. And for her it seemed the fight was not yet over: even as the *Cap Trafalgar* disappeared beneath the waves, smoke was sighted on the horizon to the north, soon to be followed by two tall masts and four funnels.

When the approaching ship was hull-up, telescopes on the British AMC's wrecked bridge identified her as another German commerce raider, the 14,908-ton *Kronprinz Wilhelm*, an ex-Norddeutscher-Lloyd ship During the duel between the *Carmania* and *Cap Trafalgar*, the *Kronprinz Wilhelm* had been some 50 miles to the north and had steamed south at full speed after having received a call for assistance from Wirth. The *Kronprinz Wilhelm* was too late to save her fellow hilfskreuzer, but she was nicely placed to exact revenge. Wearily, Grant called his men away from fighting the fires and ordered them to man the guns again

And then, just when the *Carmania*'s men had accepted that they were in a fight to the death, the *Kronprinz Wilhelm* suddenly swept round in a tight circle and steamed back the way she had come. Her commander later claimed that he had suspected that other British warships were close by, and he felt that he might be entering a trap. However, he had a burning ship under his guns, and his reason for running away without firing a shot is open to criticism

Captain Grant did not wait to question motives. The *Carmania*'s pumps were running hot and her list was increasing, while her fires on deck raged unabated. The emergency steering gear was rigged, and, making all possible speed, Grant set off to the west, anxious to clear the area without delay. During the night, using a makeshift wireless aerial, contact was established with the British cruiser *Bristol* and assistance was requested. Next morning the *Bristol* came over the horizon, followed a few hours later by another cruiser, HMS *Cornwall*, their prompt appearance doing something to justify the *Kronprinz Wilhelm*'s reluctance to intervene The two British cruisers went alongside the *Carmania* and, using their powerful hoses, soon quenched her fires. Later in the day the battered liner was escorted into Pernambuco by the AMC *Macedonia*.

The action fought by the *Carmania* and *Cap Trafalgar* was the first ever between passenger liners armed for war. Although the bravery and skill of the men manning the ships, British and German, could not be questioned, one lesson was there for all to learn. Such high-sided ships, slow to manoeuvre and without armour, are not suitable as men-of-war. It was a lesson the Germans learned quickly, but it would take another generation – and a lot more men would die – before the British Admiralty abandoned its fondness for dressing up old liners to go to war. The *Carmania* was one of the few such ships to survive the First World War. After Trinidade she was repaired and refitted in Gibraltar and was back in service within two months. When peace came again she took off her warpaint, landed her guns and returned to cosseting her passengers on the North Atlantic circuit. She was retired in 1931 and broken up at Blyth Her great forecastle head bell now hangs in the Captains' Room at Lloyds.

# 4

# Emden and Sydney

*9 November 1914*

There is a group of islands in the South Indian Ocean so remote, and so humble, that even to this day their correct name is a matter of preference The Cocos or Keeling Islands, a cluster of 27 coral reefs forming two atolls, languish in the sun 800 miles south of the Equator and 600 miles west of Sumatra They were first discovered in 1609 by Captain William Keeling while homeward bound from Java in command of the Honourable East India Company's ship *Dragon*. Keeling gave the islands his name, and then moved on, leaving it to the Company's hydrographer, James Horsburgh, to carry out a detailed survey some years later The Keelings remained uninhabited and unexploited until the 1820s, when the British adventurer Alexander Hare landed, bringing with him a party of Malaysian slaves. A later settler, John Clunies Ross, saw a potential for trade and began cultivating the coconut palms that grew freely on the islands By the time Captain Fremantle landed from HMS *Juno* in 1857 and claimed the atolls for the British Crown they were thickly covered with waving coconut palms – some 300,000 of them – leading Fremantle to christen the group the Cocos Islands. As an afterthought, having regard to the original discoverer, Keeling's name was added, and thereafter they became known as the Cocos or Keeling Islands.

In 1914 the Cocos or Keeling Islands were producing enough copra to warrant a ship calling three times a year, but their main claim to importance lay in the telegraph cable station on Direction Island. Opened in 1902 by the Eastern Extension Telegraph Company, the station was the hub of three underwater cables that came ashore on the island, one from New Zealand and Australia, the second connecting to South-East Asia through Batavia and the third reaching Europe via Rodriguez Island, Mauritius and South Africa There was also a powerful radio station on Direction, again owned by Eastern Extension The Cocos or Keeling Islands had become a centre for worldwide communications in the Indian Ocean, and of great importance in time of war However, to the British technicians who operated and maintained the equipment, the war was so far removed as to be on another planet. The climate in the islands was warm and equable; life was simple and unhurried It did not occur to these contented men that an enemy would even darken their door.

At the end of July 1914 the German East Asiatic Squadron, under the command of Konteradmiral Maximilian von Spee, lay at its Far East base at Tsingtao, on China's Yellow Sea coast. War was then imminent, and von Spee considered his ships to be in a dangerous position. Japan was at any moment expected to come in on the side of Britain and France, and her considerable fleet, which had smashed the Russians at Tsushima in 1905 under Admiral Heihachiro Togo, was just across the water. On 31 July von Spee took his squadron to sea and dispersed it. He had acted not a moment too soon, for some days later, when war had broken out in Europe, Togo arrived off Tsingtao and forced the German-built port to surrender.

Von Spee reassembled his squadron on 12 August at Pagan Island in the Marianas group, a quiet and distant anchorage. He had with him the armoured cruisers *Scharnhorst* and *Gneisenau*, the light cruisers *Leipzig*, *Nürnberg*, *Dresden* and *Emden* and various supply ships. It was obvious to von Spee that these were not waters in which he should linger, for his ships required prodigious amounts of coal in order to remain at sea and strike at the enemy. As neither China nor any other friendly country in the area could supply such coal, after consultation with his captains the admiral decided to make for South America, where Germany had friends and coal was easily obtainable. Only one ship would be left behind to create what havoc she could in Eastern waters, and the light cruiser *Emden* was chosen for this role.

Seiner Majestät Schiff *Emden*, built at Danzig in 1908 and now commanded by Korvettenkapitän Karl Friedrich Max von Müller, was a cruiser of 3,593 tons, powered by triple-expansion steam engines of 13,500 indicated horse-power which gave her a top speed of 24 knots. She mounted ten 4.1-inch guns, nine 5-pounders, four machine guns and two 18-inch torpedo tubes. Her tower, or bridge structure, was protected by 4-inch armour plate and her deck amidships by 2-inch armour. Her bunkers held 790 tons of coal, giving her a maximum range of 3,790 miles at her economical cruising speed of 12 knots or 1,850 miles at 20 knots She was small, only 387 feet by 43 feet, and highly manoeuvrable – ideally suited for her proposed role as a commerce raider and limited only by her access to supplies of coal. Her commander was equally fitted to the task ahead Born at Hanover in 1873, the son of a colonel in the Prussian Army, von Müller had 23 years' service in the Imperial German Navy behind him. He was a man of a few words, sometimes almost taciturn, but he was a strong, fair officer, a first-class navigator and a seaman who commanded the respect of his crew

Von Müller's second in command, Kapitänleutnant Hellmuth von Mücke, was also the son of an army officer. He was born in Saxony in 1881 and his naval service of fourteen years included the command of a destroyer. In direct contrast to his captain, von Mücke was a charming extrovert but again greatly respected by those who served under him Among the *Emden*'s complement of 397 officers and men was only one reservist, Kapitänleutnant Julius Lauterbach, once a master with Hamburg-Amerika Linie, well versed in the ways of merchant ships and familiar with Indian Ocean waters. Lauterbach was to prove invaluable to von Müller as an adviser on these matters and as a boarding officer for prizes Another notable on the *Emden*'s quarterdeck was her torpedo officer, Leutnant zur See Franz Joseph, Prinz von Hohenzollern-Sigmaringen, the nephew of Kaiser Wilhelm

Accompanied by the collier *Markomannia* carrying 6,000 tons of coal, the *Emden* sailed from Pagan Island on 14 August and set course to the south-west One of von Müller's first actions when at sea was to rig a dummy funnel, giving four in all With this simple addition to her superstructure he hoped that his ship might be taken for a British 'County' class cruiser should she be sighted by suspicious eyes.

Moving cautiously, and constantly on the lookout for the enemy, the *Emden* and her collier threaded their way though the Pacific islands, stopping from time to time at friendly anchorages to pick up supplies, fresh water and information. On 22 August she entered the Molucca Passage, on the 25th rounded the southern end of the Celebes and during the night of the 29th slipped through the Lombok Strait, entering the Indian Ocean unseen. By this time the *Markomannia*'s cargo was running low and von Müller's pressing need was for more coal: without fuel for her boilers, the *Emden* would menace no one, least of all the enemy

The most likely spot in the Indian Ocean to find unescorted merchant vessels was in the shipping routes that pass south of Ceylon, and, once clear of Java, von Müller set course northwards for the Bay of Bengal. As had been expected, the horizon remained empty of ships until the *Emden* drew near Ceylon. Then, during the night of 9 September, a light was sighted ahead which turned out to be the Greek steamship *Pontoporos*. This was a neutral ship, and von Müller hesitated to interfere with her, but when Lauterbach boarded he found the merchantman to be carrying 6,500 tons of coal consigned to the British naval base in Bombay. This was legitimate contraband, and the *Pontoporos*, under the command of Lauterbach, joined von Müller's convoy. Now, with ample stocks of fuel, albeit poor grade Indian coal, the German cruiser was equipped to go about her business of sinking the enemy's ships.

The war was young, and no one expected a German raider to be at large in the Indian Ocean. During the next few months the *Emden* captured and sank 23 merchantmen totalling 101,182 tons, plundering their cargoes as required. She also shelled the oil storage tanks of the Burma Oil Company at Madras, causing considerable damage and killing sixteen civilians, then entered Penang and sank the Russian light cruiser *Jemtchug* and the French destroyer *Mosquet* Wherever possible, von Müller treated the crews of the ships he sank with the greatest consideration, even going as far as to use two of the captured ships to land his prisoners in neutral ports.

When, in early October, von Müller decided that the ship was in need of a refit and his crew a short rest from the ceaseless patrolling, he boldly took the *Emden* into Diego Garcia, a remote British island south of the Chargos Archipelago. Diego Garcia had no wireless station, and only rare contact with the outside world, so the locals were unaware that Britain and Germany were at war. They co-operated willingly in the *Emden*'s refit But elsewhere in the Indian Ocean consternation reigned As a result of the German cruiser's activities, shipping in the Bay of Bengal had all but come to a standstill, the marine insurance market was in chaos, the port of Rangoon was closed for a fortnight and all troop convoys from Australia and New Zealand were delayed

Such was the mayhem caused by the *Emden* that, when she came out of Diego Garcia after a few days, a total of 78 Allied warships were scouring the ocean for her, among them the heavy cruiser *Hampshire*, the light cruiser *Yarmouth*, several AMCs and destroyers of the Royal Navy, a Japanese cruiser squadron and various Russian and French warships She had a number of narrow escapes, and at the end of October von Müller deemed it advisable to find less hazardous hunting grounds He parted company with the *Markomannia* and *Pontoporos*, taking in their place the British collier *Buresk*, recently captured to the west of Ceylon. The *Buresk* was a great prize, being loaded with 6,600 tons of best Welsh steam coal; ironically, her cargo was in transit to the British China Squadron at Singapore, which was then primarily hunting the *Emden*.

Von Müller's plan was, first, to create a diversion by attacking the cable and wireless station on Direction Island, in the Cocos or Keelings Having done so, he then hoped to make a quick dash westwards across the Indian Ocean, retracing his steps and leaving his pursuers to chase their own tails. When off the eastern approaches to the Gulf of Aden, von Müller hoped to repeat his previous success amongst shipping bound to and from the Suez Canal

With typical naïvety, it had been confidently predicted in Britain that the war would be over by Christmas 1914, but as the winter progressed it became painfully obvious that this would not be so The muddy fields of Flanders had turned into a gigantic killing ground, sucking in hundreds of thousands of men from all sides British losses were particularly heavy, and the call went out to the Empire for more men. Australia and New Zealand were among the first to offer help, and a large expeditionary force was put together consisting of 20,000 Australians and 8,250 New Zealanders. This represented the flower of the manhood of both nations, and, quite understandably, their respective governments were anxious that the men be given maximum protection on the long sea passage to Europe. The 5,000-mile crossing of the Indian Ocean, where a powerful German raider was known to be at large, particularly concerned them.

A huge troop convoy, with the Australians and New Zealanders in 36 ships, left Albany in south-west Australia in the morning of 1 November 1914. Escorting the convoy were the heavy cruiser HMS *Minotaur* and the Australian light cruisers *Melbourne* and *Sydney*. Off Fremantle two more troopships joined, and with them came the Japanese battlecruiser *Ibuki*. Captain E B Kibble, in the *Minotaur*, was Senior Officer Escort.

The convoy set course for Colombo, where the ships would refuel. It was a long haul – fourteen days at the convoy's speed of 9½ knots – but there were no German submarines in the Indian Ocean and von Spee and his East Asiatic Squadron were known to be off South America. That left only the *Emden*, and all four escorts outclassed the raider in guns, armour and speed.

Grim news of von Spee's activities came through twenty-four hours after the convoy left Fremantle. In a battle fought in a howling gale off the coast of Chile, the German Admiral had met and engaged Sir Christopher Cradock's squadron, sinking all but one cruiser. This was a humiliating defeat for the Royal Navy and it left von Spee with a free run in southern waters. It was feared that he might now take his victorious ships round the Horn and across the Atlantic to the support of German South-West Africa, which was about to be invaded by South African troops. A strong British naval presence was therefore urgently needed at the Cape, and on the 8th Kibble received orders through the wireless station on Direction Island to detach with the *Minotaur* and make for Cape Town at all possible speed The heavy cruiser left the convoy, and Captain Mortimer Silver, in HMAS *Melbourne*, took over as escort commander.

After coaling from the *Buresk* at Simaloer, a little-visited island off the north-west coast of Sumatra, the *Emden* set course for the Sunda Strait, which she reached at noon on the 4th Von Müller anticipated that, following the mayhem he had created off Ceylon, ships westbound from the Far East might be diverted to pass between Java and Sumatra, and he believed that a few days spent in the area would prove fruitful. But, although he kept a close watch on the strait, patrolling diligently within sight of the still-smoking island of Krakatoa, he saw nothing bigger than native proas After twenty-four hours he moved on, heading to the south-west.

During the night of the 7th the *Emden* was nearing the Cocos or Keeling Islands when her wireless operators picked up a coded message preceded in plain language by the one word, 'Urgent'. They listened carefully but were unable to break the code. The strength of the transmission indicated that it was coming from the British station on Direction Island, and as it was repeated at intervals throughout the night it was plainly of some importance. Around dawn the signal was at last acknowledged by a ship whose call-sign was unknown to the German cruiser's wireless office, and von Müller assumed that the vessel was a British warship. When contact was established the exchange of messages between shore and ship was brief, but long enough for the *Emden*'s operators to form the opinion that the ship in question was at least 250 miles off and moving away. Von Müller breathed a sigh of relief

The conclusions of the *Emden*'s operators were incorrect, and von Müller's acceptance of their report at face value was a grave mistake The signals overheard were in fact between Direction Island and HMS *Minotaur*: the British cruiser was at that point only 100 miles away and had just left the Australian troop convoy for the Cape of Good Hope. The convoy, meanwhile, continued to steam slowly north-north-east, keeping strict radio silence The ships and their powerful escort of a battlecruiser and two light cruisers would pass within 50 miles of the Cocos or Keeling Islands, and von Müller was blissfully unaware of their presence

Throughout the night of the 8th the *Emden* lay drifting 50 miles to the north of the islands, preparing for the attack on Direction Von Müller planned to arrive off the island at first light and send away a landing party in boats to destroy the wireless station and, if possible, cut the telegraph cables. He knew that the islands were not defended, and he did not anticipate any resistance There was a distinct possibility that the station would transmit an SOS before his men were able to destroy the radio, but, given that, in his opinion, the nearest enemy warship must now be several hundred miles away, von Müller's mind was at ease The deed would be done, and he would be long gone, heading north-westwards at 24 knots, before help came He was so confident that the raid would be carried out undisturbed that he sent the *Buresk* in to lie off the islands, intending to top up his bunkers from the collier while his men were ashore.

Shortly before dawn on the 9th the *Emden* emerged from a heavy rainstorm and von Müller, who had been on the bridge for some hours, had his first sight of Direction Island, a dark hump topped by a tall radio mast He rang for slow speed, and, with her guns cleared for action and her boats swung out, the cruiser glided silently over the mirror-calm sea towards the western end of the island At 05.30 she reached shallow water off Port Refuge, and, with the sea frothing white under her quarter as her engines went astern, she came to a halt Von Müller gave the order to let go the anchor and, with a loud rattle that seemed like a peal of thunder in the still morning air, the cable spilled out of the hawsepipe and the cruiser was brought up, swinging to the tide. There was no sign of life to be seen on shore, no indication that the arrival had been witnessed.

As the sun lifted over the horizon, a fifty-strong landing party, led by Kapitänleutnant von Mücke and embarked in the steam pinnace and two cutters, were lowered to the water and cast off. They left the ship's side with the pinnace towing the cutters crowded with men, all of them in high spirits. They might have been a party of schoolboys on a summer outing had it not been for the arms they carried, which included four light machine guns. The latter were a precaution against serious resistance being met at the wireless station, although von Müller considered this highly unlikely In the event of trouble, von Mücke had orders to abandon the raid and return to the ship; as a last resort the *Emden*'s guns would then shell the station, a step von Müller was most reluctant to take for fear of inflicting civilian casualties.

With the landing party safely on its way ashore, von Müller, anxious to make good use of the waiting time, broke radio silence to call in the *Buresk*, then lying 30 miles south of Direction. The coaling of the *Emden* would be carried out in Port Refuge while von Mücke and his men were at work ashore. Contrary to von Müller's assumption, however, the British on the island were not sound asleep. They reacted immediately the *Emden*'s wireless operator went on the air, the powerful shore transmitter demanding to know, 'What code? What ship?'

It was uncharacteristic of Karl von Müller to believe that he would not be sighted when approaching Direction Island In fact, his ship had been spotted by an early-rising Chinese worker some time before she came to anchor in Port Refuge. An unannounced ship arriving off these islands was a very rare occurrence, and the man lost no time in reporting to the British The British staff were, in fact, already on the alert. Two months earlier the light cruiser *Nürnberg*, on her way to join von Spee in South American waters, had attacked the British cable station on Fanning Island, in the Pacific, and cut vital cables, and the Admiralty had immediately warned all other isolated stations to be on their guard. It was also known by those on Direction that the *Emden* was somewhere at large in the Indian Ocean.

As soon as he was challenged, von Müller ordered his operators to jam Direction's transmitter, but the damage had already been done. The message 'SOS Emden here' had gone out over the air, and for the next fifteen minutes a report that the island was under attack went down all three submarine cables, reaching Australia, Singapore and South Africa The raising of the alarm did not worry von Müller unduly, for he was still under the impression that no enemy warship was close enough to interfere with his plans This complacency would cost him dear.

The ANZAC troop convoy was then only 55 miles off Direction Island, and the Senior Officer Escort, Captain Silver, ordered HMAS *Sydney* to investigate The *Sydney*, commanded by Captain John Glossop RN, was a *Chatham* class cruiser of 5,400 tons, launched on the Clyde shortly before the outbreak of war. She carried eight 6-inch guns, all mounted so as to give an arc of fire covering both sides of the ship, and two torpedo tubes  Her main deck was armoured against plunging fire, and her hull plates in way of the magazines and engine room were of 3-inch thick steel, extending some distance below the waterline  Of her crew of 391 officers and men, 252 were Australians  She had a top speed of 25½ knots.

Once ashore on Direction Island, von Mücke and his party, as anticipated, had met no resistance. In fact, the British staff of the cable and wireless station, taking their cue from Superintendent Darcy Farrant, were most co-operative. The only time they raised a protest was when the Germans were about to bring the wireless mast down on the island's tennis courts  As the British were unarmed, they could do little else but co-operate  They were, however, only putting on a show to discourage the Germans from making a thorough search of the station, lest they discover the reserve transmitter and receiver, which had been hidden as soon as the *Emden* was sighted  Direction Island W/T Station would be back in business within a few hours of the landing party leaving.

Having watched the boats successfully thread their way through the coral heads and shallow patches to reach the beach at Port Refuge, von Müller sent a coded wireless signal calling the *Buresk* in to begin coaling  The signal was not answered by the collier, but von Müller was not concerned, having previously impressed upon the *Buresk*'s captain the need to keep wireless transmissions to an absolute minimum  He assumed that the collier would arrive unannounced, but when there was no sign of her by 8 30 von Müller became worried and the call was repeated

At 9 o'clock, much to von Müller's relief, the *Emden*'s masthead lookout reported heavy smoke on the horizon. This was assumed to be the *Buresk*, delayed for some reason, and now coming in at all speed  Ten minutes later the lookout reported two masts and a single funnel, which matched the collier's profile, although she appeared to be coming in at very much more than her usual speed. As yet, there was still no sign of the landing party, and von Müller was becoming anxious on that account. The two hours he had given von Mücke to carry out his work of destruction were long past. He hoisted a flag signal urging the party to make haste, but no reply to the signal was seen

Von Müller's unease turned to consternation when, at 9 15, the approaching ship altered course and turned broadside-on to the anchorage, showing her full silhouette  She had not one funnel but four, and she was certainly not the harmless *Buresk* hurrying in to offer her coal: this was a sizeable warship, which, in these waters, could only be the enemy  Alarm bells shrilled throughout the *Emden*, her engine room telegraphs jangled urgently and a cloud of steam rose from her forecastle head as her anchor winch took the strain  Ten nail-biting minutes passed before her anchor was aweigh, and, with her stokers desperately working to build up the steam lost while at anchor, the German cruiser steered for the mouth of the lagoon.

Von Müller had by now identified the other ship as a British 6-inch gun cruiser, against which the *Emden*'s 4.1-inch guns would clearly be outweighed and outranged  They would also be almost certainly outfought, for von Müller now realized with a sinking heart that all ten of his gunlayers – the key men

*Emden and Sydney*   43

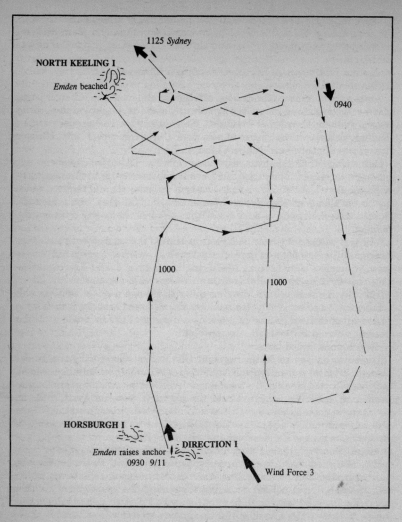

1125 *Sydney*

NORTH KEELING I

*Emden* beached

0940

1000

1000

HORSBURGH I

*Emden* raises anchor
0930 9/11

DIRECTION I

Wind Force 3

Emden *versus* Sydney, *9 November 1914*

of the guns' crews – were still ashore with von Mücke's raiding party. It seemed that the *Emden*'s luck had run out, but von Müller did not intend to give in without a fight.

The *Emden* cleared the entrance to the lagoon and, with battle ensigns flying defiantly, charged out to sea to meet her enemy. At 9.40, with the range at 10,500 yards, the German cruiser opened fire, and despite the absence of her gunlayers her first two salvos bracketed the British ship. But the odds against her winning a gun-to-gun fight with her more heavily armed opponent were very long indeed. Von Müller's only hope was to slow the enemy down with his guns and then manoeuvre into position to use his torpedoes, and to this he was committed

Captain John Glossop, on the bridge of the incoming HMAS *Sydney*, had no doubts about the identity of his adversary, or of her capabilities. He was fully aware that he outgunned the *Emden*, and he was also alert to the danger posed by her torpedoes. As soon as the other ship opened fire, he turned the *Sydney* under full helm through 180 degrees. The ships were on parallel courses, heading northwards away from the islands. Given the opportunity, Glossop intended to fight the battle at arm's length

Glossop had underestimated his enemy The *Emden*'s third five-shell salvo scored a direct hit on the *Sydney*, temporarily knocking out both the Australian ship's fire control positions. The hits also sent up dense clouds of smoke, which led the *Emden*'s cheering gunners to think they had inflicted serious damage. The German shells were indeed striking home with deadly accuracy, but the *Sydney*'s 3-inch thick armour plating easily absorbed the punishment. On the other hand, with both fire control positions out of action, and her guns firing individually over open sights, the Australian's shooting was poor. It was twenty minutes before Glossop saw his first shell strike home. This destroyed the *Emden*'s wireless office and caused a number of casualties.

The *Sydney* then veered away, opening the range, so that the *Emden*'s lighter guns were largely ineffective. Von Müller tried desperately to move in closer, but each time he altered towards the *Sydney* Glossop made a similar alteration of course away, thus keeping the two ships far enough apart to give his 6-inch guns the advantage.

There was an inevitable conclusion to this unequal battle, fought out under a blazing tropical sun and within sight of the men ashore on Direction Island. With both ships racing side by side, and with Glossop maintaining the distance between them at about five miles, the *Sydney*'s superior guns, with an emergency fire control established, slowly and precisely pounded the *Emden* to pieces Early in the action her electricity supply was cut and all communications reduced to word of mouth or voicepipe. The steering telegraph was smashed, then the steering transmission, obliging von Müller to steer his ship by the emergency gear aft. This gear, connected directly to the rudder, was so slow to turn the ship that the *Emden* was unable to dodge the shells coming her way. Then a 6-inch shell landed amongst the ready-use ammunition of the after guns, causing a massive explosion that smashed both guns and killed their crews A serious fire engulfed the emergency steering gear and all those manning it From then on von Müller's only means of steering his ship was by using his engines.

The *Emden*'s upper decks were reduced a complete shambles, with dead and wounded lying untended amongst the smoking debris and scalding steam gushing from severed pipes. At 10 45 the foremast received a direct hit and came crashing down, adding to the awful chaos. Then a salvo from the *Sydney*'s guns struck a most devastating blow, striking all three of the *Emden*'s funnels. In preparation for coaling from the *Buresk*, the funnel stays had been let go and in the ensuing panic had not been set up again All three funnels collapsed, leaving the *Emden*'s boiler fires without sufficient draught to generate the required heat. The collapse of the funnels also sent clouds of choking smoke and gases blowing back into the engine room, driving those still alive up on deck. The German cruiser's engines slowed their beat and she lost speed

While his ship was under fire, von Müller had tried valiantly to close the range to 3,500 yards, at which his torpedoes would be effective, but without success When the funnels went, he made a last desperate attempt to close the gap by altering boldly to starboard, but Glossop was ready for this and pulled the *Sydney* clear. Soon after that a British shell scored a direct hit on the *Emden*'s torpedo flat, which was below the waterline. The flat began to flood and the torpedo officer, Prinz Franz Joseph, was obliged to evacuate his men before they were drowned.

With his last real hope of survival gone, von Müller was forced to concede defeat. His ship was on fire in several places, holed below the waterline, unable to steer effectively and losing speed all the time. Of his guns, only one or two continued to fire intermittently, and to no great effect. The *Emden* was finished. Karl von Müller's thoughts now turned to his surviving men, many of whom were terribly wounded and in need of medical attention. He could not bring himself to abandon the ship, or let her go down without an effort to save those men The only answer was to run the *Emden* ashore.

At 11.15 von Müller ordered his guns to cease fire, and with the *Sydney*'s shells still hitting home he altered course directly for the reef off North Keeling Island. Approaching the reef, he stopped engines and the battered ship slid on to the coral under her own momentum with a heart-rending screech as her keel found the bottom A touch ahead on the engines, and she was hard and fast, her stern still afloat in deep water.

The *Emden* was still flying her ensign as she ran ashore, and this invited two more salvos from the *Sydney*'s guns before Captain Glossop accepted that his enemy was beyond resistance Glossop then sheered off and went in pursuit of the *Buresk*, which had chosen this unfortunate moment to put in an appearance. When the *Sydney* neared the *Buresk* the collier's crew scuttled her and abandoned ship.

The rusting remains of the German cruiser *Emden* lie on the reef off North Keeling Island to this day, a sad monument to Karl von Müller's complacency, which cost the lives of 134 of his men and landed the Korvettenkapitän and the rest of his crew in an Australian prisoner-of-war camp. Helmuth von Mücke and his party were more fortunate. After causing what destruction they could on Direction Island, they escaped in the 70-foot schooner *Ayesha*, then lying at anchor in the lagoon. Following an amazing voyage across the Indian Ocean, and a hazardous trek through Saudi Arabia by camel, von Mücke reached Constantinople on 23 May 1915, having lost only four men on the way

5

# The Falkland Islands

H aving detached the *Emden* to pursue her brief but successful sortie into the Indian Ocean, Konteradmiral Graf von Spee left Pagan Island and made his way south-eastwards across the Pacific towards the coast of Chile  His East Asiatic Squadron now consisted of the armoured cruisers *Scharnhorst* and *Gneisenau* and the light cruisers *Leipzig*, *Nürnberg* and *Dresden*  The *Scharnhorst* and *Gneisenau*, commanded by Kapitän zur See Schultz and Kapitän zur See Maerker respectively, were sister ships of 11,600 tons displacement, armed with eight 8 2-inch, six 5.9-inch and twenty 3.4-inch guns and four 17.7-inch torpedo tubes, with a top speed of 22½ knots. The *Dresden* and *Nürnberg*, commanded by, respectively, Fregattenkapitän Lüdecke and Fregattenkapitän von Schönberg, were of 3,600 tons, had a speed of 24½ knots and were armed with ten 4-inch guns, eight 5-pounders and two torpedo tubes. The *Leipzig*, commanded by Fregattenkapitän Haun, was a slightly older ship, similarly armed but capable of only 22 knots. Von Spee flew his flag in the *Scharnhorst*  With regard to fuel and supplies when in South American waters, the squadron would rely on a number of German cargo vessels stationed in various neutral ports awaiting the signal to put to sea.

News of Admiral von Spee's coming went ahead of him, causing considerable panic in shipping circles both in Britain and in America. It was feared that, after creating havoc on the Pacific coast, the powerful German squadron might then round Cape Horn into the Atlantic and succeed in cutting British trade routes with America. With this awesome possibility in mind, the Admiralty ordered Rear-Admiral Cradock to take his West Indies Squadron – redesignated the South American Squadron for the purpose – into the Pacific to challenge von Spee before he became too ambitious.

It was intended that the battleship *Canopus*, mounting four 12-inch and twelve 6-inch guns, would join Cradock in the Pacific and so, it was hoped, swing the odds in his favour. Unfortunately, the 14-year-old *Canopus*, barely able to make 18 knots, was still 200 miles away when Cradock met up with von Spee off the Chilean coast in a storm on 1 November  In view of the atrocious weather, and having only the ageing heavy cruisers *Good Hope* and *Monmouth*, the light cruiser *Glasgow* and the armed merchant cruiser *Otranto* with which to tackle the German squadron, Cradock would have been forgiven if he had chosen to fight another day. But, in the best traditions of the Royal Navy, he decided that David must challenge Goliath

The outcome of the action, which entered the history books as the Battle of Coronel, was a foregone conclusion. The *Good Hope* and *Monmouth* were hopelessly outgunned and outranged, as was the *Glasgow*; the *Otranto*, an unarmoured passenger liner masquerading as a man-of-war, might as well have not been present. In just forty minutes the *Good Hope* and *Monmouth* were sent to the bottom, along with 1,400 men, including Cradock The *Glasgow*, a 26-knot ship, acting under orders to warn the *Canopus* and the Falkland Islands, made good her escape, while the *Otranto*, apparently ignored by the Germans, also got away.

Bad news has wings, and word of the disaster off Coronel reached London within hours. The effect on the British public was a mixture of grief and humiliation. It was already reeling from the huge casualty figures coming in daily from the Western Front, and now to be told that Britannia no longer ruled the waves was a bitter blow indeed – but that was the plain message from Coronel. The Admiralty, usually slow to react, on this occasion responded with commendable speed. The battlecruisers *Inflexible* and *Invincible* were rushed into Devonport for a hurried refit and on 11 November, ten days after Coronel, sailed for South American waters. The two 17,250-ton ships, each with a maximum speed of 28 knots, mounted eight 12-inch and sixteen 4-inch guns and were protected by 6-inch armour plate on the hull and 7-inch around their gun turrets. Rear-Admiral Sir Frederick Doveton Sturdee, who flew his flag in the *Invincible*, had orders to take on coal in the Cape Verde Islands and then rendezvous with ships under the command of Rear-Admiral Stoddart off Abrolhos Rocks, near the coast of Brazil. It was expected that Stoddart would have with him the armoured cruisers *Carnarvon*, *Kent*, *Cornwall* and *Defence* and the light cruisers *Bristol* and *Glasgow*, the last fresh from repairs at Rio de Janeiro following her brush with von Spee. Once assembled, the combined squadrons, under the overall command of Sturdee, were to go south to the Falkland Islands to coal, and then through the Straits of Magellan into the Pacific. There they were to seek out and destroy von Spee's squadron, so restoring the good name of the Royal Navy.

When Sturdee's force left the Abrolhos Rocks on 17 November, von Spee was on the other side of South America and also heading south. News had reached him that Britain's ally, Japan, which possessed some very formidable heavy ships, was about to harass him in the Pacific, and he had concluded that it was time to return to Germany If the opportunity presented itself, von Spee intended to create more mayhem in the Atlantic on his way home. His first object after rounding Cape Horn was to attack the Falkland Islands, destroying the wireless station and the stocks of coal held at Port Stanley for the Royal Navy. Von Spee's intelligence was that the islands were completely undefended

The Falkland Islands, lying 300 miles off the coast of Patagonia and square in the path of the roaring Forties, are one of the more desolate outposts of British imperialism, home to penguins, seals, flocks of hardy sheep and a handful of even hardier sheep farmers. The sovereignty of the islands has always been in dispute, but it is clear that the first European to sight them was the English navigator John Davis, in 1592 Two years later Sir Richard Hawkins again sighted them, but the first man to land was a Dutch seaman, Sebald de Wert, who in 1598 found them uninhabited and named them the Sebald Islands. Another 95 years elapsed before the next man to land, Captain

Strong, of the Royal Navy, gave the islands their present name in honour of Lord Falkland, then First Lord of the Admiralty  Comte Louis de Bougainville, the renowned soldier and explorer, claimed the islands for France in 1764 and set up a colony, but this became unsustainable and was evacuated two years later. Captain John Byron, grandfather of the poet Lord Byron, then landed to re-establish the British claim, and after some years of argument between France and Spain – the latter also claiming possession – the Falklands became British by a convention signed with Spain in 1771. Apart from being a refuge for sailing ships damaged in the unending struggle to round Cape Horn, the islands did not assume any strategic importance until the advent of steam, when the Admiralty established a coaling station at Port Stanley

Von Spee was in need of coal before entering the Atlantic, and on 21 November he made a rendezvous in the Gulf of Penas, in southern Chile, some 800 miles north of Cape Horn, and refilled his bunkers and storerooms from six German merchantmen loaded with coal and stocks of food. The squadron was now amply supplied for the long voyage home; the only thing the ships lacked was ammunition, and this was not a deficiency von Spee could hope to remedy in these waters  The destruction of the wireless station on the Falklands was therefore a first priority.

A week later, during the morning of 2 December, while rounding Cape Horn in heavy weather, von Spee met up with the British barque *Drummuir*, beating her way around the cape westbound. Taking into account the weather and the urgent need to deal with the Falklands station, it would have been wise for the German admiral to have ignored this humble sailing ship, or at least to have shelled her from a distance. But von Spee was not one to pass up any opportunity of hitting the enemy  When the *Drummuir* was boarded and found to be carrying 2,800 tons of anthracite, the best steaming coal available anywhere, her fate was decided

The weather was far too rough to transfer the coal at sea, so the *Drummuir* was towed into the Beagle Channel, and there, in the lee of Picton Island, where Charles Darwin once made his observations, the coaling of the cruisers began. The transfer was a slow operation and the squadron did not sail again until 6 December, having first taken the empty *Drummuir* out to sea and sunk her. It was not apparent to von Spee at the time, but by delaying his ships for four days to plunder coal he was not really in need of, he had made a very grave mistake

By this time the battleship *Canopus*, in need of repairs to damage caused by heavy weather, had arrived in the Falklands and alerted the islands to the possibility of attack by a strong German force. After a hurried conference with the Governor, the commander of the *Canopus*, Captain H S Grant, decided to beach his ship in Port Stanley so that her big guns might be used to defend the port. Grant also set up observation posts on nearby hills, laid a minefield across the entrance to Port William, the outer harbour of Port Stanley, and landed a detachment of Royal Marines equipped with 12-pounder guns  The Governor rounded up every able-bodied man from the local inhabitants to form a defence force, while all the women and children were sent inland for safety. The Falklands stood by to await the arrival of the enemy

Such was the complete secrecy surrounding the existence of Rear-Admiral Sturdee's task force that the islanders were taken completely by surprise when, at 10.30 in the morning of 7 December, the British ships arrived off Port Stanley. The sense of relief turned to disappointment when Sturdee, who believed von Spee's squadron to be still in Valparaiso, announced that he would stay only long enough to coal his ships – forty-eight hours at the most. The coaling commenced at once, with the two lighter-draught cruisers *Bristol* and *Glasgow* entering Port Stanley while the battlecruisers *Inflexible* and *Invincible* and the cruisers *Carnarvon*, *Cornwall* and *Kent* anchored in Port William; HMS *Defence* had been detached to Cape Town on orders from London. As a precaution against a surprise attack when the ships were coaling – highly unlikely in Sturdee's opinion – the armed merchant cruiser *Macedonia* was ordered to patrol outside the port.

That evening a lookout at the *Macedonia*'s masthead reported smoke on the horizon to the south, but as twilight was then coming in, and as Sturdee was firmly convinced that no danger threatened, the report was ignored. The ships in the harbour, the long sea passage of the Atlantic behind them, settled down to pass a peaceful night in port

The morning of the 8th dawned bright and clear, with the promise of a fine summer's day to come Coaling was resumed at first light, Sturdee intending to sail that night for the Horn. With the exception of the AMC on her monotonous patrol outside, no ships were visible at sea, confirming, so it was thought, that the report of the previous night had been the work of an over-active imagination Von Spee, who was at that time approaching the Falklands from the south, was equally ignorant of the situation beyond his visible horizon. He believed Port Stanley to be undefended, except for a few obsolete guns on shore, and he intended first to send in boats to clear any mines which might be laid in the entrance to Port William The *Gneisenau* and *Nürnberg* would then enter the harbour, drop anchor and send parties ashore to destroy the wireless station, set fire the coal stocks and capture the Governor. The sea was calm, with only a light breeze blowing, and it was anticipated that the landing operation would be carried out smoothly and without due haste. Little or no resistance was expected from shore, and any that did arise would be swiftly crushed by a few well-placed salvos from the cruisers The sun was well up when the German squadron moved in on the islands, the *Scharnhorst* leading, followed by the *Nürnberg*, *Gneisenau*, *Dresden* and *Leipzig*, with the supply ships *Baden*, *Santa Isabel* and *Seydlitz* bringing up the rear.

Given Admiral Sturdee's unbelievable complacency in allowing all his ships, with the exception of the AMC, to be in port together without steam up, the scene was set for a second massive blow to be dealt to British naval supremacy. That this débâcle was avoided – though only narrowly – was due largely to the heroic action of a young woman whose name has long disappeared into the mists of time At around 7 o'clock in the morning of the 8th, the lighthouse keeper on Cape Pembroke, the southern headland of Port William, sighted a number of warships approaching from the south and, using his powerful telescope, recognized them as German. The keeper had no means of communication with Port Stanley and sent his wife on horseback to warn the Governor. The woman was heavily pregnant, and the long ride over rough roads proved too much for her. Soon after arriving at the Governor's Residence she collapsed and died, but not before gasping out news of the threat to the islands.

When word of the German threat was passed to Rear-Admiral Sturdee, he realized that he was in a most embarrassing situation, caught with his ships unready for sea and with the enemy knocking at his door He took the only action open to him, ordering all ships to raise steam immediately, and with haste. The battlecruisers used oil fuel to heat their boilers quickly, resulting in dense clouds of oily black smoke rising above Port William

The smoke was so thick that it hid Sturdee's ships from sight, and Von Spee assumed that the panicking residents of Port Stanley had set fire to the islands' stocks of coal At one time the *Gneisenau*'s first lieutenant thought he glimpsed a tripod mast through the smoke screen, indicating the presence of a battlecruiser, but his report was discounted: von Spee insisted that there could be no British battlecruiser nearer than the Mediterranean. And so, having wasted four days in needlessly relieving the *Drummuir* of her cargo of anthracite, von Spee had lost his opportunity to raid the Falkland Islands, which, twenty-four hours earlier, had been virtually undefended. Now the admiral was compounding his error by refusing to accept danger signals

On shore, the first confirmation of the arrival of the Germans came from the *Canopus*, lying beached in Port Stanley harbour When his masthead sighted the enemy ships, Captain Grant hoisted the flag signal 'Enemy in sight', but the smoke generated by the battlecruisers was rolling across the harbour and only the *Glasgow* saw the signal She attempted to contact the flagship using her 24-inch signal lamp, but it was not until she fired her 3-pounder signal gun that the warning got through to Sturdee

The German squadron continued to close the land, with *Gneisenau* and *Nürnberg* in the van, about fifteen miles ahead of the other ships. As they drew near to Cape Pembroke, the smoke lying over Port William momentarily cleared and Kapitän zur See Maerker, of the *Gneisenau*, was for the first time able to see into the harbour He was astounded by what he saw, identifying two armoured cruisers, two light cruisers and two heavier ships at anchor. Maerker immediately signalled the flagship, but von Spee refused to believe that he was facing a force any more powerful than the one he had so easily beaten at Coronel The squadron continued to advance, and at 9 o'clock a ranging shot was fired at the Port Stanley wireless station.

The first shot of the engagement brought an immediate response from the *Canopus*. Firing blind over the low hills that hid her from seawards, the battleship opened up with her 12-inch guns. Her first salvo fell short of the *Gneisenau*, then within six miles of the land, but one shell ricocheted off the water and went through the base of the German cruiser's after funnel. The shell did not explode on impact and the damage was negligible, but the mere threat of being faced by big guns caused von Spee to call off his planned attack He ordered his ships to sheer away and steam out of range.

The first British ship out of Port William was the armoured cruiser HMS *Kent* She cleared the headlands at 9.45 and found herself steaming on a parallel course with the German squadron at a range of about eight miles. *Kent* was closely followed by the light cruiser *Glasgow*, and then came the *Invincible*, *Inflexible*, *Carnarvon* and *Cornwall*, all working up speed as fast as the pressure in their boilers would allow. At 10 22 Sturdee, in *Invincible*, hoisted the signal 'General chase'

It was soon obvious that the chase would be a long one  The Germans were already making in excess of 20 knots, while the British ships, many of them with dirty bottoms through long absence from dry dock, would take some time to match this. But time was one thing Sturdee had on his side. His battlecruisers, with full steam up, were faster than the *Scharnhorst* and *Gneisenau* by a good three knots, and in these high latitudes the sun did not set in summer much before nine in the evening  At 11.15 he ordered a reduction in speed to allow the slower ships of his squadron to catch up and then sent all hands to an early dinner  Sir Frederick Doveton Sturdee was not a man to take precipitous action.

At 11.30 HMS *Bristol* sighted the German supply ships *Baden*, *Santa Isabel* and *Seydlitz* and informed the flagship. Sturdee then signalled the light cruiser to detach, taking the AMC *Macedonia* with her, to capture or destroy the merchantmen  This operation, out of sight of the main fleet, took longer than anticipated, and it was early evening before the *Baden* and *Santa Isabel*, their crews having been taken off, were sunk  The *Seydlitz* managed to escape under the cover of darkness

The main action, carried out against the snow-covered peaks of the Falklands, under a cloudless sky and on a grey, leaden sea, was a spectacular sight  Eleven powerful warships, with battle ensigns streaming astern and funnels trailing long plumes of black smoke, raced south-eastwards, six British pursuing five German, their guns questing but silent.

At 12 47, three hours after the first British ship had cleared Port William, the range had been reduced to 16,500 yards and the *Inflexible* opened the proceedings with a single shot from one of her 12-inch guns. As the 1,000lb projectile winged its way through the air, Rear-Admiral Sturdee signalled by wireless 'God Save the King', the receipt of which raised a cheer from all the British ships. The battle had begun in the heroic style in which it would be fought throughout. And, as the guns began to roar, into the midst of the opposing squadrons, like a great white ghost from another world, glided a tall-masted windjammer, all sails set. She was the *Fairport*, an ex-British ship under the Norwegian flag, homeward bound and two months out from Tocopilla, Chile. She was making very little progress in the light wind, and for the next six hours she was a silent witness to the Battle of the Falkland Islands.

The *Inflexible*, with the range tested, now brought all her big guns into play, and she was joined by the *Invincible*, both battlecruisers targeting the German light cruiser *Leipzig*, which had fallen behind  Realizing that it would only be a very short time before the *Leipzig* was blown out of the water by the British guns, von Spee signalled *Leipzig*, *Dresden* and *Nürnberg* to break away from the squadron and try to escape  As he had anticipated, when the three light cruisers altered course and ran to the south-west, three British ships, the light cruisers *Kent*, *Cornwall* and *Glasgow*, broke ranks and raced in pursuit  The main battle was to be between the big ships. Gun for gun, the British battlecruisers *Inflexible* and *Invincible*, with their eight 12-inch and sixteen 4-inch, easily outweighed the *Scharnhorst* and *Gneisenau* with their eight 8.2-inch and six 5 9-inch; they were also three knots faster  However, the ships were near enough equal for an incautious manoeuvre or chance shell hitting a vital spot to decide the day

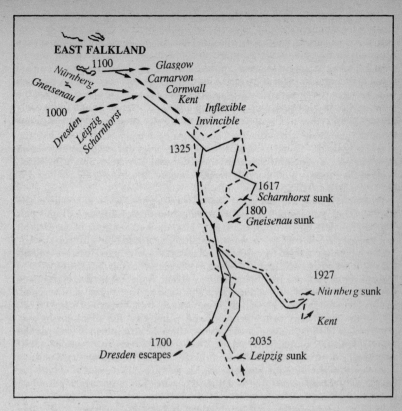

EAST FALKLAND

Nürnberg 1100 Glasgow
Gneisenau Carnarvon
Cornwall
1000 Kent
Dresden Leipzig Scharnhorst Inflexible
Invincible
1325

1617
Scharnhorst sunk
1800
Gneisenau sunk

1927
Nürnberg sunk

Kent

1700 2035
Dresden escapes Leipzig sunk

*Battle of the Falkland Islands, 7 December 1914*

Using a mixture of coal and fuel oil to feed their boiler furnaces, Sturdee coaxed his battlecruisers up to a speed of 26 knots and slowly, almost imperceptibly, he began to gain on von Spee's heavy cruisers  But now a weakness in the British ships showed up  Although the *Inflexible* and *Invincible* were newly built, they had only the most primitive aids to laying their guns  Their shells fell wide of the fleeing enemy

By 1 42 p m. the range had decreased to 13,500 yards, and it became clear to von Spee that he could not hope to get away without a fight. Maintaining speed, he abruptly turned the *Scharnhorst* and *Gneisenau* to port to present their broadsides and opened fired with all sixteen 8.2-inch guns simultaneously  The superiority of the German gunnery was immediately obvious, shells falling all around the British ships  Sturdee took up the challenge, turning his ships to match broadside for broadside, and the fight began in earnest

The big guns thundered defiance at each other, hurling their great shells across the cold, grey waters of the South Atlantic. The *Invincible* was the first to be hit, but she was not seriously damaged. Then two British shells spiralled down on to the *Gneisenau*, one striking home below the waterline. The *Scharnhorst* was also hit, but Sturdee, not wishing to give away the advantage of the longer range of his guns, now hauled his battlecruisers away

Von Spee took advantage of the lull to run to the south, hoping to get away, and Sturdee followed him round, but not fast enough The British ships had lost ground, and within twenty minutes the Germans had opened the range by 3,000 yards. It took another forty minutes of hard steaming before *Inflexible* and *Invincible* were in a position to open fire again. British shells began once more to rain down on the fleeing Germans, whose big guns did not have the reach to hit back. Then the *Scharnhorst* and *Gneisenau* suddenly turned on their pursuers and steamed straight towards them. It was von Spee's intention to close the range to 10,000 yards quickly, in order to use both his 5.9 and 8.2-inch guns in concentrated broadsides.

For the next hour the four great men-of-war fought a fierce engagement, the smoke of their guns mingling with that from their funnels to cast a gloomy pall over their lonely battleground. Then, at last, the heavier guns of the British ships began to tell, both the *Scharnhorst* and *Gneisenau* being hit repeatedly. The *Scharnhorst*'s third funnel was shot away, she was holed forward and aft below the waterline and many of her guns were knocked out, but she continued to fire back with those left Soon she was ablaze from end to end, both masts were down, her boats were reduced to matchwood and her bridge was wrecked. Yet she still fought on, her ensign flying bravely from a jury mast rigged aft. She began to list heavily to starboard, and as her guns fell silent one by one, von Spee, in one last magnificent gesture, altered course directly towards the *Invincible* to deliver a torpedo attack The torpedoes were never launched. At around 4.15 the *Scharnhorst* was still under way, and straining to get close to her enemy, when she rolled over and sank, leaving only a cloud of dispersing smoke and a clutter of wreckage to tell of her passing Konteradmiral Maximilian Graf von Spee and all his men went down with her

The *Gneisenau* continued the fight alone, but she was no match for the two British battlecruisers, which moved back out of range of the German's guns and shelled her at will. Her forward funnel was shot away, one of her main turrets was blown clean over the side and the sea poured into her hull through great holes blasted below the waterline At 5 30 she was listing heavily to starboard and appeared stopped, steam, smoke and flames enveloping her upperworks All her guns but one had ceased fire, though not because they were smashed or had given up the fight The *Gneisenau* was out of ammunition.

Before she sank, at about 6 p.m , it was reported that the German cruiser's superstructure and upper deck had been completely destroyed and 600 men lay dead or wounded. Fortunately, when she went, she capsized very slowly, giving those who survived a chance to abandon ship Typically, the British ships then expended every effort to save life. Boats were lowered smartly, but with the sea temperature not much above freezing, men who were exhausted by the long chase and battle died within minutes Of the *Gneisenau*'s total crew of 765, only 175 survived.

The remainder of von Spee's squadron, the light cruisers *Dresden*, *Leipzig* and *Nürnberg*, had earlier escaped to the south-west with the *Kent*, *Cornwall* and *Glasgow* in pursuit. Some hours passed before the *Glasgow*, the fastest of the British cruisers, caught up with the *Leipzig* and opened fire on her The range was 12,000 yards, and the two ships were evenly matched except that the Glasgow had two 6-inch guns, which she used to good effect in a running fight that lasted over an hour. The *Leipzig* scored two damaging hits on the *Glasgow*, which kept her at bay, but when the *Cornwall* arrived on the scene with her fourteen 6-inch guns the die was cast. And yet, even under the devastating combined broadsides of the two British ships, the *Leipzig* lasted for another four hours Then, emulating her admiral's flagship, she made an audacious but unsuccessful torpedo run at her opponents She lasted until dark, when, with all her ammunition expended, she gave up the fight and sank by the bows, her ensign still fluttering proudly Only eighteen of her complement of 290 survived

The *Dresden* had got away, but while the *Glasgow* and *Cornwall* were pounding the *Leipzig* into submission the armoured cruiser *Kent* was ordered to tackle the *Nürnberg*. The *Kent*, however, had been last in the queue for coaling at Port William and had been sent to sea before her turn came By this time she was running dangerously short of fuel, and when she finally brought the *Nürnberg* to action she was reduced to feeding her boats and cabin furniture to the furnaces.

The *Nürnberg* had a 1½-knot advantage over the *Kent*, and it was not until 5 p m that the British cruiser, with her stokers in a state of near exhaustion and most of the wooden fittings of the ship consumed, came within range of the *Nürnberg*. The German ship was the first to open fire, using her two stern guns with considerable accuracy at a range of 12,000 yards. The *Kent* held her fire for another ten minutes, and when the range was down to 7,000 yards opened up with rapid salvos The *Nürnberg*'s answer was to alter to port to bring her broadside to bear *Kent* followed her round and replied with her starboard guns.

For the next hour the two ships, twisting and weaving like two seasoned prize fighters, faced each other and exchanged salvo for salvo. They were on converging courses, the range shortening all the time, and as the guns thundered out so increasing death and destruction was meted out to each ship by the other As the two cruisers fought their battle in isolation, the weather, which had been fair throughout the day, began to deteriorate. Patches of rain and drizzle swept across the watery battlefield, seriously affecting visibility At one time it seemed quite possible that the *Nürnberg* would escape under cover of the rain, but, in the struggle to gain ever more speed, her engineers put too much pressure on her boilers and two of them burst, killing a number of her engine-room crew The *Nürnberg* slowly lost speed.

The *Kent* now began to gain on the German cruiser, her salvos hitting home with increasing effect as the distance between them lessened When darkness closed in, the *Nürnberg* was a mass of flames, but her guns continued to fire, briefly falling silent, as did those of the *Kent*, when another great four-master appeared from the west, glided between the duelling ships and disappeared in the gathering dusk on the other side The identity of the barque was never established, but there were many who said she was a visitation from the past, perhaps wondering why these southern waters, which had known nothing but peaceful commerce for centuries, had become a place of killing and destruction

The *Nürnberg* went down with her guns still firing at 7 27  It was said that her ensign still flew, tied to a broken oar and held aloft by a wounded man as she slipped beneath the waves. The *Kent* did all she could to save lives, but as her boats had disappeared into her boiler furnaces her efforts were largely in vain. Of the *Nürnberg*'s crew of 295, only seven men survived.

The Battle of the Falkland Islands was a complete victory for Rear-Admiral Sturdee, for of von Spee's powerful squadron only the *Dresden* escaped. She was to meet her end three months later, surprised while refuelling off the Pacific island of Masafuera by HMS *Kent* and *Glasgow*. Von Spee's foolish action in dallying off Cape Horn to seize the *Drummuir*'s cargo cost him his entire squadron and his own life, that of his two sons – one serving in the *Gneisenau*, the other in the *Nürnberg* – and the lives of 2,000 German officers and men. The British lost no ships, the damage was slight and just seven men were killed and four wounded. The only casualties ashore in the Falklands were the lighthouse keeper's wife and her unborn child, whose deaths undoubtedly saved the lives of many British seamen whose paths they had never crossed.

# 6

# Dogger Bank

*24 January 1915*

Before the Battle of the Falkland Islands it is doubtful if more than a handful of the population of Scarborough had ever heard of the islands; even fewer would have been able to point them out on a map. Yet this sleepy Yorkshire coastal spa was chosen to receive the full force of the German Navy's revenge for its humiliating defeat in the South Atlantic

When the news reached Germany of the destruction of Konteradmiral Graf von Spee's squadron off the Falklands on 8 December, there was immediate public outrage and a demand for retribution  The Admiralstab, reeling under the terrible blow to its pride, obliged with a plan to inflict a short, sharp bombardment on the north-east coast towns of Scarborough, Whitby and Hartlepool. At the same time it was hoped to entice out the British Grand Fleet – now known to be without the battlecruisers *Inflexible* and *Invincible* – and lead it into a prepared minefield laid off the Dogger Bank

At dawn on 15 December the First German Scouting Group, consisting of five battlecruisers, accompanied by light cruisers and destroyers, left its anchorage in Jade Bay and set out westwards across the North Sea, under the command of Admiral Franz von Hipper. The weather, a half gale blowing and visibility severely restricted by a mixture of drizzle and fog, was typical for the time of the year  A miserable crossing was in store for those manning the German ships, but the foul weather was a sure cloak to hide them from patrolling enemy vessels

Scarborough was at breakfast when the first shells landed, but it was some time before the realization dawned that the commotion was not caused by ships of the Royal Navy at gun practice. Half an hour and 500 shells later, with eighteen people lying dead and the local hospital overflowing with injured, Scarborough was aware of the horrors of war  Meanwhile von Hipper's ships also attacked the port of Hartlepool. In a fierce bombardment lasting over an hour, 102 civilians, mainly women and children, were killed  The German ships then moved on to shell Whitby, where another two innocents died

This attack on the civilian population of England was ill-conceived and achieved nothing but trouble for Germany  The raid was regarded as a breach of the Hague Convention and caused a great upsurge of public indignation in Britain, resulting in recruiting offices all over the country being besieged by men wishing to join up to fight in the trenches  There were some, however, including the Coroner who held the inquest on the victims in Scarborough, who asked, 'Where was the Royal Navy?' This was a fair question, for the Navy claimed to have thrown an impenetrable ring of steel around the British Isles.

It is perhaps fortunate that the British public was not aware that the Admiralty knew of the German plan to attack the ports forty-eight hours in advance yet did nothing to prevent it Naval Intelligence learned of the proposed German sortie early on 14 December, but it was decided to let the attack go ahead, the intention being to get behind the German ships and destroy them on their way back to the Jade. When von Hipper's squadron sailed on the night of the 14th, Rear-Admiral Sir David Beatty was already at sea with four battlecruisers, backed by six super-dreadnoughts of the Grand Fleet, three armoured cruisers, six light cruisers and a flotilla of destroyers. Eight submarines were also sent to take up station off Terschelling, to torpedo any German ships lucky enough to escape the British trap.

Even allowing for the deliberate sacrifice of lives in the north-east ports, it was a good plan, and it should have resulted in the complete destruction of the German squadron – had it not been for the intervention of the weather. At one point British destroyers did make contact with German destroyers, but the visibility was so poor and the sea so rough that the engagement was brief and inconclusive Meanwhile von Hipper's battlecruisers had done their work and were racing back across the North Sea before Beatty, wary of the shallow waters of the Dogger Bank and minefields reported in the area, could close the trap

The next time von Hipper ventured out into the North Sea he found that his luck had run out. As before, British Naval Intelligence had been reading the German ciphers, and when von Hipper's squadron left the Jade in the evening of 15 January 1915 a warning was immediately flashed to the Admiralty. This time there would be no provocative bombardment of civilian targets, the German admiral's orders being to make a sweep of the Dogger Bank area to create maximum havoc amongst the British fishing fleet and to attack any British naval patrols met with.

The Dogger Bank is a 160-mile long area of shoal water in the North Sea lying sixty miles out from Flamborough Head There is a minimum depth of water of around six fathoms, but much of the bank has 10–20 fathoms. Overall is an abundance of fish, making the Dogger Bank one of the richest fishing grounds in the world. Its name comes from the Dutch word *dogger*, meaning trawler. The British and Dutch fleets fought a famous battle on the bank in 1781, and in October 1904 the Russian Fleet, on its way to meet the Japanese at Tsushima, fired on a concentration of Hull trawlers, believing them to be Japanese torpedo boats. In January 1915 the Dutch and the Russians were long departed, but the Hull fishing boats were still on the bank, apparently undisturbed by the rumblings of war all around them.

At 5 45 p m. on 23 January 1915, some six hours after British Naval Intelligence had decoded his orders from the Admiralstab, von Hipper left Jade Bay for the Dogger Bank with the First and Second Scouting Groups. He flew his flag in the 24,640-ton battlecruiser *Seydlitz*, armed with ten 11-inch, twelve 5 9-inch and twelve 3 4-inch guns. The others in the First Group were the 22,640-ton *Moltke*, with an armament similar to that of the *Seydlitz*, the 28,000-ton *Derfflinger*, mounting eight 12-inch, twelve 5.9-inch and twelve 3.4-inch, and the *Blücher*, a 15,550-ton battlecruiser armed with twelve 8.2-inch, eight 5 9-inch and sixteen 3 4-inch guns The *Seydlitz*, *Moltke* and *Derfflinger* were all said to be capable of 28 knots, while the *Blücher*, no more than a large armoured cruiser by Royal Navy standards, could make only 23. The *Blücher* was the weak link in von Hipper's squadron, and she would not have been with him but for the detention in dry dock for repairs of the larger *Von der Tann*. The Second Scouting Group consisted of the light cruisers *Stralsund*, *Graudenz*, *Rostock* and *Kolberg*. Each group was accompanied by a flotilla of eleven destroyers and the complete raiding force totalled 30 ships.

Forewarned, the Admiralty saw this latest foray by the German Fleet as an opportunity to take revenge for Scarborough and Hartlepool and ordered Beatty to sail from Rosyth with his battlecruiser squadron. With him would go the 1st Light Cruiser Squadron, and three more light cruisers and 35 destroyers were dispatched from Harwich to lend support As an additional precaution, but to remain at a distance unless called in to help, Admiral Jellicoe sailed from Scapa Flow with a substantial force of battleships, cruisers and destroyers. Other destroyers, torpedo boats and submarines were ordered in to complete the net into which it was hoped that von Hipper would sail

Beatty arrived to the north of the Dogger Bank before dawn on the 24th with three squadrons of ships. The 1st Battle Cruiser Squadron was made up of the sister ships *Lion* (flag) and *Princess Royal*, each of 26,350 tons and mounting eight 13.5-inch and sixteen 6-inch guns, and the 28,000-ton *Tiger*, with eight 13.5-inch and twelve 6-inch guns. The 2nd Battle Cruiser Squadron, commanded by Rear-Admiral Sir Archibald Moore, consisted of the *New Zealand* (flag) of 18,800 tons, carrying eight 12-inch and sixteen 4-inch guns, and the similarly armed, 17,250-ton *Indomitable*. The *Lion*, *Princess Royal* and *Tiger* were 28-knot ships, while the smaller battlecruisers had a top speed of 26 knots Of the big five, HMS *Tiger*, commanded by Captain Henry Pelly, was the newest and biggest, but for some reason known only to the Admiralty she was manned by a scratch crew containing a large number of fugitives from the Navy's jails Her fitness for battle was therefore in question. Beatty's big ships were supported by the 1st Light Cruiser Squadron, the victors of the Battle of Heligoland Bight, *Southampton* (flag), *Nottingham*, *Birmingham* and *Lowestoft*, still under the command of Commodore William Goodenough.

At 7 a.m. a rendezvous was made to the north-east of the Dogger Bank with those other Heligoland veterans, the Harwich Force, commanded by Commodore Reginald Tyrwhitt in the light cruiser *Arethusa* Beatty now had at his disposal a powerful force made up of five battlecruisers, seven light cruisers and 35 destroyers As he set off on an easterly course to seek out the enemy again, the British admiral was determined not to repeat the fiasco of the previous month

The weather was unseasonably fair, with a light north-easterly wind and visibility so good that it was limited only by the curve of the horizon – a pleasant change from the usual winter murk of the North Sea. At 7.25 the light cruiser *Aurora* (Captain Wilmot Nicholson), trawling thirteen miles to the south of the main force with a flotilla of destroyers, reported by wireless that she was in touch with the enemy. A few minutes later the flashes of her guns were seen on the bridge of HMS *Lion*.

Nicholson had sighted a three-funnel cruiser accompanied by four destroyers, which he first took to be the *Arethusa* and part of the Harwich Force But when challenged by lamp the cruiser opened fire on the *Aurora*, much to Nicholson's consternation He had in fact stumbled on one of his opposite numbers, the German light cruiser *Kolberg*, scouting to the north of von Hipper's squadron.

The 4,350-ton *Kolberg*, armed with twelve 4.1-inch guns and having a top speed of 27 knots, found the range quickly and scored three hits on the *Aurora* in succession, fortunately without inflicting serious damage or casualties. Recovering from her surprise, the *Aurora* returned the German cruiser's fire, and for the next ten minutes the two ships fought a duel with their evenly matched guns. In the end, the *Aurora*'s gunnery proved superior, and she was hitting the *Kolberg* hard. The fight ended abruptly at about 7.25 when a British shell hit the *Kolberg*'s bridge, causing extensive damage and killing two men. This was too much for the German commander, who sheered away and ran for home at full speed. Nicholson was tempted to give chase, but he had sighted more enemy ships to starboard, and in accordance with his orders he turned northwards to rejoin Beatty

Beatty was already leading his ships towards the sound of the guns, increasing speed to 22 knots. In doing so, he was unwittingly steaming into the thick of a German minefield. However, by dint of good luck or defective mines – the truth will never be known – the British ships sailed through the field unharmed. Von Hipper, meanwhile, seeing the danger he was running into, had also turned for home, signalling ahead by wireless to Wilhelmshaven that he needed support from heavier ships. The Admiralstab, unfortunately, were unaware that the British had been reading their ciphers and had laid no contingency plans for supporting von Hipper's sortie The best they could do was to order the battleships of the High Seas Fleet, then lying at anchor in Jade Bay, to prepare for sea at once. Given that these big ships would take many hours to raise steam, this was a somewhat futile gesture

For the moment, however, von Hipper was not unduly concerned at his predicament He was fourteen miles ahead of the British ships, which from call signs reported by his wireless office he identified as Rear-Admiral Moore's 2nd Battle Cruiser Squadron, over which his own ships had a considerable advantage of speed Heavy smoke trailing astern from the German ships made visual confirmation of the British force difficult, but von Hipper was so confident of his advantage that he did not bother to increase to maximum speed.

It was not until 8 40 that von Hipper became aware that the British ships were steadily gaining on him, and that they were in fact Beatty's battlecruisers – ships that he could not easily outrun. He at once increased speed, but although the *Seydlitz* and *Moltke* were able to reach 27 knots, the *Derfflinger* was slightly slower and the *Blücher* was hard pressed to make 23 knots Consequently the German ships, which had been steaming in line abreast, became strung out in a ragged line astern. The *Seydlitz* was leading, closely followed by the *Moltke*, then, with an ever-widening gap, by the *Derfflinger*; the *Blücher*, her funnels glowing red hot, brought up the rear, looking and feeling dangerously vulnerable.

Beatty settled down to what might be a long chase, increasing the speed of his battlecruisers from 24 to 25 knots and then to 26. Finally he passed the order for 29 knots, knowing full well that none of his ships could achieve such a speed. But the inference was obvious – he wanted maximum effort, and this he got, the *Lion, Tiger* and *Princess Royal* eventually reaching an unprecedented 28½ knots Even the *New Zealand* and *Indomitable*, although they were still lagging behind, far exceeded their designated speeds.

To an observer looking down from the skies on this fine winter's morning – one such was the German Naval Zeppelin *L5* – the sight the two squadrons of sleek, grey ships racing each other across the North Sea must have been awe-inspiring The big ships, their guns raised to maximum elevation awaiting the order to fire, burned prodigious amounts of fuel as they strained, the Germans to escape and the British to overtake All around them, on the horizon, destroyers and cruisers of both flags hovered, uncertain of their roles.

The *Blücher*, lagging well behind the others and losing ground all the time, was the first to open fire A single ranging shot, fired in desperation, fell a mile short of HMS *Lion*, twelve and a half miles astern on the German battlecruiser's starboard quarter and gaining. The echo of the *Blücher*'s gun died away and the uneasy silence, broken only by the muffled beat of powerful engines and the urgent thrashing of propellers, descended on the sea again At 8 52, with the range at an estimated 20,000 yards, Beatty became impatient and decided to try his luck. The first shell, fired from the *Lion*'s 'B' turret, fell short of the *Blücher* but the second, fired two minutes later, fell over, thereby establishing the range with a fair degree of accuracy. Firing continued, using the same 13.5-inch gun. The fourth shot produced a cloud of yellow smoke from the fleeing battlecruiser's stern It was a direct hit, and, at just under 20,000 yards, the longest range then recorded for a hit between two ships in action This did not bode well for von Hipper's squadron

Beatty's shell had struck below the *Blücher*'s waterline, and this was to be the beginning of her end. Her speed fell off and she lagged further behind the others, eventually coming under the combined fire of the three leading British battlecruisers, the *Lion*, *Tiger* and *Princess Royal*, with the *New Zealand* joining in as soon as she was within gun range In an effort to postpone the inevitable, von Hipper ordered the rest of his squadron to open fire. Unfortunately for Beatty, the German ships were partially blinded by their own smoke streaming astern, the *Lion* being the only enemy ship of which they had a clear sight. The *Moltke*, *Derfflinger* and *Seydlitz* concentrated their fire on her.

For a while the two ships, the *Blücher* on the German side and the *Lion* on the British, took the full brunt of the opposing salvos. The *Blücher* was hit repeatedly, while Beatty's flagship had her first taste of the enemy's fire power when, at 9 30, an 11-inch German shell slammed into her hull amidships, just below the waterline. She staggered under the shock of the explosion, but luckily the hit was absorbed by one of the battlecruiser's side coal bunkers; a wing compartment was flooded, but the damage was localized and not severe

The distance between the two squadrons continued to decrease slowly but steadily, and Beatty signalled his battlecruisers to engage their opposite numbers in the German line. It was his intention that the *Lion* should tackle the *Seydlitz*, the *Tiger* the *Moltke* and the *Princess Royal* the *Derfflinger*, leaving the *Blücher* to the slower and more lightly armed *New Zealand* and *Indomitable* The plan was sound, but because of poor communications – which was becoming an all too frequent weakness in ships of the Royal Navy – it was

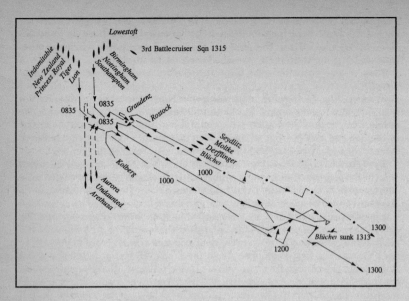

*Dogger Bank, 24 January 1915*

badly executed, with the result that the *Lion* and *Tiger* both ended up engaging the *Seydlitz* while the other battlecruisers all concentrated their fire on the crippled *Blücher*.

At 9.30 the *Seydlitz* came very near to complete destruction when one of the *Lion*'s 13.5-inch shells, nearing the end of its trajectory, plunged through her quarterdeck and pierced the 9-inch armour of her aftermost turret at the level of the working chamber. The charges then being brought up were ignited by the explosion, the flash shooting upwards in the gunhouse and downwards into the magazine. In both chambers the charges being handled caught fire. The crew of the magazine tried to escape by opening doors into the handling room of the adjacent turret and so allowed the flash to set fire to the charges there. The fire spread to the adjoining magazines and upwards as far as the gunhouse. The explosion wiped out the crews of both turrets, 160 men in all, and only prompt action in flooding the magazines saved the *Seydlitz* from being blown apart.

Von Hipper now called on his destroyers to lay down a smoke screen, and under cover of the smoke he altered course to the north, hoping to escape from the British battlecruisers. At the same time other German destroyers threatened a torpedo attack on the *Lion* and *Tiger*. Beatty foiled both plans by turning his big guns on the destroyers, which were forced to retire at high speed.

Shortly before 10.00, for some reason known only to himself Beatty ordered the *Lion*, *Tiger* and *Princess Royal* to reduce speed to 24 knots to allow the *New Zealand* and *Indomitable* to close up and take part in the battle. This was a dangerous underestimation of the capability of von Hipper's squadron: although two of his ships were damaged, most of his big guns were still firing and their accuracy was improving all the time  This was clearly shown when the *Lion* was hit by two 11-inch shells from the *Seydlitz*. One of these shells struck the flagship's 'A' turret, disabling one of the 13.5-inch guns, while the other pierced her side armour in way of the engine room, flooded the engineers' workshop and destroyed the after fire control and secondary armament circuits.

The *Derfflinger*, although on fire from one of the *Princess Royal*'s shells, now also turned her guns on the *Lion* and immediately hit her with two 12-inch shells. The shock of the double explosion was so great that those on the bridge of the flagship thought that she had been torpedoed – U-boats were believed to be in the area. The damage was serious enough. The *Derfflinger*'s shells had pierced the *Lion*'s 5-inch thick hull armour below the waterline, holed the feed tank of the port condenser and flooded it with salt water. In order to avoid even more catastrophic damage, the battlecruiser's boiler fires were drawn, and, with an 11-degree list to port, she slowed to a crawl.

The *Lion* now became an easy target for the guns of von Hipper's ships, the *Seydlitz*, *Moltke* and *Derfflinger* all hurling shells at her  Beatty's Staff Commander reported:

> The whole ship seemed to lift and shake violently as the projectiles struck us  From these reports, of armour belt pierced on the waterline in several places, switchboard room flooded, port engine reducing speed and shortly to stop, 'A' turret magazine on fire, ship making water heavily along port side, all lights gone out, it was clear that we could not continue long in action, while it was more possible that within a few minutes we should be projected heavenwards by the magazines exploding
>
> The Admiral gave the order to flood it and turned to me, saying, 'I wonder what we should do next?' Not liking to suggest hauling out of line, but feeling that we ought to do so, I replied, 'Reduce speed and repair our damage, get the fires put out, and then resume our place in the line ' The Captain was accordingly ordered to do this and we slowly dropped back, still wondering when the magazine was going to explode

Since the action had begun, the *Lion* had been hit by sixteen heavy shells and her survival was now in question  At 10.54, when Beatty personally sighted the periscope on the battlecruiser's starboard bow, he panicked and ordered the whole squadron to make an emergency turn 90 degrees to port. After a while he ordered the other ships to continue the chase, but they had by now lost precious ground and the German battlecruisers, with the exception of the *Blücher*, were drawing away. Meanwhile Beatty had taken the crippled *Lion* out of the line, and after steaming to the north-west for half an hour he called the destroyer *Attack* alongside and boarded her with the intention of re-joining the squadron.

The *Blücher*, with only two of her heavy guns in action, and on fire in several places, was straggling in the wake of the fleeing German squadron at 17 knots. Recognizing her plight, von Hipper turned the *Seydlitz* about to go to her assistance. Then he thought better of it and resumed his course. The *Seydlitz* herself was really in no fit condition to help anyone  Two of her turrets were out of action, she was holed aft and making water and she was running short of ammunition for her 11-inch guns. Rather than sacrifice two ships – for he had accepted that the battle was lost – von Hipper reluctantly decided to leave the *Blücher* to her fate.

The *Blücher*, however, was far from finished. Commodore Tyrwhitt discovered this when, as Beatty's battlecruisers made their emergency turn-away, he took his destroyers in to torpedo the apparently helpless German ship. HMS *Meteor* was the first to run in, but as soon as she came close to the *Blücher* the latter hit back like a wounded animal at bay, putting a well-aimed 8.2-inch shell into the *Meteor*'s boiler room and causing so much damage that the destroyer was put out of the fight. Tyrwhitt pulled his ships out of range, but after a while tried again, sending in three destroyers for a simultaneous attack At the same time he took the *Arethusa* to within 2,500 yards of the *Blücher* and opened fire with his 6-inch guns. This coincided with the British battlecruisers' resumption of the chase, and the *Tiger*, *Princess Royal*, *New Zealand* and *Indomitable* all opened up on the German with their big guns Anyone else within range also joined in.

Seen in hindsight the situation was farcical, with four British battlecruisers, four light cruisers and a host of destroyers all concentrating the enormous combined firepower on one rather insignificant German battlecruiser already near the end of her tether And while this was going on the bigger German ships were disappearing over the horizon, bound for the sanctuary of Jade Bay Much of the confusion was due to the absence of Admiral Beatty, who was then aboard the *Attack*, racing to re-join the action. Beatty's plan had been for the *Tiger*, *Princess Royal* and *New Zealand* to go after von Hipper's faster and heavier ships while the slower *Indomitable* finished off the *Blücher* in her own time However, Beatty had omitted to take Rear-Admiral Moore, then temporarily in command of the squadron, into his confidence.

The *Blücher*'s last remaining gun was silenced just before noon, by which time she was a inferno, having been hit by more than seventy shells and several torpedoes. At 12 10, as Beatty boarded HMS *Princess Royal* and ran up his flag, the gallant *Blücher* finally succumbed to her terrible wounds, capsized and sank in a cloud of steam as her fires were quenched by the cold waters of the North Sea Tyrwhitt immediately took the *Arethusa* in to the rescue and with the help of some of his destroyers picked up 260 German survivors, More would have been saved had it not been for Zeppelin *L5* and a patrolling seaplane from Borkum, which bombed and machine-gunned the rescue boats, killing many Germans in the process Of the 1,130 men on board the *Blücher*, 29 officers and 841 ratings lost their lives

Beatty's first thought on re-joining his squadron was to resume the chase of von Hipper's remaining battlecruisers, but they were by then so far ahead that it would have been impossible to catch them before they came under the protection of the guns of Heligoland. He therefore regrouped his ships and turned for home. When he came up with the *Lion* again, she was heading west on one engine at 12 knots and losing speed all the time. It was doubtful whether she would make Rosyth under her own steam, and left alone she would be easy prey for marauding U-boats. Beatty therefore ordered the *Indomitable* to take her in tow As darkness fell over the North Sea, HMS *Lion*, one of the Royal Navy's finest, surrounded by a protective screen of cruisers and destroyers, wallowed at the end of a long towline on her ignominious journey home

The running fight, which began off the Dogger Bank in the morning of 24 January 1915, lasted for over three hours and covered nearly 100 miles of the North Sea It provided a rare opportunity for the British Fleet to score a decisive victory over the Germans, but it was an opportunity missed. Conditions were ideal for a sea battle, and Beatty's ships outnumbered and outgunned von Hipper's squadron, yet they failed to annihilate it. A series of misread signals and an apparent inability of individual commanders to take the initiative brought the action into chaos and resulted in four large battlecruisers, armed with 12-inch and 13.5-inch guns, expending all their efforts on pounding the comparatively insignificant *Blücher* into submission In the meantime the real prizes, the *Seydlitz*, *Moltke* and *Derfflinger*, escaped Much of the blame for the fiasco can be laid on Admiral Beatty's shoulders It was his fear – almost an obsession, it was said – of a U-boat attack that prompted him to make the emergency turn when he thought he saw a periscope that resulted in the chase being abandoned. (It was later established that there was no German submarine within sixty miles of the British squadron on the 24th )

But what really decided the outcome of the day was how the shells were fired and how they landed. Although the German guns were of smaller calibre than the British, their fire was rapid and accurate. The British gunnery, on the other hand, was lamentable Before she was knocked out of the fight the *Lion* had fired 235 shells from her big guns and registered only three hits. Admittedly, one of these projectiles caused major damage to the *Seydlitz*, but the effort expended was enormous for the result achieved. In the matter of blood spilt, the German squadron came off very much the worse, losing 954 killed and with 260 wounded On the British side, the *Lion* suffered only 11 wounded, the *Tiger* lost the Squadron Engineer, Captain (E) C. G. Taylor, and nine others, with eight wounded, while four men were killed and two wounded in the destroyer *Meteor*

The loyal British press saw the Battle of Dogger Bank in a different light. On the 25th *The Times*, with typical patriotic fervour, said:

The engagement illustrates the manner in which the Fleet protects the coast, and how a much more effective reply to attempts at raiding may be made by an active patrol than by a number of scattered flotillas of no great strength Altogether, the chase and its result are a brilliant affair on which the country will concur with their Lordships in congratulating Sir David Beatty and all concerned

# 7

# Königsberg

*6 July 1915*

In July 1914, as the clouds of war gathered on the horizon to the west, the German light cruiser *Königsberg* lay in the East African port of Dar-es-Salaam awaiting orders  It was a time of worrying uncertainty for her commander, Fregattenkapitän Max Looff  The narrow approach channel to the port gave some protection from attack, but this might easily be blocked by a determined enemy, leaving the *Königsberg* to gather weed and barnacles in the warm, fecund waters of the harbour. On the other hand, there were far worse places than Dar-es-Salaam to sit out what might be a very bloody war.

Dar-es-Salaam, then the capital of German East Africa, lies seven degrees south of the Equator and in sight of the island of Zanzibar, whose ruler founded the port in 1862. The climate in the area is for the most part hot and humid, although the town does enjoy a good sea breeze. In 1914 the population of Dar-es-Salaam was 52,350, of which 200 were European, and it was the centre of a flourishing shipping industry carried on by Arab dhows trading to and from ports in the Persian Gulf. The town was well laid out with typical German precision, the buildings were clean and architecturally attractive and the streets were broad, well-kept avenues lined by rustling coconut palms. There were four good hotels and a nine-hole golf course, the Moloo Brothers offered a fine line in 'everything most fashionable and up to date' in their emporium and the extensive botanical gardens were lit at night by electric light  On the foreshore, where it enjoyed the full benefit of the sea breezes, was an excellent European hospital. The Arabic-Swahili name Dar-es-Salaam translates into English as 'Haven of Peace', and in the summer of 1914, with the world tottering on the brink of war, this must have had a special significance for many who sailed in the *Königsberg*. But, much as Fregattenkapitän Looff enjoyed the golf and his evening strolls in the illuminated botanical gardens, he knew the time had come for his ship to fulfil the role she had been created for  Looff was ready to go to sea.

SMS *Königsberg*, built at Kiel in 1905, was a light cruiser of 3,400 tons, armed with ten 4.1-inch guns, eight 5-pounders, four machine guns and two torpedo tubes. Her pair of three-cylinder, triple-expansion steam engines developed 13,200 indicated horsepower, giving her a top speed of 23.5 knots. She matched in all respects her ill-fated sister ship *Nürnberg*, at that time at Tsingtao with Konteradmiral von Spee's East Asiatic Squadron.

In July 1914 the *Königsberg* was the only German warship of any account in the Indian Ocean. When the signal was given, Looff was confident that she would create havoc among the fleets of British merchantmen that criss-crossed the ocean on their way to and from the outposts of Britannia's Empire. As to the inevitable hue and cry that would result as soon as the cruiser began her work, Looff was not unduly troubled The Indian Ocean occupied 33 million square miles and had innumerable bays, creeks, rivers and lonely islands where a fugitive ship might hide herself – and, such were Britain's commitments at the time, the ships of the Royal Navy on station were few and far-stretched. Looff's latest intelligence was that the only threat he might face would come from Rear-Admiral Sir Richard Pierse's East Indies Squadron or Rear-Admiral Herbert King-Hall's Cape Squadron, neither of which was impressive. Pierse had only the small pre-dreadnought *Swiftsure*, the light cruiser *Dartmouth* and the obsolescent cruiser *Fox*, while King-Hall had the cruisers *Astraea*, *Hyacinth* and *Pegasus*, all of them ships that had grown old and decrepit in the service of the Empire. It appeared to Looff that the greatest threat to the *Königsberg*'s success might be the scarcity of suitable coaling stations, for Germany had few friends in the Indian Ocean outside her only colony

On 31 July, four days before the outbreak of war, Looff received orders from the Admiralstab in Berlin to put to sea The *Königsberg* being already fully fuelled and provisioned, he left Dar-es-Salaam without delay His departure was not before time, for a few days later King-Hall's cruisers *Astraea* and *Pegasus* appeared off the port and began to bombard it The British cruisers were Boer War-vintage ships, each armed with eight 4-inch guns of even older origin, but they created havoc in Dar-es-Salaam. Their shells succeeded in destroying only the wireless station and the Governor's house, but in the ensuing panic the harbourmaster scuttled the floating dry dock in the entrance channel. The net result was that the *Königsberg* was denied access to the only German port in the area and suffered the loss of her local communications link. From then on, the German cruiser was truly on her own.

Unaware of the enemy raid on his home base, Looff had taken the *Königsberg* north into the Gulf of Aden, where on 6 August he captured the British merchantman *City of Winchester*, bound from Colombo to London with a full cargo of tea. The prize was escorted to the deserted anchorage of Makalla on the coast of Oman, where the *Königsberg* was joined by the German armed merchantman *Zieten*. The *City of Winchester*'s passengers were transferred to the *Zieten*, her coal and provisions were shared out between the two ships and she was then taken out to sea and scuttled She went to the bottom, taking her cargo, the entire tea crop of Ceylon for the year, with her

The capture and sinking of the *City of Winchester* caused consternation in shipping circles and resulted in all British ships being diverted away from the Gulf of Aden unless heavily escorted. The hunt was also on for the *Königsberg*, and Looff was obliged to move south again to avoid discovery. For the next six weeks the cruiser lay hidden in the delta of the River Rufigi, a maze of salt-water creeks, with good cover provided by mangroves, some 80 miles south of Dar-es-Salaam The decision to lay up the *Königsberg* in this muddy backwater for such a long period is hard to understand Her removal from active service coincided with the arrival in the Indian Ocean of the *Emden*, and had these two formidable ships joined forces they would undoubtedly have created mayhem among Britain's vital trade routes As it was, the *Emden* did very well on her own, sinking seven ships, totalling 34,000 tons gross, in the time the *Königsberg* was laid up.

It was 19 December before Looff put to sea again, and he did so then only because an opportunity arose to exact revenge for the British bombardment of Dar-es-Salaam in the previous August. Word had reached Looff that HMS *Pegasus*, one of the two cruisers involved, was anchored off Zanzibar cleaning her boiler tubes, an operation involving the complete immobilization of a ship's engines This was a chance too good to miss, and Looff left the Rufigi before sunset on the 19th, arriving off Zanzibar at daybreak on the 20th.

Zanzibar's harbour provides a good, safe anchorage for large ships, being protected from the weather by the island itself in the east and by the mainland of Africa, only sixteen miles away, in the west. This being so, Commander John Ingles, with two anchors down, had no hesitation in immobilizing the *Pegasus'* engines while his crew went ahead with the boiler cleaning. The anchorage was not crowded, the only other occupants being the collier *Kilwa* and a handful of dhows and small native craft. Ingles had no reports of any enemy warships in the area, but, like many others, he was puzzled by the apparent disappearance of the *Königsberg*, and as a precaution against the unlikely event of a surprise attack he stationed an armed tug on patrol outside the harbour.

It may have been that the men manning the guard ship shared Ingles' opinion of the unlikelihood of an enemy attack, for they were certainly not fully alert before dawn on the 20th. The boarding party from the *Königsberg* caught them completely unawares and they were staring down the barrels of German rifles before they could lift a finger to raise the alarm

At 05.15, in the first light of the dawn, Commander Ingles was rudely awakened by the sound of gunfire and ran out on deck to find shells from the *Königsberg*'s 4-inch guns sending up fountains of water all around the anchored *Pegasus*. Ingles sent his bewildered men to action stations and the British ship's guns began to shoot back, but the advantage was with the *Königsberg* Unable to use her engines, the *Pegasus* was an easy target, and her guns were silenced one by one. Only fifteen minutes after the action started the British cruiser was on fire and taking water through several holes in her side, and many of her crew were lying dead or wounded. Commander John Ingles suffered the humiliation of having to haul down his flag to save those still living.

The *Pegasus* was listing heavily and appeared to be in imminent danger of sinking when Ingles ordered his men to abandon ship This they did, first lowering the wounded into the boats with German shells still bursting all around them. Looff appeared not to have seen the British flag lowered, or else he chose to ignore it. He did not cease fire until he saw the boats leaving the side of the *Pegasus*. Then, presumably satisfied that he had done enough to avenge Dar-es-Salaam, the German commander steamed away

As soon as the enemy was out of sight, Ingles lost no time in reboarding his battered ship He then used the collier *Kilwa* to tow the *Pegasus* across the harbour to a sand spit, where she grounded bow-on But the old cruiser had fought her last battle. The sand spit was steep-to, and she slipped off, capsized and sank. Her casualty list was heavy – 42 killed and 60 wounded. When news reached the Admiralty in London of this audacious attack on a British ship in a British harbour, there was an immediate call for revenge: the *Königsberg* must be found and dealt with once and for all

Max Looff was fully aware that his foray into Zanzibar harbour would cause a furore, and he returned at once to the shelter of the Rufigi delta, taking with him a supply ship, the small merchantman *Somali*. It was now found that the *Königsberg*'s engines required a major overhaul, involving the machining of some parts in the workshops at Dar-es-Salaam. This meant a prolonged immobilization, and Looff had no intention of allowing his ship to suffer the same fate as the *Pegasus*. With this in mind, he took the *Königsberg* further up river to a secluded creek, where she would be well hidden from seaward and under the protection of German land forces in the colony.

Long before the outbreak of war, the German Government had accepted that its territory in East Africa would be cut off from all outside help, except from the sea. To the west was the Belgian Congo, to the north British East Africa and to the south Rhodesia and Portuguese East Africa, all potentially hostile. It was therefore given to Colonel Paul von Lettow-Vorbeck, the Military Governor, to recruit and train a local force for the defence of the colony His task was not difficult The white male population was around 3,500, most of them young men, while there were over 7 million natives, from predominantly warlike tribes By the summer of 1914 von Lettow-Vorbeck had at his disposal a force comprising 2,000 German officers and up to 20,000 Askaris, armed with rifles, 70 machine-guns and 40 field guns British troops, striking south from British East Africa, attacked the port of Tanga in early November but suffered heavy casualties when they met up with von Lettow-Vorbeck's army and were forced to withdraw Another fourteen months would pass before the frontier was crossed by British troops again Meanwhile the *Königsberg* rested safe in her jungle hiding place

The mangrove swamps of the Rufigi delta are not a place for the white man to linger The climate is hot and oppressive, with the rumble of thunder constantly in the air, and rain is frequent and torrential In 1914 malaria was rife in the delta, the plague, sleeping sickness and smallpox were endemic and there was the added danger of rampant syphilis among the local population In the shallow water of the creeks, crocodiles up to fourteen feet in length cruised with watchful eyes, ready to devour scraps of food thrown overboard, and any unfortunate human who should be foolish enough to take to the water On shore a dozen different varieties of highly poisonous snakes lurked in the mangroves In these circumstances Looff did not propose to hold his ship in the higher reaches of the delta a day longer than necessary.

While the *Königsberg* languished in her uninviting hide-out, far across the seas, on the Western Front, the Allies found themselves waging a war they might well lose The Belgian Army, poorly trained and equipped, had collapsed before the German steamroller, while British and French troops, dug in on a line that ran from the Channel to Verdun, fought with a courage born of desperation to halt the advance of the Kaiser's rampaging army The line held, but the Allies were outnumbered four to one and the dead piled up obscenely on the narrow strip of scorched earth separating the trenches The British Expeditionary Force, 160,000-strong when it landed in France, had suffered huge casualties and was urgently in need of reinforcement. The only seasoned troops available were in India, and they must be brought home, but so long as the *Königsberg* was at large in the Indian Ocean the risk to any ships carrying them was great. The Admiralty was ordered to find the German raider and put an end to her without delay.

Another seven weeks went by before a squadron was assembled in the Indian Ocean with the specific aim of seeking out the *Königsberg*. This was under the command of Captain S. R. Drury-Lowe and consisted of the light cruisers *Chatham*, *Weymouth* and *Dartmouth*, each armed with eight 6-inch guns and having a top speed of 25½ knots  The cruisers took only ten days to trace the *Königsberg* to her lair in the Rufigi delta, but it was immediately obvious to Drury-Lowe that the destruction of the raider would not be easy.

Looff had chosen his hiding place well  Although the *Königsberg* was in deep water and only a dozen miles from the sea, the thick mangroves concealed her so well that the British cruisers had no clear target on which to sight their guns  As for making a closer approach, it would only be possible for Drury-Lowe's ships to cross the bar of the river, four miles from the sea, at high water springs, the highest high water of the month. An additional hazard lay beyond the bar in the form of a minefield laid by the *Königsberg*'s boats. For the time being the British had to be content with keeping the German raider cooped up in the river while they patrolled outside

After Coronel the Admiralty at one time feared that von Spee might bring his victorious squadron across the Atlantic to the aid of the *Königsberg*. Drury-Lowe was accordingly warned to be on his guard against the raider making a break for the open sea to join up with the German admiral. It was then decided to sink a blockship in the channel leading to the *Königsberg*'s lair, so that, short of the use of a great deal of explosives, she would have no access to the sea. The Admiralty collier *Newbridge* was commandeered, and on 10 November, escorted by armed steam launches and under cover of a bombardment laid down by the cruisers outside, she entered the Rufigi. Commander R. Fitzmaurice, the *Chatham*'s first lieutenant, was in command of the operation.

Looff had been anticipating some such move and had deployed a number of his crew, armed with rifles and machine-guns, on the river banks. They put up a withering fire when the *Newbridge* and her escort approached, but Fitzmaurice was successful in sinking the collier across the channel. Three of his men were killed and a number injured before the expedition withdrew

At the cost of a valuable Admiralty collier and three men, it seemed that the *Königsberg* was now bottled up in the Rufigi for good. But what Captain Drury-Lowe did not know was that the German ship could, with a little careful manoeuvring, still make her escape through another deep-water channel  However, Looff was not ready, for the *Königsberg* had suffered a serious blow during the *Newbridge* action. A 6-inch shell, lobbed blind by one of the cruisers offshore, had hit the supply ship *Somali* and set fire to her  She was burnt to the water, with the loss of all her precious coal and provisions.

Looff had some coal left in lighters, and he used most of this to take the *Königsberg* even further up-river, where, although still within range of the British guns, she was better concealed  The German captain then settled down to what might be a very long siege. But first he needed to attend to the morale of his men, which in this malaria-infested hell-hole of a jungle was in danger

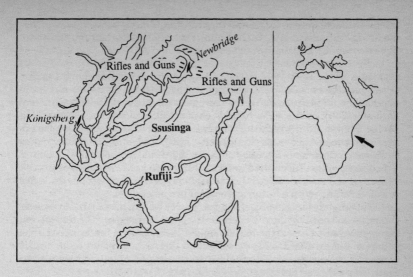

*The End of the* Königsberg, *6 July 1915*

of collapsing  And so he put them to work, some painting ship, others surveying the labyrinth of channels in the river but most of them ashore cutting wood for the ship's boiler furnaces  More than a ton of wood was required every 24 hours, just to keep the *Königsberg*'s pumps and generators working. This was hard, dangerous work – poisonous snakes and hungry crocodiles lurked at every turn – but it allowed the men no time to dwell on their plight.

While Looff may have been content with the stalemate, the Admiralty in London were far from happy. Three of their best light cruisers were tied up watching one enemy ship, and yet, with the havoc created by the *Emden* in mind, it would be the height of folly to call off these watchdogs  Any attempt to mount an assault by armed men in small boats was out of the question, for the *Königsberg*'s crew of 400 had by now been joined by several hundred of von Lettow-Vorbeck's Askaris, who were dug in on the river banks with 37mm guns  The only solution seemed to lie in establishing the exact position of the *Königsberg* and then bombard her into submission from seaward. This would require the services of a spotter aircraft

In 1914 air warfare was in its infancy and the few aircraft involved were, to say the least, primitive. However, in response to Drury-Lowe's request, a Royal Naval Air Service seaplane was sent from Cape Town aboard the *Kinfauns Castle*, a merchantman requisitioned by the Admiralty  The life of the tiny aircraft was short, for although it succeeded in pin-pointing the *Königsberg*'s hideout on the Rufigi and did some spotting for the British gunners, it was soon shot down by fire from the German cruiser.

Christmas 1914 brought little cheer to either side  The British, being out at sea, were spared the mosquitoes, but with the temperature at noon reaching 90°F and the nights only marginally less hot and sticky, the spirit of Yuletide was difficult to conjure up. The Germans sang 'Stille Nacht' and the British 'O Come All Ye Faithful', but, with a distinct lack of Christmas fare on both sides, the celebrations were muted and short-lived.

Early in the New Year, no doubt as a result of the destruction of von Spee's squadron off the Falklands, Berlin ruled that the *Königsberg* must somehow break out and return home. Given that the three British cruisers and a flotilla of smaller craft were outside the Rufigi, and that 'home' lay 9,000 miles away through totally hostile waters, this was an ambitious if not impossible undertaking. However, the *Königsberg* would go nowhere without coal for her boilers, and in an attempt to remedy this shortcoming the collier *Rubens* left Hamburg in February 1915 and slipped out into the Atlantic via the north of Scotland. The master of the *Rubens* had orders to rendezvous with the *Königsberg* 300 miles east of Zanzibar on 8 April – it being assumed that by that time the raider would have cleared the Rufigi and eluded her jailers.

Unfortunately for the collier, and for the *Königsberg*, the Admiralty's code-breakers had been reading the Admiralstab's signals again. The *Rubens* was intercepted and sunk in the Mozambique Channel only a few hundred miles south of the arranged rendezvous. The collier was caught by the cruiser *Hyacinth*, then northbound from Cape Town carrying Admiral Herbert King-Hall, whom the Admiralty had ordered to take charge of the operation off the Rufigi When the *Hyacinth* arrived, the *Chatham* left for Mombasa to coal and the *Dartmouth* returned to the Cape

Admiral King-Hall brought with him a new spotter aircraft, which on 25 April found the *Königsberg* again in the mangrove swamps She had moved to a position nearer to the sea and apparently had steam up, ready to break out In fact Looff had indeed been about to attempt an escape, but he was overruled by the Military Governor, Colonel von Lettow-Vorbeck The colonel, in desperate need of men to stem a British invasion from the north, had commandeered all but 220 of the *Königsberg*'s crew to form a naval defence force. This left Looff with just enough personnel to man his ship but insufficient to take her to sea. When the British spotter plane sighted the *Königsberg* she was preparing to move back up-river, where Looff meant to surround her with defences If his ship was doomed to end her days in this African swampland, then he was determined to hold out for as long as possible. In doing so he would tie up valuable British warships sorely needed elsewhere.

Admiral King-Hall had other ideas. He requested the Admiralty to send out more aircraft and two shallow-draught monitors, with which he intended to mount a combined air/sea assault on the *Königsberg*. The Admiralty responded by dispatching two 'River' class monitors, HMS *Severn* and HMS *Mersey*. These two ships, each of 1,260 tons displacement, 290 feet long and 42 feet in the beam, drew only five feet of water and were ideally suited to penetrate far up the Rufigi They each mounted two 6-inch guns and a 5-inch howitzer, the combined firepower of which would be devastating When it came to a long sea voyage, however, the monitors, designed for work in the English Channel, faced great difficulties Their top speed was only 12 knots (and this they could maintain for only short periods), they carried less than 300 tons of fuel and they were notoriously unstable. On the voyage out to East Africa, via the Mediterranean and the Suez Canal, the *Severn* (Commander Eric Fullerton) and the

*Mersey* (Commander R. A. Wilson) were towed by four ocean-going tugs and accompanied by the auxiliary cruiser HMS *Kent*. It was a long and arduous voyage, and it was 2 June before the small convoy arrived off the Rufigi to join King-Hall and his ships already assembled there.

Within a few days of the arrival of the monitors came the armed merchant cruiser *Laurentic*, a 14,892-ton ex-White Star liner, carrying four Royal Naval Air Service aircraft of improved design and four pilots experienced in aerial spotting. To accommodate the new aircraft an airfield was built on Mafia Island, and they began exercising with the monitors, occasionally flying inland to keep an eye on the *Königsberg*. The heat and humidity proved a great trial for the aircraft, and within a week two of them were unserviceable.

Looff received word of the arrival of the monitors from lookouts on the coast, and the reconnaissance by the aircraft confirmed for him that an attack would not be long in coming In the circumstances there was little he could do in preparation other than be doubly vigilant. Ammunition was kept close to the guns and the observation posts ashore were manned, but otherwise life went on much as it had done for months past, with those not on watch occupied in hunting, fishing and cutting fuel

On 6 July Admiral King-Hall, whose offshore force had been reinforced by the cruisers *Pyramus* and *Pioneer*, judged all his preparations to be complete and dispatched the *Laurentic* to create a diversion by shelling Dar-es-Salaam. He then entered the history books by mounting the first ever combined air and sea operation. That night, as soon as it was dark enough to hide their movements from enemy eyes ashore, the *Severn* and *Mersey*, accompanied by a fleet of thirteen small craft manned by men armed with rifles and machine guns, began a slow approach to the mouth of the Rufigi At about midnight the expedition entered the delta. The vessels anchored until an hour before dawn next morning, when they began a stealthy advance up-river.

Commander Fullerton, who was in command of the expedition, planned to penetrate the river as far as Gengini Island, which was within 10,000 yards of the *Königsberg*'s anchorage From there, with the help of the RNAS spotter planes, it was Fullerton's intention to lob 6-inch shells on to the enemy without coming in range of her smaller-calibre guns. At around 5 20, with the first flush of dawn lightening the sky astern and the mangroves on either bank beginning to take shape out of the shadows, the task force was very near its objective Then von Lettow-Vorbeck's Askaris, who were dug in on both sides of the river, opened up with rifles, machine guns and light field guns.

Fullerton was not taken unawares and immediately returned the fire, using 5-pounder guns mounted on the monitors, while machine guns on the steam launches joined in But the attacking flotilla had been caught in an open stretch of water, and the small boats took heavy punishment before they reached the shelter of Gengini Island. Three boats were sunk and a number of men were killed outright while others, wounded, fell overboard and were swept away by the fast-flowing river.

It was now almost full daylight, light enough for the spotter aircraft to be called in, and they arrived overhead, the roar of their engines adding to the cacophony of gunfire and the terrified screeching of wild animals fleeing the area in blind panic When the cruisers *Weymouth*, *Hyacinth*, *Pyramus* and

*Pioneer* opened up from offshore with their 6-inch guns, even the crocodiles slithered away to find refuge in the thickest mangroves.

At 6.23 Fullerton's monitors, hidden from up-river by Gengini Island, began lobbing shells at the *Königsberg* at a range of about 11,000 yards The spotter planes circled the German cruiser, but they were obliged to fly low and were forced to take violent evasive action to avoid the fierce concentration of small-arms fire coming up at them. Effective communication with the monitors was impossible, and Fullerton's shells went wide. Fregattenkapitän Looff, on the other hand, was better served, being in direct communication by field tele-phone with an observation post on the river bank near Gengini Island. When the *Königsberg*'s guns returned the British fire, the first shells landed on the island only yards short of the two monitors Within minutes they were bracketing the *Severn*.

But the *Mersey* was first to receive a direct hit. At 7.40 a 4-inch shell from the *Königsberg* destroyed her forward 6-inch gun, killing four men and wounding four others. Fire broke out on deck and threatened the ready-use ammunition The monitor was saved from complete destruction only by the brave action of a fire party, which dumped the shells overboard. For the time being at least, the *Mersey* was out of the fight

Fifteen minutes later, the spotter aircraft being at last in communication with the ships, the *Severn* scored the first hit on the *Königsberg*, disabling one of her 4 1-inch guns and killing two of its crew Three more hits followed quickly, one of which demolished the German cruiser's bridge, wounding Looff, two of his officers and a signalman.

Meanwhile, Commander Wilson had turned the *Mersey* about so that she could continue firing with her after gun For a while it looked as though the monitors were gaining the upper hand, but then came a catastrophe, when both the RNAS planes developed engine trouble and were forced to return to their base on Mafia Island. The aircraft were no sooner out of earshot when the *Königsberg*'s fire became so accurate that it was necessary for both the *Severn* and *Mersey* to retire down river before they were sunk.

The monitors continued to shell the *Königsberg* from their new position, but without aerial observation their bombardment was a waste of ammunition. At about 3 o'clock in the afternoon, when the sun was beating down with such intensity that men were collapsing with heat exhaustion, and after the monitors had fired over 600 shells with no appreciable result, Commander Fullerton decided to call it a day. On the way down-river German field guns concealed on the north bank opened fire and the *Mersey* was hit again, but this time the damage was negligible Just before sunset the battered flotilla regained the open sea it had left twenty-four hours earlier, taking back to Admiral King-Hall the news that the *Königsberg* had defeated their efforts

The Admiral was not pleased, but he resolved to try again. In the morning of the 11th, with the RNAS aircraft again airborne, Fullerton entered the Rufigi at 10 40 with the *Severn* and *Mersey* under tow by tugs. The bar was crossed at 11.35 and the monitors came within range of the *Königsberg*'s guns around noon. Looff, guided by observers hidden on the river bank, at once opened fire Again the unfortunate *Mersey* was the target, and she was hit by two 4.1-inch shells, one of which silenced her after gun and wounded two men

Seeing the *Mersey*'s plight, Fullerton signalled Wilson to retire and then manoeuvred the *Severn* in under the shelter of Gengini Island Here she came under intense fire from the *Königsberg* and suffered considerable damage, but she was still able to hit back with the aid of the spotter aircraft The fight that followed was savage and impersonal. Neither ship could see the other: they were like two duellists lobbing hand grenades at each other over a high wall. The *Königsberg* began to get the worst of it and was soon down to four guns as the monitor's shells, spiralling down out of the sun, began to pound her to pieces.

On the German cruiser's shattered bridge Max Looff, already wounded and with shells bursting all around him, ordered his remaining guns to continue firing until their ammunition was gone – he could do no more Soon after he gave this order, a 6-inch shell ploughed into the *Königsberg*'s after magazine, which caught fire and then blew up, turning the after deck into a smouldering scrapheap. The next shell landed on the bridge, severing all communications with the shore and again wounding Looff. The fire control tower was hit, most of its occupants being wounded, and so all co-ordination of the cruiser's remaining guns was lost The end was near.

The fire on the *Königsberg*'s after deck continued to burn fiercely, sending into the air a tall column of black smoke which was visible on the other side of Gengini Island. The *Severn*'s gunners no longer needed the assistance of spotter aircraft to assist in their work of destruction Much of the *Königsberg*'s ammunition had gone up when the magazine was hit, and her two guns still firing were down to a few rounds each The flames from aft began to creep forward, and when Looff went aft to direct firefighting operations a shell landed close by and he was once more wounded, this time seriously

By now the *Königsberg*'s last remaining gun was out of action and Looff gave the order to abandon ship Scuttling charges were laid in the cruiser's engine room, and as her boats pulled away from the ship's side there was a muffled roar. The burning ship settled on the bottom with her ensign still flying

The *Königsberg*'s war had been short and largely unproductive, her only victim being the unfortunate *City of Winchester* She had lost a total of 22 killed and another 48 men had been wounded, but those who survived carried on the war ashore, forming a naval detachment under Colonel von Lettow-Vorbeck. It was said that they salvaged some of the *Königsberg*'s guns and put them to good use against the British in the struggle for control of German East Africa, which continued for another three years

Fregattenkapitän Max Looff recovered from his wounds. It must have been of some satisfaction to him as he lay in his hospital bed that, although he had lost his ship, he had not lost the battle. For ten months the threat posed by the presence of the *Königsberg* in the Rufigi had immobilized much of the British fleet in the Indian Ocean.

# 8

# The Destroyers

*April–December 1917*

On a fine early summer's evening at the end of May 1916 the main battle fleets of Britain and Germany met in the North Sea 80 miles west of the Danish peninsula of Jutland. This, the fleets' first and only confrontation of the war, was a hard-fought, brutal clash in which the British lost three battlecruisers, three armoured cruisers and eight destroyers. German losses were only one old battleship, one battlecruiser, four light cruisers and five destroyers Numerically, then, the Battle of Jutland was a victory for Germany, but its end result was that her High Seas Fleet never again ventured out to challenge the Royal Navy For the remainder of the war the U-boats carried the flag for the Imperial Navy, and did so with such ruthless efficiency that they came near to severing Britain's maritime lifelines

Following the sinking without warning by a U-boat of the Cunard liner *Lusitania* in May 1915 with the loss of 1,198 lives, some of them American, the United States Government threatened to break off all diplomatic relations with Germany This was a threat not to be ignored, and the Admiralstab ordered all U-boats to thereafter conduct the blockade strictly in accordance with the rules laid down in the 1907 Hague Convention. This specified that a submarine must challenge a merchant ship on the surface before sinking her. At the same time the British had blocked off the Dover Strait with anti-submarine nets and mines, thus denying the U-boats easy access to the Irish Sea and Western Approaches, where their best hunting grounds lay. They had no alternative but to go north-about, thus reducing the time they could spend at sea by up to a week. The net result of all this was a considerable blunting of the U-boat weapon. British shipping losses alone fell by 20 per cent, to less than 57,000 tons a month.

After Jutland the Admiralstab ordered the U-boats to revert to unrestricted warfare against Allied merchant shipping and to force the passage of the Dover Strait whenever possible. In order to assist the U-boats to run the gauntlet of the strait, the German destroyer force based in the Belgian ports was doubled and deliberate attacks were mounted on the Royal Navy's Dover Patrol to divert its attention

The Dover Strait, gateway to the Continental ports, has always been one of the world's busiest through waterways In 1916 the through traffic was reduced to the occasional convoy, but a constant stream of ships flowed between Dover and Calais and between Folkestone and Boulogne, carrying men and munitions to feed the insatiable appetite of the Flanders battlefields. At the eastern end of the strait, tucked in behind the South Foreland, lies the sheltered anchorage of the Downs, then in use as an assembly area for convoys and often full of merchant shipping. The Dover Patrol, formed in 1914 to protect these vital waters, at first consisted of a motley collection of armed trawlers, but by the autumn of 1916, under the command of Vice-Admiral Reginald Bacon, it had become a powerful force comprising two light cruisers, 24 destroyers, eight fast patrol boats and a number of armed trawlers and drifters Also under Bacon's command were fourteen monitors each mounting two 15-inch guns and used for bombarding German shore installations

German attacks on shipping in the Dover Strait and the Downs took the form of fast hit-and-run raids, destroyers based at Zeebrugge taking advantage of the dark hours to dash in, create havoc and race home again before being challenged. In early 1917 the Admiralty Listening Service succeeded in breaking the German destroyer codes and was able to give warning to the Dover Patrol of their approach Some British successes followed, raids being repulsed during the nights of 22/23 January and 17/18 March However, in the second raid the destroyer HMS *Paragon* was sunk, and this prompted the formation of a special force of four destroyer flotilla leaders, HMS *Botha*, *Broke*, *Faulkner* and *Swift*. Two of these ships were to patrol the Dover Strait around the clock, on the lookout for German hit-and-run raiders On 20 April it was the turn of the *Swift* and *Broke* to take the night watch.

At 2,170 tons HMS Swift was closer to a light cruiser than a destroyer. She was one of an experimental class launched by Cammell Laird of Birkenhead in 1907, with 30,000 shaft horsepower engines giving her a top speed of 36 knots In addition to four 4-inch guns, she also mounted a 6-inch gun forward Her commander was 41-year-old Commander Ambrose Peck, a gunnery specialist with 26 years' service in the Royal Navy. HMS *Broke* was also in a class of her own Built by Vickers-Armstrong in 1912 for the Chilean Navy as the *Almirante Uribe*, she was requisitioned by the Admiralty at the outbreak of war and renamed after Sir Philip Broke, who served with Nelson at Trafalgar The *Broke* was of 1,850 tons displacement and carried a crew of 214, including a detachment of Royal Marines – almost unheard of in destroyers of her day She was armed with six 4-inch guns and four 21-inch torpedo tubes and had a top speed of 31½ knots. In command was 37-year-old Commander Edward Evans, who had sailed as navigator and second-in-command to Scott in the *Terra Nova* when the explorer made his ill-fated bid to be first at the South Pole in 1910.

On 20 April 1917 the *Swift* and *Broke* left Dover at 7.45 p.m. on their ninth successive night patrol, both having spent the daylight hours coaling ship – a dirty, back-breaking operation involving every member of the crew Nor did the work finish when the last bag of coal was emptied into the bunkers: the first hour at sea after clearing the harbour breakwaters was spent washing down ship with hoses to clear away the thick layer of coal dust that covered every square inch of paintwork and threatened to clog up guns and vital equipment By the time this work was finished and the exhausted deck parties had gone below to wash the dust off themselves, the destroyers were abreast of Dunkirk and nearing the eastern limit of their patrol

The Dover Strait, being littered with wrecks, shoal patches, sandbanks and rocks, is at the best of times a navigator's nightmare; in wartime, with ships unlit at night, buoys and lightvessels off station and shore lights extinguished or on reduced power, the strait was a challenge not to be faced lightly On the night in question the fog and mist that so often shroud these dangerous waters were mercifully absent, but the sky was heavily overcast With no moon to light the way, the Dover Strait was as black as the inside of a coal mine.

At midnight the destroyers were off the Sandettie Bank and on the westbound leg of the patrol. The sea was a flat calm, and in the total darkness only the phosphorescent glow of their bow waves betrayed their presence as they steamed at easy speed, with *Swift* in the lead. It was five hours to dawn, half way through a long, tension-filled night, and an undeniable lethargy was beginning to creep over the ships. Then gun flashes were seen dead ahead, in the direction of Dover, and suddenly every man was alert. Commander Peck, the senior officer, ordered full speed and the two destroyers leapt forward, their 30,000 horsepower turbines winding up an urgent crescendo The long wait to come to grips with the enemy might at last be over.

Forty minutes passed, and the two ships were off the South Goodwin, seven miles east of Dover, when several darker shadows showed up on the *Swift*'s port bow, range 600 yards and closing rapidly. A flotilla of German destroyers, fresh from shelling Calais and Dover, was making good its escape to the east.

So still was the night that those on the bridge of the *Swift* heard the fire gongs sounding down the line of German ships before they all opened up together, the multiple flashes of their guns momentarily turning night into day. The *Swift* returned fire at once, but the combined speed of approach of the opposing ships was in excess of 60 knots, and even at the close range no hits were registered on either side.

It was a time for split-second decisions; and Commander Peck made his without hesitation, ordering the wheel hard to port with the intention of ramming the leading enemy ship. The gunlayer on the *Swift*'s forward 6-inch chose that moment to fire, and the brilliant flash from the gun directly in front of the bridge temporarily blinded Peck. He missed the first German ship, narrowly avoided being run down by the second, then slewed round on to a course parallel to that of the enemy and let fly with a brace of torpedoes. Peck had the satisfaction of seeing at least one of his torpedoes strike home before he reversed course and went chasing after his original target, the leading German destroyer.

On the bridge of the *Broke* Commander Evans sighted the enemy only a fraction of a second later, and as the *Swift* cut through the line Evans launched a torpedo at the second ship and opened fire with all guns. The *Broke* immediately became a target for a dozen enemy guns – and a comparatively easy target at that, for a ball of burning cordite landed on her open bridge, lighting her up for all to see The shells homed in on her, scoring a series of direct hits Four of the crew of her forward 4-inch were killed, her torpedo crew died in the act of firing and a shell penetrated her boiler room and carried away the main steam line. A dozen men were scalded to death.

Feeling his ship losing her momentum as the pressure in her boilers fell away, Evans gave the order 'Stand by to ram', and turned on full helm towards the third ship in the German line. The *Broke* struck her – she was the destroyer *G24* – squarely in way of her after funnel with an impact that jarred both ships to a sudden halt.

Locked together, with the *Broke*'s sharp bows buried deep in the German's hull, both ships continued to fire with all guns that could be brought to bear. It was absolute point blank range and the carnage was terrible to behold, the screams of the dying and wounded audible above the crash of gunfire and the rattle of small arms. Then the German destroyer, fires raging on deck, wrenched herself clear of the *Broke* and drifted away, her list increasing as the sea poured into the hole left by the British destroyer's bows

Two enemy destroyers now remained in sight, and they both turned their guns on the *Broke* She was already a wreck above the waterline from the close-quarters fight, and more bursting shells added to the mayhem On the open bridge Evans narrowly escaped being killed by shrapnel; his quartermaster, below in the wheelhouse, was seriously injured, although he continued to steer the ship despite being on his knees And in the midst of all this came the cry 'Repel boarders!' – a call to arms not heard in the Royal Navy for a century or more

It appears that a number of Germans from the *G24* had clambered on to the *Broke*'s forecastle head when their ship was rammed, and now, either stricken with panic or with intent to carry on the fight, they swarmed aft They were met by Midshipman Donald Gyles, the officer in charge of the forward guns, who, although blinded in one eye, confronted them, revolver in hand. Others seized the cutlasses and rifles with fixed bayonets kept handy by the guns and the German boarding party was quickly dealt with Some jumped over the side; others were made prisoner Commander Evans later expressed the opinion that he thought the so-called boarders were only trying to escape from their sinking ship – which seems a likely explanation. But, in the heat of the moment, the decks being littered with dead and wounded and the only light being the flash of guns, who was to know?

Evans now turned to ram the last German destroyer in the line, but, with her main steam line severed, the *Broke*'s engines were only just turning over, and the chance was lost. Drifting, but not completely out of control, she then closed the destroyer *G85*, previously torpedoed by the *Swift* and now stopped and on fire. Evans had given the order to lower the boats to pick up survivors, when the German's forward gun opened up on the *Broke*. Evans replied with four rounds of 4-inch and a torpedo The *G85* went down, leaving her survivors crying for help in the water as the *Broke* moved away. The *Swift*, also with engine-room damage, had lost her original quarry. Then, searching around in the darkness for another target, she came upon the crippled *G24* just as she was sinking. In this instance Commander Peck could safely stop his ship to pick up survivors

The total number of German destroyers engaged in the Dover Strait on that night by *Swift* and *Broke* has never been clearly established. Some say it was as many as twelve; the Admiralty Court of Inquiry gave the number as five What is certain, however, is that two of the enemy, the *G24* and *G85*, were sunk and the British destroyers picked up 140 survivors between them The *Swift* was not severely damaged and had only one man killed and four wounded. The *Broke*, on the other hand, was badly mauled, with 21 dead and 27 wounded. She was towed into Dover, where her dead were buried on the hillside overlooking the port.

The Battle of the Dover Strait was a close broadside-to-broadside action, fought on the run and worthy of the best traditions of the fighting frigates of Nelson's day. For his part in the action Commander Edward Evans earned the title 'Evans of the Broke', by which he will be forever known. An official statement issued in Berlin on 25 April and published in *The Times* on the 26th gives a somewhat different version of the incident:

> The sinking of the enemy leading destroyer, which was mentioned in our report on the 21st, was clearly observed by the crews of the whole of our torpedo boat flotilla The enemy vessel was hit amidships by a torpedo from one of our torpedo boats and sank stern foremost within a few minutes with a big explosion Five minutes later another big explosion occurred in another British destroyer, probably owing to a torpedo hit by one of our boats which has not returned This was also clearly observed by the crews of several torpedo boats and, to judge from the severity of the explosion, it is highly probable that this vessel also sank Another British destroyer which passed astern of our torpedo boats was badly holed in the port bow by one of our guns Her bridge was also shot to pieces and the wreckage hung over the side She was also afire astern Another leading vessel received two gun hits forward just behind the bridge It is unnecessary to enter into discussion regarding the British assertion as to the insignificance of the loss of life It will be sufficient to mention the British material losses and the German hits on the British vessels and the reports in the foreign Press, according to which in the market hall of Dover a great number of British dead have been placed beside our dead

As the summer of 1917 wore on it became evident that the German Navy needed more than a victory contrived by propagandists. All was not well in the High Seas Fleet: poor food, harsh discipline and a sense of impending defeat had led to a series of mutinies. Before the winter took hold in earnest, Admiral Scheer decided to make a spectacular strike against British shipping in the North Sea – and what better target than the Scandinavian convoys?

The Scandinavian convoys were a comparatively recent innovation, brought about by the activities of German U-boats in the North Sea. There was then a considerable trade between Britain and neutral Norway and Sweden and convoys sailed daily from the Shetland Islands for Bergen under the protection of the Royal Navy. The route was short – no more than fifteen hours' steaming – but it was within easy striking distance of the High Seas Fleet, then kicking its heels in Jade Bay. Nevertheless the Admiralty saw fit to use only destroyers and armed trawlers as escorts, cruiser squadrons being kept handy in case they were needed. When the convoys had been running for six months without any attempt by German surface warships to interfere, it was inevitable that a sense of complacency should creep into the British ranks, both afloat and ashore.

When, on 15 October, a convoy of twelve merchant ships left Lerwick for Bergen, escorted by the destroyers *Mary Rose* and *Strongbow* and the armed trawlers *Elsie* and *P. Fannon*, there was a strong smell of disaster in the air that seemed to go unnoticed. That morning the Admiralty's Listening Service had detected preparations to sail powerful German minelaying cruisers and informed the Admiralty. The North Sea patrols were alerted, but no instructions were given to the convoy escorts concerning the action to be taken if they were attacked. Consequently, for Lieutenant-Commander C. L. Fox, in command of the *Mary Rose*, and Lieutenant-Commander Edward Brooke in the *Strongbow*, this was just another routine run across the North Sea They had two immediate worries: it was the autumn equinox and the weather would inevitably be foul, and the U-boats were known to be unusually active. As to the former, the *Mary Rose* being of only 1,017 tons displacement and the *Strongbow* even smaller at 898 tons, this would mean a rough, uncomfortable passage; with regard to the U-boats, the two 35-knot destroyers, each armed with three 4-inch guns, a 2-pounder and four torpedo tubes, were amply equipped to cope

Contrary to expectations, the eastbound passage was unusually smooth, and the next day, when within a few miles of the Norwegian coast, the escort was split, the *Mary Rose* and *Elsie* peeling off to meet the next westbound convoy off Marsten The *Strongbow* and *P Fannon* continued with the eastbound ships to cover their dispersal off Bergen, after which the two warships would rejoin the *Mary Rose* and the westbound ships at sea This they did on the evening of the 16th, rendezvousing twenty miles west of Marsten. The convoy was a mixed bag, consisting of twelve merchantmen, two British, one Belgian, one Danish, five Norwegian and three Swedish; since it was made up largely of neutral ships and was sailing from a neutral port, any attempt at secrecy was a wasted effort and, as usual, Berlin was informed of details of the convoy within an hour or so of its sailing

On the 15th Admiralty Intelligence signalled Admiral Beatty, 'Minelayer *Brummer* leaves Norman Deep tomorrow 16th to northward, probably for minelaying. She should be intercepted.' The *Brummer*, commanded by Fregattenkapitän Leonhardi, was more than just a minelayer: she was in fact a brand new, 3,800-ton light cruiser, equipped for minelaying, certainly, but armed with four 5 9-inch guns and capable of a speed of 34 knots. She left Norman Deep, an anchorage on the west coast of Denmark, just before noon on the 16th, in company with her similarly armed sister ship *Bremse* (Fregatten-kapitän Westerkamp), with specific orders to attack the *Mary Rose* convoy Support was to be provided by the cruiser *Regensberg* and a flotilla of destroyers, which would be at sea off the North Frisian Islands. With so many German ships at sea, all U-boats in the area were warned to be particularly careful in identifying a target before attacking.

As a cold, grey dawn broke on the morning of the 17th the convoy was just seventy miles to the east of Lerwick and, being so near to its destination, the tight discipline of the passage was easing. The *Mary Rose* had gone on ahead and was out of sight, while the armed trawlers *Elsie* and *P. Fannon* were straggling astern. When, soon after 6 a.m., the *Brummer* and *Bremse* came charging over the horizon from the south-east, only the *Strongbow* was guarding the merchant ships, and it must have been that her lookouts were not at their best. Perhaps the outline of the German cruisers was such that they could easily be mistaken for British ships, but the *Strongbow* should not have been caught so obviously unprepared. Although it was near dawn, her guns were not even manned, and before she could do anything about this she was hit by a double salvo from the German cruisers

It was all over in a few chaotic minutes The *Strongbow*'s main steampipe was fractured, her engines were immobilized and most of her engine-room crew were killed The bridge also received a direct hit and Lieutenant-Commander

Brooke was wounded, although he refused to leave his post Not that there was much left for him to command. The *Strongbow*, without steam, was helpless, lying stopped, on fire and gradually breaking up under the weight of the enemy's 5 9-inch shells. When he had seen all confidential books and papers destroyed, Brooke ordered scuttling charges to be laid and passed word to abandon ship. It was his intention to go down with her, but his men carried him from the bridge, lashed him to a Carley float and put him over the side, then followed. The *Strongbow* went down at 7.30 with her flag still flying, having fired only a few ineffective shells in defence of the convoy under her protection.

The *Mary Rose* heard the gunfire astern and immediately raced back at full speed to re-join the convoy. She was greeted by salvos of 5.9-inch shells as soon as she came in sight Lieutenant-Commander Fox made a brave attempt to launch a torpedo attack on the German cruisers but his ship was blown from under him before a torpedo could be fired. Fox and most of his crew died in the cold waters of the North Sea when the wreck of the *Mary Rose* spiralled to the bottom

In the absence of any clear orders, the convoy had not dispersed at the first sign of attack as it should have done. The merchant ships, stunned by the sudden and savage destruction of the destroyers, were still huddled together after the *Mary Rose* and *Strongbow* went down The trawlers *Elsie* and *P. Fannon* hovered nearby, but it would have been suicidal for them to have intervened. The *Brummer* and *Bremse* were therefore free to take their time in disposing of the unfortunate merchantmen. Only three ships, the two British and the Belgian, made good their escape. The other nine, all neutral flag, were sunk, dispatched like frightened rabbits by a brace of stoats When the German cruisers had completed their work and steamed away, the trawlers moved in to pick up survivors. When the final reckoning was made, it was found that the short, brutal engagement had cost the lives of 250 men, most of them dying in the *Mary Rose* and *Strongbow*.

It is known that the *Mary Rose* sent off a sighting report before she sank, but this was jammed by the *Brummer*. As a result of the jamming, news of the attack on the convoy did not reach the Admiral Commanding Orkneys & Shetlands until 4 p.m. that day, by which time the German cruisers were half way home and it was too late to catch them. The ships of the Grand Fleet and the Harwich Force patrolling in the North Sea at the time – some eighty ships in all – might just as well have been in port.

In British naval circles, the loss of the *Mary Rose* and *Strongbow*, along with nine merchant ships, had little effect other than to produce a cry for more destroyers to be built for escort duty. It did, however, result in clear instructions at last being issued to escort commanders regarding the action they should take when faced with a superior enemy force, and that was to do what a destroyer does best – to harry the enemy from a safe distance while calling for help. But such advice, wise though it may be, ran contrary to the Royal Navy's tradition and it was unlikely to be followed

In Germany the success of the raid on the Scandinavian convoy encouraged the Admiralstab to try again, especially when it became clear that no increase in escorts for these convoys was envisaged At daybreak on 11 December, a flotilla of eight of Kapitän zur See Heinrich's newest and fastest destroyers sailed from Wilhelmshaven and steamed northwards. That afternoon, undetected by the Admiralty's Listening Service, the force separated, four destroyers under the command of Kapitän zur See Heinecke altering to the north-west while the other four, under Korvettenkapitän Kolbe, continued to the north.

Heinecke's orders were to attack shipping off the Firth of Forth This he did, sinking two stragglers from a convoy bound south that night. In the early hours of the 12th the German destroyers surprised a fleet of British trawlers and sank four of them. At sunrise Heinecke turned for home leaving confusion behind him, the Admiralty being under the impression that all six ships had been sunk by a U-boat

Kolbe's force, pushing north to look for victims on the Lerwick–Bergen route, ran into a strong north-westerly gale, which brought the speed of the destroyers down to 9 knots It was after dark on the 12th before they reached the latitude of Bergen and, battling against heavy seas, began a sweep westwards. Emerging from a heavy rain squall some six hours later, they ran into an eastbound convoy of six merchantmen escorted by the destroyers *Pellew* and *Partridge* and four armed trawlers. Some distance to the west, and out of sight, was a British covering force of the 3rd Light Cruiser Squadron, consisting of two cruisers and four destroyers On sighting the enemy Lieutenant-Commander R. H. Ransome, commanding HMS *Partridge*, transmitted a warning to the covering squadron, signalled the merchant ships to scatter and turned to engage the German force. HMS *Pellew* (Lieutenant-Commander J. R. C Cavendish) followed with her guns blazing

The British destroyers, rolling and pitching in the heavy seas and dodging from rain squall to rain squall, fought like ferocious terriers to protect their flock but the German guns, outnumbering them two to one, were too much Hoping all the time that the covering force would arrive in time to save the merchantmen, Ransome and Cavendish fought their superior enemy valiantly for more than an hour – but in vain *Partridge* put a torpedo into the German destroyer *V100* but it failed to explode and the British ship was herself hit by three torpedoes which did explode Stopped and rolling helplessly in the swell, and with her decks in ruins and her communications smashed, she continued to fight her guns until the sea closed over her

HMS *Pellew*, hit by gunfire, with her port engine room flooded and unable to manoeuvre, could do nothing to prevent the German destroyers from picking off the helpless merchant ships one by one They all went to the bottom. The *Pellew* was saved by a dense rain squall that drifted across and hid her from the enemy; when she emerged from the rain she was alone on the heaving sea. Kolbe, anxious to clear the scene before the arrival of British reinforcements, was making tracks for home.

As 1917 drew to a close, although the big ships of Germany's High Seas Fleet chose to shelter behind the minefields of Heligoland, her destroyers and U-boats continued to taunt the might of the British Grand Fleet . .

# 9

# Rawalpindi and Scharnhorst

*23 November 1939*

T he autumn of 1918 provided a suitable finale for the ill-conceived plans of Kaiser Wilhelm II. It was a dank, miserable season, one of the wettest ever known in Western Europe. The battlefields of Flanders became a morass of clinging mud, through which the defeated German Army floundered eastwards as it sought to regain the borders from which it had advanced with such arrogance in the late summer of 1914 In Kiel the men of the High Seas Fleet, ordered to take their ships to sea to fight one last glorious battle against Britain's Navy, turned to mutiny For them it was all over, save for the final ignominy of that shameful procession into Scapa Flow with ensigns lowered Then, in the early morning of 11 November, a Canadian battalion of the British Army advanced through the driving rain into the ancient Belgian town of Mons, where the first shots had been fired four years, two months and nineteen days earlier. At 11 o'clock that morning the Great War came to an end Nothing of any great moment had been gained, and some 20 million people had lost their lives

The peace that followed was an uneasy one. Under the Treaty of Versailles Germany lost all her possessions overseas, her heavy industries were laid waste, foreign troops occupied the Rhineland and she was ordered to pay £6,000 million in reparations to the Allies It was a complete humiliation of a proud people, and it led directly to the rise to power of Adolf Hitler In a few short years, he turned a beaten and resentful nation into a mighty war machine the like of which the world had not then seen. History, as it will do, repeated itself, and in September 1939, almost twenty-one years after those Canadians sought shelter from the rains in the ruins of Mons, the big guns were being rolled out again

Hitler had been long aware that the greatest obstacle in the way of his search for 'Lebensraum' was Great Britain, and to defeat her he had first to sever the vital sea lanes through which much of her food and raw materials flowed. As things stood when the Reich Chancellor came to power, this was an impossible task, for under the Treaty of Versailles the German Navy was limited to six armoured ships of 10,000 tons, six light cruisers of up to 6,000 tons and a handful of torpedo boats. But British politicians in peace are notoriously gullible souls, and in June 1935 Hitler persuaded them to sign the Treaty of London This allowed the German fleet to expand to one-third the size of the Royal Navy

It was the opportunity the German admirals had been waiting for, and by the summer of 1939, most of the ships of the Royal Navy being then obsolete, the

German Navy, although smaller, was superbly equipped. Their fleet had grown to two battlecruisers, three 'pocket battleships', three heavy cruisers, five light cruisers, 57 submarines and a host of destroyers, minesweepers and auxiliary craft – all of them brand new.

The names of the two battlecruisers, *Scharnhorst* and *Gneisenau*, were a link with past glories but they were a vast improvement on their predecessors At 32,310 tons displacement, they were armed with nine radar-controlled 11-inch guns, twelve 5.9-inch and fourteen 4.1-inch guns and sixteen 37mm and eight 20mm anti-aircraft guns. Their maximum speed was 31½ knots, and they had a cruising range of 10,000 miles at 17 knots The so-called pocket battleships, *Deutschland*, *Admiral Scheer* and *Admiral Graf Spee*, were really heavily armoured cruisers of 12,193 tons. They mounted six 11-inch and eight 5.9-inch guns and eight 21-inch torpedo tubes. Their side armour was 4 inches thick, and they were powered by diesel engines, giving them a prodigious range and a top speed of 26 knots.

Hitler and his Naval Chief of Staff, Admiral Erich Raeder, with the lessons of the Falklands and Jutland in mind, had no intention of challenging the Royal Navy in big fleet actions The battlecruisers and pocket battleships were built as powerful, sophisticated commerce raiders, designed to roam the seas alone, striking at Allied merchant shipping wherever and whenever the opportunity presented itself The *Admiral Graf Spee* and *Deutschland*, each accompanied by a supply ship, left Wilhelmshaven on, respectively, 21 and 24 August 1939 and under the cover of fog slipped past the north of Scotland undetected and into the North Atlantic. The *Graf Spee* had orders to make for the east coast of South America while the *Deutschland* was to lose herself in mid-Atlantic until the call for action came

Following the fall of Poland on 6 October 1939 the land war in Europe became a confrontation of arms that stopped short of active aggression. The German Wehrmacht peered over the ramparts of the Siegfried Line while, facing them in the Maginot Line, the French kicked their heels and dreamed of glory. The 500,000-strong British Expeditionary Force, with no purpose-built defences to man, searched out decent billets for the coming winter, content in the knowledge that the RAF was bombarding the enemy with threatening leaflets The 'phoney war' of the closing months of 1939 was well named.

At sea, out on the broad wastes of the North Atlantic, the war was real enough. There had been no long-drawn-out prelude to the fight: the killing began nine hours after the declaration of war, when Fritz-Julius Lemp's *U30* sent the British passenger liner *Athenia* to the bottom with the loss of 112 lives. Then, as if they had been waiting for the crack of the starter's pistol, the German U-boats ran wild, sinking in the first two months of the war 331,000 tons of Allied and neutral merchant shipping. The Royal Navy, once the symbol of Britannia's omnipotence, was overwhelmed by the brutal efficiency of this attack from beneath the waves And as if the threat of the U-boats were not enough, it then became known that the *Deutschland* was at large in northern waters and stalking unescorted merchantmen Her success was less spectacular, for by the middle of October she had sunk only two Allied ships and captured – with some resulting embarrassment – the American freighter *City of Flint*. The Admiralty then decided that it was time to act before the pocket battleship increased her score further As the *Deutschland* had been at sea for almost three months, it was thought she might be close to making a dash for home by the northern route. With a view to preventing her return, a substantial British force was positioned across her likely path.

The Denmark Strait was covered by the 8-inch gun cruisers *Norfolk* and *Suffolk*, with three armed merchant cruisers in support, while four smaller cruisers and another AMC patrolled between Iceland and the Faeroes. Three 'C' class cruisers were positioned to the south of the Faeroes, while the cruiser *Glasgow* and two destroyers were to the north-east of the Shetlands. Also at sea, returning from patrol off Iceland, was the 6-inch gun cruiser *Sheffield*, accompanied by three more 'C' class cruisers Under the sea, five submarines also kept watch for the *Deutschland*, and standing by in the Clyde with steam raised were the battleships *Nelson* and *Rodney*, the cruiser *Devonshire* and seven destroyers. At Rosyth, on the east coast of Scotland, the cruisers *Southampton*, *Edinburgh* and *Aurora*, with two destroyers, were also ready to put to sea. In all, 40 British warships were on the alert to deal with one German pocket battleship By sheer bad luck it fell to one of the weakest links in the chain to make the first contact with the enemy.

It would seem that the Admiralty had not taken heed of one of the more obvious lessons of the First World War, that being the total unsuitability of large ex-passenger liners for service as armed merchant cruisers. These ships, as proved by the loss of seventeen of them in action in that war, presented too big a target for the enemy's guns, were too slow, lacked manoeuvrability, had thin-skinned hulls and were, by necessity, invariably armed with old guns surplus to the Navy's requirements. Yet in the autumn and winter of 1939 the Admiralty again commandeered passenger liners, fitted them with the usual obsolete guns and sent them out to face an enemy equipped with the best. In defence of the admirals, however, it must be said that, owing to the short-sighted policies of successive British governments between the wars, they had been left with too few ships for the job they faced. They had little alternative but to use merchant cruisers, but they should have dropped their preference for the elegant passenger liners and requisitioned smaller, faster ships, fruit carriers in particular.

Germany's resources were vast, and increasing as she expanded her borders in Europe, but there remained many essentials, such as oil, rubber and certain mineral ores, that she had to import from overseas Before the war her large merchant fleet carried a regular flow of these materials through the English Channel to the ports of Hamburg, Bremen, Rotterdam and Antwerp. War and the Royal Navy's blockade denied the Channel route to them, leaving only the longer and less convenient access via the 250-mile wide gap between Iceland and the Faeroes and into the North Sea. In the absence of sufficient Coastal Command aircraft for long-range reconnaissance, it fell to the Northern Patrol to police these inhospitable waters, which lie within six degrees of the Arctic Circle and right in the path of the worst of the Atlantic depressions. At best, in the short summer of these regions, it is a cold and dreary place, often blanketed by thick fog; in winter it is a place of the damned, a sea to match the Wagnerian legend. The wind moans a steady force 10, the waves are angry green mountains and rain, snow and sleet lash the face and freeze in the rigging It was this way when, in the afternoon of 23 November 1939, His Majesty's Armed Merchant Cruiser *Rawalpindi* moved towards the completion of her fourth miserable day on patrol. There were many on board this ship who longed for a return to the balmy days of not so long ago, when they had sailed this same ship through the warm, untroubled waters of the Indian Ocean

The 16,697-ton *Rawalpindi*, built in 1925 for the Peninsular & Oriental Steam Navigation Company and named after India's foremost military outpost in the days of the British Raj, had spent all her life carrying passengers between Britain and the East. These were heady days, when travel by sea was at its height and the great liner companies of Europe vied with each other to provide ever faster and more comfortable passages for a discerning clientele The *Rawalpindi* had then been at her best, the pride of P&O's fleet, her spotless teak decks, spacious cabins and elegant lounges playing host to many thousands of passengers in a year This idyllic life of flawless blue skies, steamer chairs and gin and tonics at sundown came to a sudden end in October 1939 when the *Rawalpindi* and 49 of her contemporaries were commandeered by the Admiralty. She was taken into a shipyard on the Clyde, where gangs of dockyard workers, indifferent to her illustrious past, stripped her of much of her sumptuous but highly inflammable interior fittings. Her well-used triple-expansion steam engines and their auxiliaries were given a thorough overhaul This improved their reliability, but nothing could be done to improve on the liner's top speed of 17 knots. Gun emplacements were erected on her decks, and eight 5.9-inch guns were hoisted aboard and mounted, giving her the appearance, at least, of a substantial man-of-war But the guns were old and obsolete, salvaged from the breakers' yards where ships of the First World War had ended their days. There were no asdics, nor depth charges for detecting and dealing with U-boats, and the ex-liner's thin shell plating was not reinforced with armour at the waterline When the refit was finished, HMS *Rawalpindi*, guns apart, was still the same high-sided, vulnerable merchantman she had always been. She would hold her own against the German blockade-runners, but she would also present an unmissable target for the U-boats – and she was certainly not up to taking on a real warship.

But there was one man who would have no ill said of the *Rawalpindi*. In September 1939 sixty-year-old Captain Edward Kennedy RN had for seventeen years been in retirement in the Buckinghamshire village of Farnham Common and was resigned to spending his remaining years between the potting shed and the golf course. A distinguished career on the China Station and with the Home Fleet had been marred when, in 1921, he fell foul of the Admiralty through his adjudged lenient treatment of a mutinous crew The war had come again, but Kennedy saw little possibility of being recalled to active service. This did not, however, deter him from pestering Their Lordships with demands for a ship The news that he was to be given the *Rawalpindi* came through while he was in his garden pruning roses, and it was typical of the man that he finished the job in hand before giving vent to his delight. An armed merchant cruiser might not exactly be a fighting ship of the line, but she was a command – and that was all Edward Kennedy needed to justify his existence

The men manning Kennedy's new command when he joined *Rawalpindi* on the Clyde were a brave wartime compromise, a mixture of naval reservists, pensioners and merchant seamen, the last predominating. When it came to the take-over of the passenger liner, her serving crew were given the option of staying with her. In response, three of her navigating officers, sixteen engineer officers, her boatswain, carpenter and lamp-trimmer and 104 sailors, firemen and stewards had volunteered to become temporary members of the Royal Naval Reserve. To all intents and purposes, then, while the Navy manned her guns, much of the day-to-day running of the *Rawalpindi* remained in the hands of the men who had always been responsible for it. But, with a total crew of 306, a mixture of Royal Navy and Merchant Navy – men whose background and training were poles apart – it would require all of Kennedy's qualities of command to mould the merchant cruiser into a tight and efficient ship. It was to his great credit that she was exactly this when she sailed from the Clyde on 17 November, with orders to join the Northern Patrol.

At 1500 on the 23rd the *Rawalpindi* was 95 miles off the east coast of Iceland and on the south-easterly leg of her patrol. Behind a menacing canopy of cloud, which stretched from horizon to horizon, the last rays of the setting sun were quickly smothered by the advancing gloom of night. The wind was astern of the AMC, north-north-westerly force 5 and rising The sea, glinting black and flecked with running white horses, heaved ominously, matching the moan of the strengthening wind in the rigging. It was already bitterly cold, four degrees below freezing, and as the night advanced the thermometer continued to fall.

Below, in the wardroom, once a passengers' dining saloon, it was warm and snug and stewards balanced themselves good-naturedly against the roll of the ship as they laid the tables for the evening meal This was one time when their lowly status was a privileged one: to them, cocooned in the liner's accommodation with no watches to keep nor guns to man, the harsh outside world was another planet. Their daily routine was little changed from those not-so-distant days when they attended to the needs of fare-paying passengers. Only if the ship was in action would they be required to vary this routine to man the sick bay – and, with the *Rawalpindi* engaged in chasing unarmed blockade-runners, the chance of this happening was remote.

High on the *Rawalpindi*'s navigation bridge, the watch retreated deeper into their thick duffle coats to wait out the last half-hour before eight bells brought the change of watch. In the chartroom abaft the bridge Captain Kennedy studied the dead-reckoning position marked on the chart and debated its accuracy. Several days had now passed without the opportunity to take sun or star sights, and the currents in the area were uncertain. Kennedy returned to the wheelhouse and peered through the forward windows at the fading horizon With the wind and sea rising, and the darkness coming in, he judged it unlikely that they would sight any enemy blockade-runners that night. He tried to relax, but he was plagued by thoughts of the *Deutschland* Before leaving the Clyde he had been warned by Admiral Forbes, C-in-C Home Fleet, that the pocket battleship might at any time attempt to return to Germany by the northern route. Kennedy harboured no doubts as to what he should do if the German ship hove in sight, but he feared that the *Rawalpindi*'s ancient 5.9s were no match for such a formidable opponent.

Kennedy's fears regarding the *Deutschland* were unfounded. Unknown to him – indeed, to anyone on the British side – the pocket battleship had returned to Germany a week earlier and was then safely tied up in Kiel The results of her two-month sortie into the North Atlantic had been disappointing, and the capture of the *City of Flint* had almost led to a complete breakdown of relations between Germany and the United States ≈ the last thing Hitler wanted. Added to that, the *Deutschland*'s engines began to give trouble, and, fearing that the loss of this patriotically named ship would have a serious effect on German morale, she was recalled. Before sailing again, her name would be changed to *Lützow*

It was now the turn of the *Scharnhorst* and *Gneisenau* to try their luck in the North Atlantic These two 32,000-tonners, with Vizeadmiral Wilhelm Marschall flying his flag in the *Gneisenau*, left Wilhelmshaven on 21 November and sailed up the coast of Norway unseen by British ships and aircraft. Marschall's brief was to break through the Iceland–Faeroes gap under cover of darkness, make a quick feint at the North Atlantic shipping routes and then haul up into the Denmark Strait and run for home again at high speed via the north of Iceland. Presumably the object of the exercise was not to sink ships but to put the fear of God into the British Admiralty In reality, it was a farcical operation, with two powerful warships acting like a pair of circus clowns waving red rags to taunt a snorting bull. The bull turned out to be an ageing cow wearing borrowed horns

In the afternoon of the 23rd the German battlecruisers, steaming in line abreast with the *Scharnhorst* to the north, were well into the Iceland–Faeroes gap and steering a west-north-westerly course at 18 knots At 1507 the twilight was deepening when the lookout in the *Scharnhorst*'s foretop reported an unidentified ship fine to starboard at about twelve miles The report was passed to the *Gneisenau*, and Vizeadmiral Marschall ordered Kapitän zur See Kurt Hoffman, commanding the *Scharnhorst*, to alter course to investigate and increase to 24 knots This Hoffman did, signalling the *Gneisenau* ten minutes later that the stranger was a large ship with two masts and one funnel, possibly an enemy auxiliary cruiser Both German ships went to action stations.

The hail rattling at the *Rawalpindi*'s wheelhouse windows and blotting out the horizon suddenly cleared, the clouds drew back and the first of the evening stars were visible The weather appeared to be improving. Seconds later the bell of the bridge telephone rang, rudely disturbing the quiet routine of the watch. The call came from the lookout in the crow's nest, reporting a ship fine on the *Rawalpindi*'s port bow

Kennedy moved swiftly out to the port wing of the bridge and joined the officer of the watch, who was already searching the horizon with his binoculars. Kennedy raised his own glasses and eventually focused on a dark shadow on the line between sea and sky The shadow became the outline of a ship, some seven or eight miles off and crossing the *Rawalpindi*'s bow from port to starboard at high speed It was difficult to tell in the poor light, but she had the look of a blockade-runner Kennedy ordered his first lieutenant to muster the boarding party and altered course to intercept

The distance between the two ships narrowed rapidly, and suddenly a bright light winked out at the *Rawalpindi* across the heaving waves. The message held an unmistakable threat: 'To British cruiser Heave to. Do not use your radio What ship? Where from and where bound? Do not use your wireless '

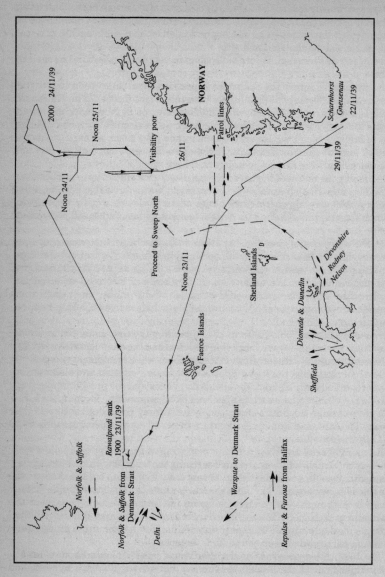

*The Cruise of the Scharnhorst and Gneisenau and the Loss of the Rawalpindi, November 1939*

The warning to remain silent came too late, for the *Rawalpindi*'s operator was already transmitting Kennedy had by now recognized the distinctive clipper bows, cowled funnel and tall fighting top of a German pocket battleship. It could only be the *Deutschland*. The threat that had been with him constantly throughout the long days of the patrol was about to become reality The cold night air took on the chill of death.

It was a deliberate policy of the German naval planners to build all their big ships with a similar silhouette in order to confuse the enemy, as it had done so on this occasion. And being under the impression that the *Deutschland* was still at sea, Kennedy might be forgiven for his wrong identification Not that it made much difference whether it was the *Deutschland* or the *Scharnhorst* the *Rawalpindi* was faced with. Hand-me-down 5.9s against 11-inch guns backed by radar was suicide whichever way you looked at it It was perhaps just as well that Edward Kennedy was not aware that the *Scharnhorst*'s equally powerful sister was lurking in the gathering darkness

In order to gain time Kennedy informed the *Scharnhorst* by lamp that he was about to heave to Meanwhile he sent his men to action stations and ordered his wireless operator to inform the Admiralty that he was under attack by the *Deutschland* This being done, he rang for emergency full speed and put the helm hard over to present the liner's stern to the enemy. Smoke floats were rolled over the side and, with her ex-merchant service engineers coaxing every last revolution out of her gleaming pistons, the *Rawalpindi* ran for her life.

The gods were not on Edward Kennedy's side that night. The strong wind whipped away the smoke screen before it was formed and the fleeing liner lay cruelly exposed to her pursuer. The time was 1540, it was quite dark and a brilliant moon had appeared from behind the clouds to cast its cold light on the arena

Aboard the *Scharnhorst* the main batteries had reported ready for action, but Hoffman decided to give his quarry one more chance to surrender The battlecruiser's 21-inch signal lamp clattered away, its light flashing across the intervening stretch of water between the two ships an uncompromising message: 'Stop or we sink you.'

Kennedy's answer was to drop more smoke floats and call for yet more speed As before, the wind, now nearing gale force, dispersed the smoke as fast as it was generated, and, although the ship rattled and shook as she surged forward at a hitherto unknown speed, there seemed little hope of escape The enemy was gaining remorselessly.

Suddenly rain squalls began to close in around the *Rawalpindi* and Kennedy dared to hope for a miracle Then he saw the other ship looming up out of the night His heart sank, for this was clearly another enemy warship. Without reference to books – there was no time for this – Kennedy identified the newcomer as either the light cruiser *Emden* or the heavy cruiser *Admiral Hipper*, and he informed the Admiralty of this. He was, of course, wrong again: the *Gneisenau* was moving in to back up her sister.

At 1600, the range being down to 9,000 yards, Hoffman ordered one of his 4 1-inch guns to put a shot across the *Rawalpindi*'s bows This was ignored, and a few minutes later, having complied with all the niceties of International Law, and more, the German captain opened fire with his main armament

The *Scharnhorst*'s first salvo was a near miss, but close enough to bring home to Kennedy the hopelessness of the situation he was in. His choice was either to be blown out of the water while running away or to turn and face the enemy and go down with pride. He chose the less humiliating option, altering course to bring his starboard guns to bear. At 1607 the *Rawalpindi*'s four starboard 5.9s barked and recoiled in unison, and it said a lot for the skill of the British gunners that one shell from this first broadside landed on the *Scharnhorst*'s quarterdeck The impression the shell made on the battlecruiser's armour plate was negligible.

The *Scharnhorst*'s big guns roared again, and once more her shots fell short. The *Rawalpindi*'s gunners could not repeat their first strike, but they were loading and firing as fast as the shells could be passed, and they were close to getting the range, their salvos falling only 100 yards short of the *Scharnhorst*.

This was a fight that could have only one ending. Riding high out of the water, the *Rawalpindi* was an easy target, and the German gunners, having the added advantage of radar, homed in on the AMC with increasing accuracy, demolishing her superstructure and blasting holes in her thin, unarmoured sides There was a brief respite when the *Rawalpindi* was momentarily hidden by a heavy rain squall But, as she came out of the rain, she took a direct hit in the generator room and lost all electrical power. In complete darkness, and with their ammunition hoists still, Kennedy's gunners, many of them by now wounded, struggled heroically to keep their guns firing.

The events that followed were confused, but it is believed that at this point the *Gneisenau* came up on the *Rawalpindi*'s port side and added the weight of her 11-inch guns to those of the *Scharnhorst*. The British gunners did their utmost, dividing their shot between the attacking ships, but the odds against them were overwhelming. For every shell they fired over their open sights five came back with unerring accuracy

The *Rawalpindi*'s senior wireless operator had switched to his emergency battery transmitter and was tapping out a call for help when a flurry of German shells crashed down on the AMC's bridge, silencing him for ever Wheelhouse and chartroom were wiped out, and there were no witnesses to tell the tale, but it is probable that at this point Captain Edward Kennedy was killed, along with his merchant seamen navigating officers.

Just ten minutes after the first shot was fired by the *Scharnhorst*, the *Rawalpindi*, caught in a deadly hail of shells from both sides, was a blazing wreck, further torn by the explosion of her own ammunition. Her captain and most of her officers were dead, other dead and dying lay everywhere at their posts, yet she did not lower her colours Only one 5.9-inch gun, manned by two men, continued to fire spasmodically, and it is said that other men returned the German fire with rifles and machine guns – a glorious but ineffectual gesture of defiance. At 1612 the last gun fell silent and the crippled ship lay hove-to, a funeral pyre rolling awkwardly in the trough of the waves. The German battlecruisers continued to pound away at her for another ten minutes

When the senseless bombardment finally stopped up to 100 men were still alive on the *Rawalpindi*, many of them grievously wounded. Someone – no one was sure who it was – gave the order to abandon ship, but when the survivors came to lower the boats they found all but three had been destroyed in the battle and one of these was holed  While the wounded were being loaded into the remaining boats the ship was shaken by a series of explosions and it was feared that her main magazine would soon go  Those who were able to do so went over the side into the icy water

It was evident that the gallant fight put up by the *Rawalpindi*'s men had earned the respect of Vizeadmiral Marschall. He was aware that the AMC's wireless transmissions might bring every Royal Navy ship within 100 miles down on him, but he still observed the code of the sea  The three lifeboats were clearly visible in the light of the flames as they left the burning ship's side, and without hesitation Marschall took his ships in to the rescue. With great difficulty in the heavy seas the *Gneisenau* picked up twenty-one men from one boat, the *Scharnhorst* six from another. The third boat, containing eleven men, was rowing towards the *Scharnhorst* when the flagship signalled her to break off and clear the area immediately.

The *Rawalpindi*'s wireless operators, all three of whom were killed, had not given their lives in vain  Marschall's sudden departure had been prompted by the arrival of the 6-inch gun cruiser HMS *Newcastle*, then sighted through a break in the rain by the *Gneisenau*'s lookouts  The *Newcastle* was no match for two German battlecruisers, but her arrival had warned Marschall that the game was up: other, bigger ships might be on the way.

The 9,500-ton *Newcastle*, commanded by Captain J. Figgins, was the nearest ship of the Northern Patrol Line to the *Rawalpindi* and had steamed at maximum speed to the support of the AMC. The cruiser was not equipped with radar, and she came out of the rain and all but ran into the German battlecruisers  Unwilling to commit suicide by tackling two capital ships alone, Figgins sheered off to the north and took refuge in a handy rain squall  He planned to shadow the Germans until Admiral Forbes sent in his big guns, but ten minutes later the rain turned to snow and shut down the visibility to two cables. Figgins lost sight of his quarry

For the next twenty minutes the *Newcastle*, on reduced speed, searched in vain for the enemy. Then, at 1845, the snow cleared as quickly as it had come down and Captain Figgins saw flames to the south-east that he assumed must be the *Rawalpindi*  He was about to alter towards her when his lookouts reported a light low down on the horizon to the west  Believing that this might come from one of the German ships, Figgins increased speed to 25 knots and altered course to investigate

Whether the light seen was a product of an overtired lookout man's imagination or the result of the careless action of someone aboard one of the German ships will never be known, for nothing was seen after steaming for twenty minutes  Figgins, accepting that he had lost contact with the enemy and was unlikely to regain it, now steamed back towards the *Rawalpindi*  He arrived just in time to see the AMC capsize and sink  A search was made, and the eleven men in the lifeboat abandoned by the *Scharnhorst* were found and lifted aboard, more dead than alive. An upturned boat was also found  The two men clinging to it were covered with ice several inches thick but were still alive

Captain Edward Kennedy, 41 of his officers and 226 men lost their lives in the *Rawalpindi*'s courageous stand against a vastly superior enemy  It may be that the liner's guns scored only one hit on the German battlecruisers, but her action resulted in two of Hitler's newest and finest ships running for home like scared rabbits. The shame that must be forever borne by the Admiralty is that the only honour Edward Kennedy received for his sacrifice was a posthumous Mention in Dispatches

10

# Renown and Gneisenau

*9 April 1940*

A t the Battle of Warsaw in 1920, the invading armies of the newborn Union of Soviet Socialist Republics were hurled back from the gates of the city and then slaughtered in their hasty retreat homewards. This was the end of an ill-conceived venture that, not surprisingly, led to a lasting hatred between the two countries  The Poles eyed Russia's every move with suspicion, while the Russians licked their wounds and plotted vengeance

Long before the outbreak of war in September 1939 the Soviet Union was well aware that it would soon be a target for Hitler's Panzers, and to buy time Josef Stalin concluded a pact of non-aggression with Germany. The Russian dictator then set about creating a series of buffer zones to protect his country from the assault he knew must surely come from the west. He began, as might be expected, with Poland

On 17 September 1939, while the Poles fought heroically to stem the advance of the steamrollering German Panzers, Soviet troops crossed the lightly defended frontier in the east and marched rapidly westwards on a wide front Twenty-four bloody hours later they met their new German allies at Brest-Litovsk, and so had created a moat almost 200 miles wide between Russia's borders and those who might wish to invade them

Stalin then turned his eyes to the north and, ignoring a non-aggression pact he had signed with her, marched into Finland. However, this second incursion in search of land did not prove as effortless as the first. The Finns, fiercely independent, put up a stiff resistance, but with no powerful allies willing to come to their aid it was all over by the spring of 1940. Now, with the Russian divisions massed on Finland's northern border, it was the turn of the painstakingly neutral Sweden to feel uneasy, as did her next door neighbour Norway. These virtually undefended lands had good cause to fear, but the threat to their neutrality would not come from the Russians, who were then more interested in bringing the Baltic republics of Latvia, Estonia and Lithuania into the Communist fold

In 1940 Sweden was one of the world's largest producers of iron ore, and one of her biggest customers was Germany, whose massive war production industry had an insatiable appetite for the mineral  Most of the iron ore came from mines in Lapland, in the far north of Sweden, some 10 million tons a year being shipped to German foundries  In the summer months the ore went via the Baltic from the port of Lulea, at the head of the Gulf of Bothnia. This was a safe, sheltered route, beyond the reach of British ships and aircraft  Winter was less simple  From October to the end of April the Gulf of Bothnia freezes over and

Lulea is icebound. To overcome this handicap a rail link was built from the Swedish mines to the northern Norwegian port of Narvik, which is ice-free all year round. German ore carriers had no option but to use the outside route in winter, loading in Narvik and making a high-speed dash down the west coast of Norway in neutral territorial waters and into the Skagerrak. Much of this 750-mile passage lay inside the string of small islands off Norway known as the Leads, but the threat posed by British surface ships, submarines and aircraft was still great. As there was no way in which the German war effort could be sustained without a regular supply of Swedish iron ore, Hitler concluded that he must take control of Norway before Britain and her allies did so He laid his plans accordingly

Within a few weeks of the outbreak of war Winston Churchill, then Britain's First Lord of the Admiralty, had warned of the need to put a stop to the shipments of Swedish iron ore to Germany through Norway. He strongly advocated the immediate mining of the approaches to Narvik, but, unwilling to violate Norway's neutrality, the Cabinet refused to sanction such an operation It was not until late in March, when both Poland and Finland had fallen, that permission was given for the Royal Navy to seal off Narvik.

Coincident with the preparations being made in London to cut off his supply of Swedish iron ore, Hitler was laying plans for the invasion of Denmark and Norway. The German landings in Norway were scheduled to take place in the early hours of 9 April, and merchant ships carrying troops and their equipment left ports in the Baltic on the 3rd. They were followed a few days later by warships, also carrying troops, which would escort the merchantmen on the final run-in to the landing ports.

On the 5th the British Government, ever obsessed with diplomatic niceties, informed the Norwegian and Swedish governments of its intention to put a stop to the German iron ore traffic by laying minefields in Norwegian waters. The Germans, committed to total war, did not reciprocate by divulging their plans, and the first Britain knew of the intended German invasion was during the morning of the 7th, when reconnaissance aircraft sighted a large enemy naval force heading north from the Skagerrak. In the lead were the battlecruisers *Scharnhorst* and *Gneisenau* – a rare sight at sea since their brush with the *Rawalpindi* – and behind them ten destroyers carrying a regiment of the crack Third Mountain Division, bound for Narvik. They were followed by the heavy cruiser *Admiral Hipper* and four destroyers with another 1,700 troops, their destination Trondheim The British aircraft bombed the German ships but no hits were observed The presence of the invasion force was then reported by radio, but the message was not received by any British station.

Meanwhile, unaware that the Germans had stolen a march on them, the ships of Operation 'Wilfred', as the British minelaying project was designated, had set sail for Norway on the 6th. It was intended that a minelayer, escorted by four destroyers, would lay mines in the Leads between Bergen and Trondheim and, at the same time, two other destroyers would mark out a dummy minefield off the port of Trondheim. Four other minelayers were to sow mines in the Vestfjord, the long, deep-water approach to Narvik. A squadron under the command of Vice-Admiral W. Whitworth consisting of the battlecruiser *Renown*, the cruiser *Birmingham* and fourteen destroyers would provide cover for the Vestfjord undertaking, which was the primary object of Operation 'Wilfred'

The Norwegian Sea has a record of persistent bad weather and the spring of 1939 showed no exception. On the night of the 7th, with a rapidly falling barometer, the cloud base lowered and the wind rose steadily, and by the time Whitworth's force was approaching Vestfjord in the early hours of the 8th it was blowing a full gale from the south-west. Mist and driving snow added to the difficulties of the operation, but by 0500 the mines had been laid and the ships stood out to sea with the weather worsening all the time. Anxious to clear the coast before sunrise, Whitworth called for full speed and the 26,000-ton *Renown* began to bury her broad bows in the rising seas The small, narrow-beamed destroyers found the going too hard and fell back one by one, unable to maintain speed without incurring serious damage

The 1,350-ton *Glowworm*, commanded by Lieutenant-Commander Gerard Roope, was one tenaciously holding her position, corkscrewing violently and slamming into the oncoming waves with hammer blows that threatened to loosen every rivet in her flimsy hull But she refused to give in, until a heavy sea swept her decks and the cry of 'Man overboard!' went up.

It did occur to Gerard Roope, as he looked down into the maelstrom from the *Glowworm*'s open bridge, that to put his ship about in such weather was to court disaster for them all. But it was one of his men out there, fighting for his life in the cold, angry sea He hesitated only for a brief moment, then, choosing the right time, hauled the destroyer around, using helm and engines to full effect. The *Glowworm* slid sideways into the trough, and for one awful moment it seemed that she would disappear for ever under the next wave as it reared menacingly over the ship. It was a close run thing, and Roope's knuckles were white as he gripped the bridge rail, but the gallant little man-of-war seemed to know what was required of her. When the white-topped mountain of green water struck she was on her new course, and she lifted her stern high as the wave passed underneath.

Miracles sometimes do happen at sea; certainly for the poor wretch who had gone overboard from the *Glowworm*'s deck some form of divine intervention happened that morning He was a tiny speck of human flotsam in a limitless expanse of angry ocean, but Roope's lookouts spotted him and he was still alive when the boat's crew pulled him from the icy water. The most difficult part of the operation was recovering the rescue boat, as the fury of the sea threatened to smash it against the ship's hull each time it came alongside When at last the boat was hoisted in and its exhausted crew and the rescued man were safe below sipping hot rum, it was after 0800. The *Glowworm* was completely alone and 150 miles to the south-west of Vestfjord. Roope had orders to keep complete radio silence, and he could do no more than resume his original course, increase speed as much as the weather allowed and hope to regain contact with the *Renown* before nightfall

The sea was not as empty as it appeared to be when the *Glowworm* began to bury her forecastle into the waves again. The storm that had all but wrecked Whitworth's minelaying operation had also played havoc with the German invasion force heading for Trondheim. At that moment, unknown to Roope, the 14,000-ton *Admiral Hipper* and her troop-carrying destroyers were scattered all around the *Glowworm*, hidden in the passing rain and snow squalls and all attempting to re-establish contact with each other At 0830 the inevitable happened. Emerging from a blinding rainstorm, the British destroyer found herself face to face with two 'Von Roder' class destroyers, formidable opponents of 2,400 tons armed with five 5-inch guns The smaller *Glowworm*, with only four 4.7-inch guns, was hopelessly outclassed, but she had the precious advantage of surprise and she made the best of it.

Roope attacked without hesitation, throwing the *Glowworm* at the nearest enemy ship with all guns blazing. The German destroyer was caught completely unawares, and after firing two salvos at the *Glowworm*, both of which went wide, she took refuge in the rain Roope then rounded on the other ship, the *Bernd von Arnim*, which, being crowded with troops, also fled. The *Glowworm* went after her like a snarling terrier and a running fight ensued, during which the *Bernd von Arnim*, in her bid to escape, increased speed too quickly and slammed headlong into a particularly heavy sea, which stove in her bows. The German, making water fast, was forced to slow down and fight it out

In spite of her heavier firepower, the *Bernd von Arnim* was hard put to defend herself against the *Glowworm*'s aggressive attack. Two other German destroyers came rushing to her aid, but they too failed to take account of the power of the sea One lost several men overboard and both suffered weather damage, neither then being in a state to challenge the British destroyer Just as it seemed likely that the *Glowworm* might win the day, the 13,900-ton *Admiral Hipper* appeared out of the rain.

Roope at first mistook the *Admiral Hipper* for a British cruiser, and in the few moments he hesitated the *Glowworm* was hit by a salvo of 8-inch shells. The damage was fortunately superficial, and now would have been the time for the *Glowworm* to use her full 36 knots to run for the nearest rain squall. But Gerard Roope was not one to shirk a fight, no matter how one-sided He called for more speed and, with the *Glowworm* cleaving her way through the storm-tossed seas in a welter of spray and foam, charged in to make a torpedo attack on the *Hipper*.

It was a brave attempt, but one doomed to failure The *Glowworm* delivered her torpedoes, but in doing so she steamed straight into the full might of the *Hipper*'s big guns. The two German destroyers, taking heart from the arrival of their powerful consort, joined in the fray

The *Glowworm* staggered under the weight of shells thrown at her and, with the dead and wounded piling up all around him, Roope ordered his engineers to make smoke and pulled back. He was not running away, but buying time to contact the Admiralty and warn them of the presence of the *Hipper* and her troop-carrying destroyers When this was done Roope turned his ship about and threw her back into the smoke screen she had laid. When the *Glowworm* emerged on the other side of the foul-smelling, oily cloud she was making 38 knots.

Dead ahead and broadside-on lay the *Hipper* The German cruiser immediately opened fire with all the guns she could bring to bear and, fearing another torpedo attack, turned her bows towards the British destroyer to present a smaller target The *Glowworm* was taking savage punishment from the German's massed guns and hitting back bravely with her own puny armament, but Roope knew that, gun-to-gun, he had no chance against the heavy cruiser. He resorted to the only effective weapon left in his armoury – the ship herself He threw the destroyer across the *Hipper*'s bows, spun her around under full helm and charged for her exposed side The *Glowworm* struck the enemy cruiser amidships like a high-speed battering ram, pierced her armoured hull and sliced it open for 150 feet as she slid aft

The *Glowworm* fell away from her wounded adversary, her bows stove in and the sea pouring into her hull through the smashed plates. She was a complete wreck from the punishment she had taken at the hands of the *Hipper*'s gunners and ablaze from stem to stern, but she still had a gun or two that barked defiance. For fifteen minutes or so she lay rolling in the trough, then the flames reached her main magazine and she blew apart.

This audacious attack by the destroyer *Glowworm* on an enemy ten times her size was not made without grievous loss, for over 100 men went down with her. But it had been a brave and glorious act, and one which the German seamen, lately on the wrong end of the destroyer's guns, fully appreciated. Despite the tremendous seas now running, they made every possible effort at rescue, eventually snatching forty survivors from the water Lieutenant-Commander Gerard Roope, the last man to be hauled up the *Hipper*'s side, lost his grip, fell back into the water and disappeared. His bravery earned him the posthumous award of the Victoria Cross The *Admiral Hipper* limped into Trondheim and was out of action for many weeks to come The supreme price paid by Gerard Roope and so many of his men was not entirely in vain

HMS *Renown*, in company with the destroyers *Hardy*, *Hunter*, *Havoc*, *Hotspur*, *Hostile*, *Icarus*, *Ivanhoe*, *Impulsive*, *Esk* and *Greyhound*, was only a little over fifty miles to the north of the *Glowworm* when Roope signalled that he was in contact with the enemy. Vice-Admiral Whitworth's first reaction was to go to the *Glowworm*'s aid, and he was on the point of turning south when he was ordered by the Admiralty to maintain his patrol off Vestfjord to intercept any enemy ships attempting to enter the fjord The *Renown*'s sister ship, the *Repulse*, the cruiser *Penelope* and four destroyers, the Admiralty said, were on their way to the *Glowworm* These ships were much further away, however, and would arrive too late.

Whitworth maintained his watch off Vestfjord, intending to steer westwards until midnight, and then eastwards, in order to be off Skomvoer Light, at the entrance to the fjord, at dawn A strong south-westerly gale was blowing as a result of a deep trough of low pressure crossing the area. The trough line went through early in the evening, the wind veering quickly to the north-west and increasing to strong gale The seas, already running high, began to tumble and streak with the force of the wind. Blinding sleet and snow squalls reduced the visibility to nil at times. During the course of the night the destroyers became unmanageable, and at 2207, after consulting with the *Renown*'s commander, Captain C E. B Simeon, the admiral altered course to the north-west and reduced speed to 6 knots. The squadron was then, in effect, hove-to with the wind and sea on the bow, the most comfortable position to adopt in the circumstances

At 0200 on the 9th the wind moderated and veered more to the north The short Arctic night was almost at an end, and in the north-east, where the first

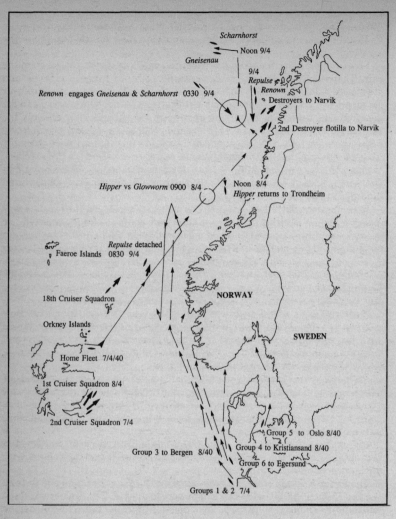

Scharnhorst *and* Gneisenau *versus HMS* Renown, *April 1940*

streaks of dawn were showing, the horizon was sharp and clear between the
squalls. Speed was increased to 10 knots at 0240, and the *Renown* came round
on to a south-easterly course, the destroyers following and forming up in line
astern.

Soon after 0330, with the light improving all the time, two large unidentified
ships were seen in a gap between two squalls to the north-east. The sighting
was brief and the ships quickly merged back into the rain, but not before it had

been established that they were at a range of ten miles and on a north-westerly course. Whitworth, certain that he was in contact with the enemy, increased to 15 knots, then to 20 knots, and came round to steer for the position of the sighting

Five minutes later the ships were sighted again as they emerged from the rain. They were then on the *Renown*'s starboard beam, range nine miles, and steering a parallel course The battlecruiser's turrets swung around to cover the strangers while Whitworth and his staff studied the silhouette cards. In the poor light and the atrocious weather prevailing, identification was difficult, the targets moving through the rain squalls and at times disappearing completely below the wave tops The best that could be said was that they were probably a battlecruiser of the *Scharnhorst* class and a heavy cruiser of the *Hipper* class Whitworth had in fact stumbled on the famous sisters *Scharnhorst* and *Gneisenau*, back at sea again and on their way north after covering the German landings at Narvik.

In comparison with these modern German battlecruisers, the *Renown* was a very old ship Built in 1916 for another war, she had already reached her quarter century, but between 1936 and 1939 she had gone through an extensive refit in which she was more or less rebuilt from the hull up At a cost of £3 million, only £30,000 less than her original cost, the battlecruiser, originally of 26,500 tons, had been given new engines and boilers, her armour belt increased to six inches and the elevation of her six 15-inch guns improved. Her secondary armament was uprated to twenty 4 5-inch guns, two 3-inch anti-aircraft guns, four 3-pounders and eight 18-inch torpedo tubes. Her new engines gave her a top speed of 30 knots. She was now a ship to be reckoned with, but against her the *Scharnhorst* and *Gneisenau*, each of 32,310 tons and with a maximum speed of 31½ knots, mounted a total of eighteen 11-inch, twenty-four 5 9-inch and twenty 4 1-inch guns.

At 0405 the *Renown*'s fire gongs clanged and her great guns thundered out and recoiled in unison, momentarily checking the ship's way through the water and filling the air with the acrid stench of burning cordite. Three times in as many minutes the guns roared, each time sending six 2,000lb high-explosive shells arcing across the storm-laden sky, probing for the enemy The third salvo found the range, bracketing the *Gneisenau* This stirred the German battlecruiser into action and she fired back, her first salvo finding its mark with uncanny accuracy.

The *Renown* was bracketed by the enemy in turn, but by pure good fortune the two 11-inch shells that struck home were not lethal. The first wrecked the midshipmen's quarters and the officers' baggage store but failed to explode; the second struck the foot of the foremast, bringing down the wireless aerials but causing only minor damage on deck

Much to Whitworth's great surprise, the enemy ships now turned away, as though reluctant to fight. He took the *Renown* after them, increasing to 26 knots, but at this speed the seas began to break over the forward turrets, making them impossible to work Speed was eased to 23 knots and rapid salvos were fired at the retreating enemy. The British destroyers, anxious to join in the fight, had thrown caution to the winds and risked setting back their bows to draw abreast of the flagship They opened fire at the extreme range of their

4-inch guns and were highly unlikely to score hits, but the gesture was a boost to morale and no doubt caused some consternation aboard the German ships After a few salvos Whitworth, concerned at the damage the destroyers might inflict on themselves as they battled against the heavy seas, called a halt. He ordered them to break away and patrol the approaches to Vestfjord, which were then undefended. The admiral was still not aware that German troops had landed at Narvik.

Both the *Scharnhorst* and *Gneisenau*, despite their combined superiority of firepower over their lone pursuer, were now zigzagging wildly, their salvos ragged and poorly aimed Whitworth decided to concentrate on the *Gneisenau* with his 15-inch guns while his starboard 4 5s engaged the *Scharnhorst*, which was to the east at a range of between 18,000 and 20,000 yards. At this distance the fall of shot from the 4 5s was difficult to spot in the breaking seas and *Renown*'s gunnery officer resorted to firing blind ladders across the best range obtainable by rangefinder. Again this was only a gesture, but it was effective in keeping the *Gneisenau* on the defensive

At 0414, *Renown*'s sixteenth 15-inch salvo was rewarded with a bright orange flash near the *Gneisenau*'s bridge. The German battlecruiser's guns then ceased fire, probably because her fire control had been knocked out. Two minutes later another hit was indicated by a sudden eruption of smoke amidships that came neither from the German's funnel nor her guns. More hits were observed, then the *Gneisenau* increased speed and presented her stern to the *Renown*, dropping all pretence of putting up a fight. In the words of Captain Simeon, the effect of the final hits 'was to make a reluctant enemy into a hurriedly retiring one'

As soon as the *Gneisenau* broke off the action and turned away the *Scharnhorst* began to make smoke and swung across her consort's stern, apparently in an effort to cover her escape. Whitworth then switched the fire of the *Renown*'s main armament to the *Scharnhorst* When the first 15-inch salvo fell dangerously close to her, she also sheered away and took to her heels, occasionally swinging to fire a broadside at the *Renown*. It was now that an 11-inch shell from the *Scharnhorst*'s guns caused the only casualty of the action aboard the *Renown*. Lieutenant-Commander Martin Evans, the battlecruiser's navigating officer, was hit in the left foot by a shell splinter from a near miss and lost two toes. Although in considerable pain, Evans refused to leave the bridge and continued to con the ship throughout the rest of the action.

The wind had now veered to the north-north-east and was strengthening all the time, bringing on its wings frequent squalls of icy sleet that lashed at the ship vindictively. The seas, steep and angry, marched in from the far horizon like battalions of avenging warriors And into this the *Renown*, striving to close the gap with the enemy, steamed at 26 knots, her broad bows slamming into each incompressible wall of green water with a resounding crash that sent shock waves running from stem to stern. Accurate gunnery was impossible, and Whitworth reluctantly reduced to 20 knots.

The chase continued for the next hour, with the *Renown*'s guns continuing to hurl salvos after the rapidly disappearing enemy. The *Gneisenau* replied with an occasional salvo from her after turret, which was clearly under local control, while from time to time the *Scharnhorst* swung around to fire an ineffective broadside  At 0600 the German ships, having increased their lead to 16½ miles, disappeared into a rain squall and all contact was lost  Whitworth was unwilling to give up the chase and increased to 29 knots at the risk of serious damage to the flagship, but when the rain finally cleared an hour later the horizon was empty of ships

Ironically, although the *Renown* was little affected by the enemy's shells, a combination of the fierce blast from her 15-inch turrets and the pounding she took when slamming into the seas at speed caused considerable damage. Her fore hatch was blown in by the gun blast, and the seas breaking over the forecastle head found their way below, flooding several compartments. Of the other side, it was later learned that the *Renown*'s big guns had scored three hits on the *Gneisenau*, crippling her main fire control, putting one of her forward 11-inch turrets out of action and causing extensive damage to her superstructure

Both the Admiralty and Vice-Admiral Whitworth remained in ignorance of the true situation in Narvik, and when the Admiral was ordered to concentrate his efforts on preventing enemy forces from reaching the port he decided that a reconnaissance was required  Captain B. A W. Warburton-Lee, who had commanded the earlier minelaying operation, was therefore directed to take five destroyers of his flotilla into Vestfjord to assess the situation  That evening Warburton-Lee, flying his pennant in HMS *Hardy*, led the *Hunter*, *Havoc*, *Hotspur* and *Hostile* into the fjord as far as the pilot station at Trangy. Here he was warned by the Norwegians that six German destroyers and a U-boat had earlier passed up the fjord and that the entrance to Narvik harbour was mined. Warburton-Lee signalled this information to Whitworth, adding that he intended to enter Narvik harbour and attack the enemy at dawn

With *Hardy* in the lead, the destroyers left Trangy soon after midnight and an hour later entered the narrow waters of Ofotfjord. It was a dark, moonless night, shrouded in mist and filled with driving snow  With the steep sides of the fjord closing in on them, the ships steamed slowly in line ahead, every eye straining and every ear cocked for any sign of danger  At first light, about 0400, they were off the entrance to Narvik harbour  A fine mist still clung to the land, but the snow had cleared away

Five German destroyers were visible at anchor in the harbour, all larger and more heavily gunned than the British ships, but, leaving *Hotspur* and *Hostile* on guard outside, Warburton-Lee led the others in  The Germans were caught napping  The *Hardy* blew the bottom out of the enemy flotilla leader with a torpedo, while another German destroyer was hit by two torpedoes fired by *Hunter* and *Havoc* and sank before its crew could reach their guns  The remaining three German ships were subjected to such a hail of shells from the British guns that they were all disabled before they could offer resistance.

Having disposed of the German destroyers, Warburton-Lee called in the *Hotspur* and *Hostile* to assist in the destruction of the 23 merchant ships in the harbour  Eight of these, all German, were sunk before the British destroyers withdrew without loss or damage to themselves

His luck having held so far, Warburton-Lee considered that it would be unwise to tempt Providence further and led his ships out of the harbour  As they cleared the breakwaters three German destroyers were sighted coming out of Herjangs Fjord at high speed, obviously intent on joining battle. This the British could have coped with, but out of the mist ahead now appeared two other German destroyers, which had been anchored unseen in Ballangen Fjord. The newcomers opened fire with all guns as they advanced

Warburton-Lee's escape route to the sea was cut off and he now had no alternative but to fight his way out. The odds against the British ships were too great. The *Hardy* quickly came under fire from the heavier German guns, one shell landing squarely on her open bridge, mortally wounding Warburton-Lee and killing most of those with him. Only one man, Lieutenant Stanning, was unhurt He took the wheel and, when a shell exploded in the engine room, beached the stricken destroyer on the nearest shore. Warburton-Lee's last signal before he died was 'Continue to engage the enemy.'

In accordance with the Captain's last wish, the fight went on, developing into a furious battle reminiscent of the days of fighting sail, so close were the opposing ships as they slugged it out in the fjord. The *Hunter*, commanded by Lieutenant-Commander L. de Villiers, was sunk; *Hostile* and *Hotspur* were damaged, but with *Havoc* they shot their way out of the trap to the open sea. As they were fleeing, the German supply ship *Rauenfels* entered Vestfjord, bound for Narvik. She was loaded with ammunition for the invasion force, and when the *Havoc* opened fire on her she blew up with a spectacular display of pyrotechnics that provided a suitable finale to a magnificent naval action.

Warburton-Lee and his men did not die unavenged At noon on the 13th the battleship HMS *Warspite*, accompanied by nine destroyers, went back into Ofotfjord, sank the seven German destroyers remaining there, and withdrew without loss to themselves.

# 11

# Cape Matapan

*28 March 1941*

In spite of the heroic efforts of the Royal Navy, and a belated landing by British and French troops, the German invasion of Norway ended in unqualified success. By mid-June the whole country, from Oslo to the North Cape, was in German hands, the Allied troops having been forced into an ignominious retreat back to their ships. Meanwhile Holland, Belgium and Luxembourg had also fallen to the swift-moving Wehrmacht, and before the month was out the unthinkable happened. France, with her supposedly impregnable Maginot Line breached and her two million-strong army in disarray, surrendered to the advancing enemy. Britain now stood alone, awaiting the invasion barges to cross the Channel.

At sea, in the Mediterranean, another terrible catastrophe threatened  For more than a hundred years the British and French fleets had jointly controlled these almost landlocked waters, ensuring that they were kept open to legitimate commerce  Now the French Mediterranean Fleet had declared for the Vichy Government and might soon come under German control. This Britain could not countenance, and she called on the French ships to surrender to the Royal Navy. The French refused to bow and took refuge under the guns of their Mediterranean base at Mers-el-Kebir, near Oran  Here they were besieged by a British naval force under Admiral Sir James Somerville and on 3 July, having declined to surrender, were systematically destroyed by the big guns of their erstwhile ally. Nearly 1,300 Frenchmen died in a foolish stand for a cause that was without honour

The threat posed by the renegade French Fleet in the Mediterranean had been removed, but there still remained the Italians, who two weeks before the fall of France had thrown in their lot with the Germans. On paper the Italian Fleet was an impressive force which included six modern battleships, nineteen equally modern cruisers, 120 destroyers and over 100 submarines  All were based in ports within easy striking distance of British merchant shipping passing through the Mediterranean  Fortunately, although the Italian ships were in many cases superior to those of the Royal Navy, the crews who manned them lacked the stomach for a fight when the odds were equal

The two fleets first clashed on 8 July 1940 when the Italians put to sea intent on attacking a British convoy bound from Alexandria to Malta. This was an important convoy, and it was escorted by the battleships *Warspite* and *Malaya*, the aircraft carrier *Eagle*, five cruisers and eighteen destroyers. Although the Italian attackers were, if anything, numerically superior, when the British warships rounded on them they put up only a token fight before running away.

The *Warspite* and *Malaya* chased them to within 25 miles of the Italian mainland and in a long-range action damaged one Italian battleship and two cruisers without suffering so much as chipped paintwork themselves. Ten days later the Royal Australian Navy cruiser *Sydney* and two destroyers met the 40-knot cruisers *Bartolomeo Colleoni* and *Giovanni delle Bande Nere* off the island of Crete. Although the *Sydney* was outclassed and outgunned, the Italians again turned tail and ran, relying on their superior speed to take them out of danger. They were not quite fast enough HMS *Sydney*'s accurate gunnery crippled the *Bartolomeo Colleoni* and she was finished off with torpedoes by the destroyers. The other Italian cruiser made good her escape, but not before being severely pounded by the *Sydney*'s guns

Italy invaded Greece in October 1940, expecting a short and victorious campaign. However, the tenacity and ferocity of the Greek resistance soon had the Italian armies facing complete disaster In March 1941 Germany felt obliged to come to the aid of her incompetent ally and moved troops into Bulgaria, preparatory to crossing the frontier into Greece Britain responded by sending her troops in, a mistake that was to rank with her ill-fated adventure in Norway in the spring of 1940 and would seriously affect the fortunes of the North Africa campaign But, once landed in Greece, the British troops could not be easily withdrawn, and keeping them supplied, via the Cape and the Suez Canal, became a major problem for the Royal Navy It was on the final 500-mile passage from Port Said to Piraeus that the merchant ships proved to be most vulnerable, for on this leg they were within easy reach of German and Italian land-based aircraft. Only with heavy escorts did the British convoys fight their way through.

Although their own surface ships had shown little inclination to challenge the Royal Navy in the Atlantic, the Germans were secretly disgusted that the largely unused Italian Fleet made no attempt to attack the British convoys Pressure was exerted by Admiral Erich Raeder, C-in-C of the German Navy, on his Italian opposite number Admiral Riccardi, but Riccardi procrastinated, claiming that without aircraft carriers he could not guarantee air cover for his ships When Raeder offered German aircraft, Riccardi pleaded a shortage of fuel – and so it went on The truth was that the Italian dictator Mussolini was already harbouring doubts about which way the war would go and hesitated to commit his fleet

The pressure on the Italians was increased, and in desperation Admiral Riccardi agreed to make a token sweep into the Eastern Mediterranean in force The operation, to be led by Admiral Angelo Iachino, was planned as a sortie by a squadron of heavy cruisers, supported by the battleship *Vittorio Veneto* and with air cover provided by German land-based aircraft. The cruisers were to split into two sections when approaching Crete, the northern section steaming as far as the eastern end of the island while the southern section would turn back on reaching Gavdhos Island. Any enemy ships met with would be attacked. At best this was only a half-hearted gesture, but the Germans were satisfied that at long last the Italian Fleet was to put to sea with aggressive intent

Admiral Iachino sailed from Naples during the night of 26 March, flying his flag in the *Vittorio Veneto* and accompanied by an escort of four destroyers The

41,377-ton battleship, not long from the builder's yard, had a top speed of 30 knots, mounted nine 15-inch guns and was herself alone a match for anything the British had afloat in the Mediterranean. She was joined later in the day from other Italian bases by the 10,000-ton cruisers *Bolzano, Fiume, Pola, Trento, Trieste* and *Zara*, all armed with 8-inch guns, the two 6-inch gun cruisers *Luigi di Savoia Duca degli Abruzzi* and *Giuseppe Garibaldi* and nine destroyers The assembled squadron was an impressive display of naval might and inspired Admiral Iachino to go in search of British supply convoys.

The Italian ships passed through the Straits of Messina at dawn on the 27th, rounded the toe of Italy and then steamed south-east towards Crete As the day wore on Iachino became more and more apprehensive as there was no sign of the promised Luftwaffe air cover and the Mediterranean was living up to its image with fine, clear weather. He felt dangerously exposed, and his fears were realized at around noon that day when 75 miles east of Sicily A Sunderland flying boat of RAF Coastal Command at Malta, nearing the end of its maximum flying time and about to return to base, sighted three of the Italian cruisers which had detached to sweep north of Crete. The game was up.

Admiral Sir Andrew Cunningham, British C-in-C Mediterranean, had been warned by Naval Intelligence as early as the 24th that a major Italian fleet operation was planned for the Aegean or Eastern Mediterranean He was not unduly surprised when the Sunderland's report came in It seemed likely that the Italians were about to attack convoys ferrying Australian and New Zealand troops between Port Said and Piraeus, and Cunningham at once ordered all these convoys to return to whichever port was nearest. More air reconnaissance was set up, and Vice-Admiral H. D Pridham-Wippell, who was then at sea off Crete with the 2nd Destroyer Flotilla, was ordered to join up with a cruiser force also at sea and take up a position south of Gavdhos Island Under cover of darkness on the 27th Cunningham left Alexandria with the 1st Battle Squadron, comprising the battleships *Warspite, Barham* and *Valiant* and the aircraft carrier *Formidable*, screened by nine destroyers of the 10th and 14th Destroyer Flotillas. Cunningham's battleships were all of 1916 vintage and hard pressed to make 25 knots, but they each mounted eight 15-inch and fourteen 6-inch guns. The plan was for Pridham-Wippell to lure the Italians to within range of these guns

Admiral Iachino, through his cypher breakers on the *Vittorio Veneto*, was aware that his northern force had been sighted by the Coastal Command Sunderland. On the evening of the 27th, after consulting with Naval Headquarters in Rome, he therefore cancelled the sweep to the north of Crete and gathered all his ships together. A surprise attack on a British convoy was now out of the question, but, mindful of the pressure the Germans were exerting for a fleet action of some kind, Iachino was reluctant to turn back

At dawn on the 28th the Italian fleet was forty miles to the west of Gavdhos and making 18 knots on a course of 130 degrees The ships were deployed in three separate formations, the *Vittorio Veneto* and four destroyers to the south, the cruisers *Zara, Fiume, Pola, Abruzzi* and *Garibaldi*, with six destroyers, thirty miles to the north and the *Trieste, Trento* and *Bolzano* and three destroyers in the middle. As soon as it was fully light the *Vittorio Veneto* launched her spotter aircraft, which an hour later reported sighting four enemy cruisers and four destroyers. The enemy ships were then some sixty miles ahead of the Italian force and steering a similar course. Assuming that these warships were the escort for a convoy not yet visible, and calculating that the odds were heavily in his favour, Iachino increased to 30 knots and prepared for action.

There was no convoy. The ships Iachino's aircraft had spotted were Vice-Admiral Pridham-Wippell's squadron, which comprised the cruisers *Orion* (flag), *Ajax*, *Gloucester* and *Perth* and the destroyers *Hasty*, *Hereward*, *Ilex* and *Vendetta*. It had been planned that Cunningham's 1st Battle Squadron would be in close support, but the Admiral was still 95 miles to the south, the *Valiant* having clipped a sandbank on sailing from Alexandria, clogging her main intakes and reducing her speed to 20 knots. Meanwhile Pridham-Wippell's ships, not one of them with a gun larger than 6-inch calibre, were on their own.

It was fortunate for the British cruiser squadron that the *Vittorio Veneto*'s spotter plane was not the only one in the air at that time The carrier *Formidable* had also put up reconnaissance aircraft at dawn, one of which, at 0722, reported sighting four cruisers and four destroyers steaming on a south-easterly course. Cunningham, not surprisingly, assumed that the aircraft had sighted Pridham-Wippell's ships and took no action. In fact, the ships seen were part of Iachino's fleet.

The battle might never have been joined had the *Orion* not sighted the Italian cruiser *Trieste*, which was then lagging behind Iachino's main force. Pridham-Wippell increased speed to intercept and soon had two other enemy cruisers in sight. The Vice-Admiral was now in a dilemma, for his identification charts told him that the Italian ships were much superior in firepower. Rather than attack directly, he put on more speed and drew closer to the Italians. When he was sure he had been sighted and recognized, he led his ships round on to a southerly course. The enemy cruisers followed Pridham-Wippell was leading them into a trap.

At 0812 the Italian cruisers opened fire at a range of thirteen miles. Their shells fell short of the British ships, but the faster Italians were closing the gap and in another fifteen minutes the range was down to twelve miles HMS *Gloucester*, bringing up the rear of the British cruiser force, came in for the full fury of the Italian guns and was forced to zigzag wildly to avoid being hit She opened up with her after turret, and while her 6-inch salvos fell short they appeared to be enough to persuade the enemy cruisers to fall back out of range.

For the next half hour both sides were content with the occasional ranging shot as the British drew the Italians to the south-east. All this time Pridham-Wippell was in touch with Cunningham on board the *Warspite*, advising the admiral of the progress of the action. Pridham-Wippell, believing that the pursuing Italian cruisers were the only enemy ships in the area, was content to keep his distance, but this was becoming increasingly difficult The Italians clearly had a speed advantage of several knots over his ships.

At 0855, without warning, the roles of the British and Italian ships were suddenly reversed Admiral Iachino, who for some time had been having misgivings about this incursion deep into enemy waters, decided to go no further. He ordered the cruisers to reverse course and return to base, and while the manoeuvre was being executed he continued to the east with the *Vittorio*

*Veneto* to cover their rear. As soon as the Italians turned for home Pridham-Wippell followed them around, intending to keep visual contact while remaining out of range of their guns. Unwittingly, he now put his ships in danger of being caught between the retreating cruisers and the *Vittorio Veneto*. The battleship, with her accompanying cruisers and destroyers, was then to the north-east of the British ships and beyond visual range.

The day had become typically Mediterranean, with a warm sun shining down out of a blue sky dotted with fine-weather cumulus like balls of cotton wool, and the sea as calm as a mirror. Even though the enemy was in sight, the war seem far removed and the mood in the British ships was relaxed and unhurried. Teacups rattled on bridges, guns' crew sunbathed outside their turrets and the unoccupied leaned over rails to gaze down into the shimmering blue water. Then the 41,000-ton *Vittorio Veneto* appeared on the horizon to the north-east and opened up with her 15-inch guns.

The Italian battleship was sixteen miles off the leading British ship, Pridham-Wippell's flagship HMS *Orion*, and her fire was heavy and accurate. Tall geysers of water erupted all around the *Orion*, shattering the illusory peace. Pridham-Wippell, realizing that he was in an extremely dangerous position, at once sheered off to the south and increased speed to 30 knots. The *Vittorio Veneto* and her entourage followed him, and when the range came down to twelve miles Iachino's cruisers added their 8-inch guns to the battleship's salvos, concentrating their fire on the *Orion*; the *Gloucester*, plagued with engine trouble and falling back, also came under fire. Pridham-Wippell ordered all ships to make smoke, which they did very effectively, completely hiding the squadron from the Italians, and after a few parting salvos Iachino gave up the chase and turned his ships back to the west.

Pridham-Wippell's ships, all miraculously undamaged, joined up with Admiral Cunningham's battle fleet at 1230 and the combined force then set off after the retreating Italians. Unfortunately, the *Valiant* still had problems with her condenser and could make only 22 knots; the *Barham*, feeling her great age perhaps, also could manage no more.

The action seemed likely to turn into a long stern chase, which the Italians, with their vastly superior speed, must surely win. Cunningham's only real hope of bringing Iachino to battle now lay in the use of air power. RAF Blenheims were called in from Greece and found Iachino's ships ninety miles south of Cape Matapan, the southernmost point of Greece. During the course of the day the Blenheims dropped a total of 23,750lb of bombs on the Italian fleet, but apart from a few near misses on the cruisers *Garibaldi* and *Zara* this was largely a wasted effort. Torpedo bombers flown off the *Formidable* had more success. One Albacore penetrated a horrific curtain of fire, including a 15-inch splash barrage, and survived long enough to put a torpedo into the *Vittorio Veneto*.

The torpedo struck the battleship on the port side aft, the explosion ripping a great hole in her hull. The sea poured in, flooding the port engine room, and the *Vittorio Veneto* slewed to a halt, listing heavily to port. Damage control parties rushed into action, and within the hour much of the water had been pumped out and the *Vittorio Veneto* was again upright and under way on her starboard engine, making 15 knots. She later worked up to 19 knots, and, with

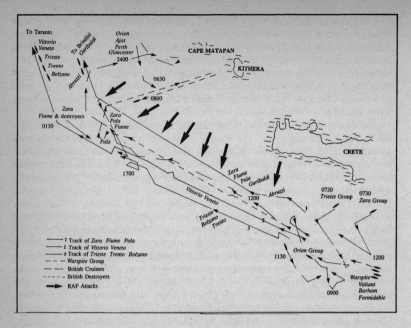

*Battle of Cape Matapan, 28 March 1941*

the heavy cruisers *Trieste*, *Trento*, *Fiume*, *Zara*, *Bolzano* and *Pola* forming a tight screen around her, she pushed on to the west.

With sunset only a few hours away, Cunningham knew he now had little hope of catching up with the Italians before dark, but he was determined to keep in visual touch or he would lose them altogether. To avoid this he ordered Vice-Admiral Pridham-Wippell to make contact once more with the enemy. At the same time the admiral called for a final strike by the *Formidable*'s torpedo aircraft. Six Albacores went in with the last of the daylight and were again met by a fierce anti-aircraft barrage, the Italian ships letting fly with every gun they could bring to bear. The British aircraft were not deterred and flew steadily on, skimming the surface of the water. The primary target, the *Vittorio Veneto*, escaped further harm but one British torpedo struck the 10,000-ton cruiser *Pola*. She was seen to slow down and then stop, dropping rapidly astern of the other ships.

Being under the impression that the British ships tracking him were a long way astern, and confident that the coming darkness precluded any more air attacks, Admiral Iachino felt relatively safe. He sent the cruisers *Zara* and *Fiume* back to stand by the damaged *Pola* and carried on to the west. He was, as yet, completely unaware that Cunningham's battleships were on his trail and was confident that Pridham-Wippell's cruisers, even if they regained contact, would not attack again before next morning. By this time the Luftwaffe would be overhead

110   *Salvo!*

Iachino was also not privy to the knowledge that Admiral Sir Andrew Cunningham was a keen exponent of the night action – even if some of his officers were not Furthermore, Cunningham was well aware that German aircraft would arrive at the crack of dawn to threaten his ships. At 2037, having returned to the *Warspite*'s bridge after supper, Cunningham received a report that the Italian fleet was only 33 miles ahead of his ships and steaming at an estimated 13 knots. The admiral signalled his destroyers to move in to attack with torpedoes

The 2nd and 14th Destroyer Flotillas, with Captain Philip Mack leading in HMS *Jervis*, shot ahead at 28 knots like hounds let off the leash Mack planned to cut across in front of the Italians and then attack from the north Unfortunately, he was acting on false information: the *Vittorio Veneto* and her escorts were in fact 57 miles to the west and moving away at 19 knots It was a dark, moonless night, with only moderate visibility, and Mack's destroyers passed astern of the Italians without sighting them.

Pridham-Wippell, whose flagship *Orion* was equipped with an early form of radar (then known as RDF), had meanwhile made contact with the enemy At 2100 he reported: 'One unknown ship 240 degrees five miles apparently stopped. My position is 35-20N 21-06E.' Thinking that the stationary ship, which was no more than an unidentifiable blip on the RDF tube, might be the *Vittorio Veneto*, Pridham-Wippell decided to leave her to Cunningham's battleships He slipped past the stationary ship in the dark and continued on, hoping to come up with the rest of the Italian fleet The vice-admiral, being, like Captain Mack, under the mistaken impression that the Italians were making only 13 knots, did not increase speed above 20 knots

On receipt of Pridham-Wippell's report, Cunningham altered course to investigate, forming his three battleships and the carrier into a tight line ahead, with three cables between each ship The *Valiant*, the only ship with RDF, was in the lead At 2203 she reported an RDF echo at three points on her port bow, distance eight miles and stopped. The *Valiant*'s radar operator estimated the target ship to be over 600 feet long, and hopes ran high that this was the *Littorio* class battleship earlier reported to have been hit by the *Formidable*'s aircraft.

The tension mounted as Cunningham brought his ships around to port to head directly for the enemy in line abreast, a move considered by some on the bridge of the *Warspite* to involve a high degree of risk When some of his staff warned against the action, Cunningham said, 'If that's the enemy, we will turn towards them and find out what sort they are and how soon we can sink them ' One eye witness later commented: 'It thus occurred for the first time in a night encounter either in peace or war [that] a battle fleet turned towards an unknown force of enemy ships.'

The carrier *Formidable*, being highly vulnerable, was ordered out of the line and dropped astern. The battleships, *Valiant*, *Warspite* and *Barham*, with the *Valiant*'s radar reports being passed by radio to the flagship, now moved in with all guns manned, their attendant destroyers keeping station on either side At 2220 the target still had not moved and the range was down to $4^1/_2$ miles. Cunningham signalled the destroyers on the port side to move over to starboard, to give his big guns a clear field of fire.

The first visual sighting of the target was at 2223, by the Australian destroyer *Stuart*. Seconds later night glasses on the bridge of the flagship picked out a shadowy outline which was indentified as a *Zara* class cruiser. She was in fact the *Pola*, the other victim of the *Formidable*'s torpedo bombers The unfortunate cruiser had been lying dead in the water while her engineers worked frantically to repair her damaged engines. Like all Italian warships the *Pola* had no radar, and she was completely unaware of the large British force moving in on her.

At 4,000 yards, with the Italian cruiser still exhibiting no sign of having seen the approaching ships, Cunningham used starboard helm to bring the three battleships back into line ahead, their crouching gun turrets swinging silently to port on oil-filled bearings to lock on to the target. The night came suddenly alive when, at 2228, the destroyer *Greyhound* snapped on her 21-inch searchlight and the battleships followed suit. Caught in the blinding swathes of light, the *Pola*, listing heavily and down by the stern, was cruelly exposed, defenceless and bewildered. And then, as the probing beams swept from side to side, two more cruisers – the *Zara* and *Fiume* – and four destroyers were revealed close by. All the enemy ships had their guns trained fore and aft, and so complete did the surprise appear to be that it was as though the British had stumbled upon a gathering of sleepy fishermen with their nets down. Engine-room telegraphs jangled urgently, propellers thrashed the water and steel decks vibrated to the thump of running feet

The Italian awakening came too late. The *Warspite*'s firing gongs rang, a brilliant orange flash turned night into day and the battleship shuddered as six of her 15-inch guns thundered out as one. The huge 2,000lb shells showed up momentarily in the searchlight beams, and then the exposed side of the *Pola* disappeared from view in a welter of smoke and flame.

The other battleships joined in, and broadside after broadside slammed into the helpless Italian cruisers, none of which fired back (the excuse given for this was that the cruisers had no flashless propellant for their guns). Whatever the reason, first the *Pola*, then the *Zara* and then the *Fiume* were reduced to blazing wrecks without firing a single shot in their own defence.

As the flames on board the cruisers lit up the night sky and billows of black smoke rolled back to the horizon, the Italian destroyers recovered sufficiently to launch a torpedo attack. Cunningham immediately pulled his big ships out of the way, leaving the British destroyers to deal with their opposite numbers The fight was fierce and chaotic, with the air filled with bursting shells and the sea alive with streaking torpedoes When it was all over fifteen minutes later the Italian destroyers *Giosue Carducci* and *Vittorio Alfieri* were on fire and sinking.

The *Fiume* sank in flames less than an hour after being pounded by the 15-inch guns of Cunningham's battleships, taking with her most of her complement of 705 men. The *Zara*, abandoned by her crew, was torpedoed and sunk at 0240 on the 29th by the destroyer flotilla leader *Jervis*. It was also left to the *Jervis* to finish off the *Pola*, which was still afloat at 0400 that morning. Her crew had taken to the water soon after she was first hit but had re-boarded when it appeared that she might stay afloat. Had these men then set about putting their ship in order, it may have been possible for the damaged cruiser to slip away in the dark. It would seem, however, that the rough handling they had received at the hands of the British battleships, followed by the shock of immersion in the water, was too much for them  Once back aboard they broke open the *Pola*'s wine locker and indulged themselves unwisely  When Captain Mack put the *Jervis* alongside and sent over a boarding party armed with cutlasses, the surrender was quick and final  Mack decided to tow his prize back to Alexandria, but the dawn brought with it the expected large force of German dive bombers and the *Pola* was hastily abandoned by friend and foe alike  She was despatched by a torpedo from the destroyer *Nubian*

Thus ended the running fight known as the Battle of Cape Matapan  It had cost the Italians three heavy cruisers and two destroyers, along with the lives of 2,400 men, including Vice-Admiral Cattaneo, commanding the heavy cruiser squadron  The British, who had suffered no damage or casualties in the ships and had lost only two aircraft, picked up 905 enemy survivors, among them 35 Germans. They would have saved more but the arrival of the German dive bombers put an end to rescue operations. As he was leaving the area Admiral Cunningham radioed the Chief of Italian Naval Staff, giving the position of the survivors still in the water, and advised that a hospital ship was needed

At sunrise, the British ships then being only forty miles off Cape Matapan, Cunningham decided to continue the search for the *Vittorio Veneto*, which he believed was still being shadowed by Pridham-Wippell. The admiral was unaware that, when, during the bedlam of the night, he had signalled all ships not engaged with the enemy to withdraw to the north-east, the cruisers had taken him at his word  Admiral Iachino, seeing the reflection of gun flashes in the sky, had meanwhile made for home as fast as his one engine would carry him.

Cunningham was disappointed that he had been cheated of the chance to meet Iachino in battle, but as he turned his ships to return to Alexandria he was well satisfied at having won the day  The fleet was attacked by German bombers as it steamed south, but these were beaten off by the *Formidable*'s fighters.

Matapan was the first fleet action fought by the Royal Navy in the Mediterranean since the Battle of the Nile in August 1798. As a result of Cunningham's decisive victory, the powerful Italian surface fleet never again took the offensive, and the defence of convoys supplying Rommel's troops in North Africa was thereafter left to German U-boats and aircraft. More importantly, when it became necessary to evacuate the British expeditionary force from Greece at the end of April, the total absence of Italian warships in the area undoubtedly saved thousands of British lives

# 12

# Kormoran and Sydney

*19 November 1941*

A wave of national pride swept through Australia when in November 1914 the cruiser HMAS *Sydney* sank the German commerce raider *Emden* off the Cocos or Keeling Islands. Although the *Sydney* was commanded by an Englishman and almost half her crew were from the mother country, she earned a very special place in the Australian history books. When the *Sydney* was scrapped after the war her fighting top was erected on Bradley's Head in *Sydney* harbour to remind succeeding generations of the Royal Australian Navy's past glory. A few yards away from the old mast stands a sad memorial to the 645 men who lost their lives in another HMAS *Sydney,* twenty-seven years after the *Emden*.

The third warship to bear the name of Australia's principal city – the first was a sailing ship of 100 tons launched in 1813 – was built at Swan Hunter's yard at Wallsend-on-Tyne in 1934 for the Royal Navy She was to be named HMS *Phaeton*, but before completion she was bought by the Australian Government and commissioned as HMAS *Sydney* in 1935 The new *Sydney* was a *Leander* class cruiser of 6,830 tons displacement, with four oil-fired turbines designed for a top speed of 32½ knots Her armament, eight 6-inch and four 4-inch guns, four 3-pounders, three quadruple .5-inch machine-guns and eight 21-inch torpedo tubes, was supplemented by a catapult-mounted Walrus amphibian

On the outbreak of yet another world war, in September 1939, Australian-born Captain John Collins took command and the *Sydney* became an all-Australian ship. She spent some time patrolling Indian Ocean waters but in May 1940, when the fall of France was imminent and Italy seemed certain to enter the war on the side of Germany, she was transferred to the Mediterranean

Within a few days of the collapse of France and Italy's entry into the war, the *Sydney* was involved in her first brush with the enemy. On 9 July 1940, when on patrol to the north of Crete in company with the British destroyers *Ilex* and *Hyperion*, she sighted the 40-knot Italian cruisers *Bartelomeo Colleoni* and *Giovanni delle Bande Nere*. The Italian ships, named after two great military heroes in their country's history, failed to live up to their assumed mantles, taking flight as soon as the *Sydney* appeared. The Australian ship gave chase and opened fire at a range of eleven miles, concentrating on the *Bartolomeo Colleoni*. The *Sydney*'s gunners had learned their trade well and so crippled the *Colleoni* that the destroyers easily finished her off with torpedoes The *Sydney* then turned her guns on the *Bande Nere* and she also sustained damage, but she succeeded in escaping under cover of a smoke screen. Italian bombers joined in the fight, but in spite of their attentions the *Sydney* and her destroyers rescued 545 enemy seamen from the water.

Over the next six months the *Sydney* took part in a number of major actions in the Mediterranean that earned her well-deserved honours. When, in February 1941, with the Japanese threat looming on the horizon, the cruiser returned to Australian waters, the welcome she received was ecstatic. On her arrival in Sydney harbour she was greeted by an armada of small craft which escorted her to a berth packed with cheering crowds. After a triumphal parade through the city streets, Captain Collins and his crew were given a civic reception by the Governor-General and the Lord Mayor, and then presented with a bronze plaque commemorating the sinking of the *Bartolomeo Colleoni* The Australians, with most of their fighting men serving in a war so far away that it was difficult to relate to, needed heroes to acclaim, and they had found them in HMAS *Sydney*.

While the *Sydney* was afloat in the more agreeable waters of the Mediterranean, 38-year-old Korvettenkapitän Theodor Detmers was feeling the icy lash of the north wind off the coast of Norway Throughout the campaign to invade and subdue this frigid land, Detmers had been in command of the destroyer *Hermann Schoemann*, riding close escort to the *Scharnhorst* and *Gneisenau* It was a time of savage battles fought against two unbending enemies, the British and the Arctic weather, to which had been added the extra burden of the unpredictable behaviour of the newly built destroyer's experimental engines. When, on 17 June 1940, Detmers brought the *Hermann Schoemann* back to Wilhelmshaven, he welcomed the change of command he was offered

Detmers experienced not only a change of command but also a change of vocation: he was appointed to an ex-merchant ship His new command, *Hilfskreuzer 41*, had been built by Krupps at Kiel as the *Steirmark* for Hamburg-Amerika's East Indies service and requisitioned by the German Navy as a commerce raider in the summer of 1939 She was a ship of 9,400 tons gross, powered by four diesel engines driving twin screws, which gave her a service speed of 18 knots and a maximum range of 70,000 miles at 10 knots As a Far East trader in times of peace, the *Steirmark* would have had few equals When she emerged from the Deutsche Werft in Hamburg later in the year after an extensive conversion she would still pass as an innocent merchantman, but she was in reality a ship of war to be reckoned with The *Kormoran*, as the Kriegsmarine had renamed her, was armed with six 5.9-inch guns, two 37mm and five 20mm cannon and four 21-inch torpedo tubes The 5.9s were behind counter-weighted steel shutters and the smaller guns under canvas covers, while two of the torpedo tubes were below the waterline and the others concealed on deck Also cleverly hidden from prying eyes were a large motor launch designed for minelaying, two Arado 196 spotter seaplanes and, for the first time on any German auxiliary cruiser, a radar system

The *Kormoran*'s conversion to her new role and her subsequent working up into a state of readiness for war proved to be a lengthy process, and it was 3 December 1940 before Korvettenkapitän Theodor Detmers and his crew of 397 took her to sea with 5,200 tons of fuel oil, 300 mines, 20 torpedoes, ample ammunition for her guns and her hold filled with stores and equipment. Some of the equipment was intended to be handed over to other raiders and U-boats already at sea. Disguised as the Russian ship *Vyacheslav Molotov*, the *Kormoran* slipped through the Denmark Strait during the night of 13 December and then headed south for the busy shipping lanes of the South Atlantic, where many Allied ships still sailed unescorted.

Detmers was pleasantly surprised to fall in with his first victim even before crossing the Equator, and even more surprised to find how easy it was to ply his new trade. The 3,729-ton Greek cargo ship *Antonis*, bound from the Bristol Channel to the River Plate, surrendered without resistance when the *Kormoran* stopped her on 6 January 1941 some 700 miles west of Freetown. To an earlier generation of German raider the Greek's cargo of 4,800 tons of Welsh coal would have been manna from Heaven, but Detmers had no use for it and he ordered the ship and cargo to be scuttled before going on his way.

The *Kormoran*'s second victim, encountered twelve days later, was the 6,889-ton tanker *British Union*, bound for Trinidad in ballast She was by no means as supine as the Greek, immediately turning stern-on when challenged and opening fire on the *Kormoran* with her 4-inch as she zigzagged away. As she fled, the tanker's radio operator tapped out the 'RRRR' signal, signifying that she was under attack by a surface raider. Detmers sank the *British Union*, but in the circumstances he thought it best not to linger. He chose wisely, for, shortly after the *Kormoran* dropped over the horizon, the British armed merchant cruiser *Arawa* appeared in answer to the *British Union*'s call for help.

Detmers had learned early in his new career that commerce-raiding was not without risks. The lesson was repeated on 29 January when he met up with the 11,900-ton refrigerated British meat carrier *Afric Star* and, a few hours later, another British ship, the 5,723-ton *Eurylochus*. Both ships, each armed only with a single 4-inch mounted aft, put up a stiff fight before being sunk and the *Eurylochus* succeeded in getting away an 'RRRR' signal.

The *Kormoran* spent three not particularly fruitful months in the South Atlantic She sank three more ships, captured another and replenished her stores and ammunition several times from the support ship *Nordmark* Throughout, the raider was constantly plagued by engine problems caused by overheating propeller-shaft bearings. Detmers, having been elevated to the rank of Fregattenkapitän, then decided that the time had come to try his luck elsewhere He rounded the Cape of Good Hope in heavy weather during the night of 1 May and moved into the Indian Ocean, where three other German raiders, the *Komet*, *Pinguin* and *Orion*, were then operating with some success. As soon as the weather allowed, the *Kormoran* was repainted, and she assumed the identity of the Japanese ship *Sakito Maru*.

In 1941, Japan's annual production of oil was around 400,000 tons while her annual rate of consumption was 5 million tons, her huge (but currently idle) navy using 12,000 tons a day. Hitherto she had imported the bulk of her oil from America, but when Japanese troops invaded Indo-China in July of that year the United States suspended all trade with Japan, including oil This was closely followed by an international oil embargo, which prevented all but a trickle entering Japan. As Germany had seized the Romanian oil fields for her own needs in October 1940, so Japan now cast an acquisitive eye around the Pacific

Less than 2,000 miles to the south, in the Dutch East Indies, over 8 million tons of oil were being extracted annually – more than enough to supply Japan's needs – to say nothing of an abundance of rubber, tin and iron ore. Japan had then recently signed a pact of non-aggression with Russia and so, she hoped, bought security for her northern coasts. This left her free to strike in the south, when the time was right When HMAS *Sydney* returned to her home waters in February 1941 the Japanese war chiefs were working on their plans for an air attack on the American naval base of Pearl Harbor in Hawaii

The *Sydney* spent the autumn and winter of 1941 on patrol and escort duties in the Indian Ocean. It was a boring, repetitive assignment, unrelieved by the stimulus of combat, but it did have its compensations. The cruiser spent a good deal of time in Australian ports, which suited her crew admirably. In May Captain Collins was relieved by Captain Joseph Burnett, a 42-year-old Australian who had served with the Royal Navy before becoming Assistant Chief of Naval Staff with the RAN

Spring turned to summer, and while the storms of Cape Leeuwin were abating the *Sydney* was employed escorting Singapore-bound merchantmen from Fremantle as far as the Sunda Strait On 11 November Burnett took the cruiser out of the Western Australian port on what looked like being another routine voyage. The *Sydney* was escorting the 6,683-ton *Zeelandia*, carrying troops of the 8th Australian Division for the garrison at Singapore The *Zeelandia*, a British ship, was manned by a particularly troublesome Australian crew whose antics had resulted in her being thirteen days late in leaving Fremantle On passage north the troopship's firemen did not give of their best, resulting in another twenty-four hours lost, and it was the 17th before the *Sydney* finally handed over her charge to the cruiser HMS *Durban* off the Sunda Strait. These malicious and unnecessary delays engineered by the *Zeelandia*'s militant crew were largely responsible for the tragic events that followed

It seemed that the *Kormoran*'s fellow raiders had stirred up a hornet's nest in the Indian Ocean, for she arrived to find the Royal Navy unusually active The scores of vulnerable merchantmen sailing alone Detmers had expected to find were not in evidence, all Allied shipping in the western part of the ocean having been organized into convoys under escort In early June, having spent a fruitless and uncomfortable month in the stormy seas and driving rain of the South-West Monsoon, Detmers decided to try more hospitable waters in the east

The well-used route between the Straits of Malacca, the gateway to the Far East, and the bunkering station at Colombo proved equally barren. The *Kormoran* came across only one likely victim, and she somehow managed to escape. In the third week in June Detmers had decided to go deep into the Bay of Bengal to mine the approaches to the port of Calcutta, when the sighting of a patrolling British armed merchant cruiser changed his mind.

Over the next few days Detmer's luck improved dramatically with the sinking of the *Velebit*, a 4,153-ton Yugoslav ship, and the *Mareeba*, a 3,472-ton British steamer loaded with 5,000 tons of sugar However, the loss of these two ships alerted the Royal Navy, and the cruiser *Enterprise* and the aircraft carrier *Hermes* were sent out to search for the culprit They looked in vain, for

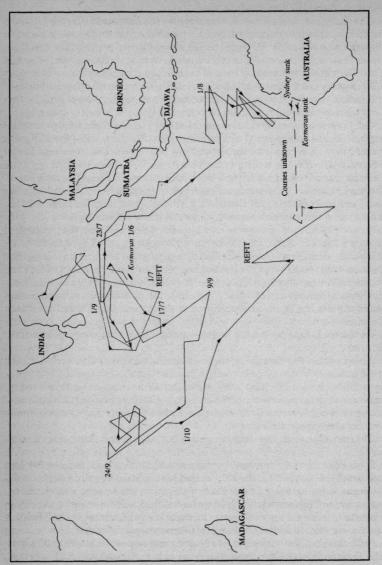

*The Cruise and Loss of the Raider Kormoran*

Detmers had already moved south, where, in the shelter of an uninhabited island off the west coast of Sumatra, the *Kormoran* assumed the disguise of the Dutch motor vessel *Straat Malakka*

The change of identity did little to improve the *Kormoran's* fortunes. In the next three months, during which she patiently scoured the seas between Western Australia and the Sunda Strait, she sank only one ship, the 3,941-ton Greek steamer *Stamatios G Embriricos* As they saw the year drawing to a close without the spectacular successes they had envisaged, Detmers and his crew experienced a great deal of frustration  In the six months they had cruised the Indian Ocean, they had sent to the bottom just three Allied ships with a total tonnage of just over 11,500 tons

On 18 October the *Kormoran* met the supply tanker *Kulmerland* to refuel and transfer her prisoners  Owing to difficulties with the pumps, the oiling was a painfully slow operation, and it was the 26th before the two ships parted company  The *Kormoran* still had on board the 300 mines brought out from Germany, and Detmers now considered laying these in the shipping lanes off Western Australia  For reasons not recorded he changed his mind, and with her lethal cargo of high explosives still occupying space in her after cargo hold the *Kormoran* continued her monotonous patrolling of an empty sea

In the afternoon of 19 November, while the real *Straat Malakka* languished in port 4,000 miles away in Portuguese East Africa, her impersonator, the *Kormoran*, was off the west coast of Australia, near the Tropic of Capricorn  The German ship was experiencing a recurrence of her shaft bearing problem and steaming at easy speed on a north-north-easterly course  It was a fine, clear day, with a calm sea and low swell, and any of the raider's crew not on duty had found a place out of the sun and were resting, including Fregattenkapitän Detmers.

At 1600, when the heat of the day was on the wane and the ship was emerging from her afternoon siesta, the lookout high on the *Kormoran's* foremast reported a ship to the north. Detmers was quickly on the bridge and searching the horizon with his powerful Zeiss binoculars. He focused on a white speck showing up fine on the port bow, which he took to be a sailing ship – not an uncommon sight in these parts  Then, as the distance lessened, the outline of a moderate-size steamer took shape  For the first time in many weeks Detmers felt the adrenalin running.

Detmers estimated the other ship to be at a distance of about fifteen miles and on a reciprocal course, in which case the meeting would take place within half an hour. He sent his men to their action stations and, bracing his legs against the rise and fall of the ship, raised his binoculars again. Only then did he begin to feel uneasy. The outline of the approaching ship was changing, losing some of its innocence  Then, as he watched, the ship veered slightly to starboard, opening up her silhouette to reveal the twin funnels and tall fighting top of a warship. It did not take long for Detmers to establish that he was facing a *Perth* class cruiser with eight 6-inch guns and a speed in excess of 30 knots  The *Kormoran*, on reduced speed because of her overheating shaft bearings, was caught in the open with no bolt-hole to run to

The ship bearing down on the *Kormoran* was the *Sydney*, returning south after handing over the troublesome *Zeelāndia* at the Sunda Strait  Captain

Burnett, anxious to recover the time lost, was making good speed for Fremantle.

Detmers first, and instinctive, reaction was to ring for emergency full speed and alter course due west to run at right angles to the oncoming ship. As the *Kormoran* leaned under full helm in a tight turn to port, so the bows of the enemy cruiser followed her round, the froth of her bow wave visibly increasing as she put on speed.

In response to Detmer's repeated calls for more and more speed, the beat of the *Kormoran*'s four diesels rose to a frenzied tattoo – a slight alteration of course and her stern was to the enemy, and, as though she realized she was running for her life, she surged forward Engine revolutions mounted steadily, and then, for the first time ever, the ex-merchantman, shaking like a thing possessed, reached a speed of 19 knots.

Darkness was less than two hours away, and Detmers had his hopes pinned on a miracle, when the engine-room telephone shrilled The news from below was as bad as it could be. A cylinder of No 4 diesel was running hot, probably due to a jammed exhaust valve. There was no argument: that engine must be shut down or else the damage would be irreparable. The raider lost her new-gained momentum and began to limp along at 14 knots.

There was now nothing left but to play the game of bluff at which the *Kormoran* had become so practised – only this time the other participant was no innocent merchantman unversed in the guiles of war With his guns manned behind their shutters and torpedoes at the ready, Detmers hoisted the Dutch ensign, and when, with the gap between the two vessels down to seven miles, the *Sydney*'s lamp flashed a challenge, he instructed his yeoman of signals to play for time What followed was a masterly performance, mimicking exactly what Detmers, as a Navy man, would expect of a stupid foreign merchant ship The reply given by Yeoman Ahlbach on the lamp was slow and unintelligible, so that the *Sydney* was obliged to repeat her challenge over and over again. She eventually lost patience and demanded that the Dutch ship hoist her signal letter flags. Ahlbach continued the act and after a long delay hoisted a string of flags in an unreadable tangle. The flags were lowered, and again hoisted in the same condition, then once more lowered. This ridiculous farce was acted out until Detmers judged he had gained all the time possible, then the flags were untangled and the four-letter signal identifying the ship as the *Straat Malakka* flew plain at the *Kormoran*'s yardarm.

If the German raider had been disguised as an old Greek tramp, then the bluff might have worked. But she was impersonating a cargo liner owned by the prestigious Royal Dutch Interocean Line, whose crews were highly trained professionals, adept at using signal lamp and flags Detmers, being ignorant of the ways of merchant ships, had overdone it and Captain Burnett of the *Sydney* was not taken in. The cruiser converged on the *Kormoran* at full speed, all her guns trained. At her port yardarm she hoisted the two-letter flag signal 'IK'.

Ahlbach was puzzled by the flag signal. In the International Code of Signals manual the two-letter signal 'IK' read 'Prepare for a cyclone, hurricane or typhoon', which in the circumstances was nonsensical. Detmers, when consulted, was equally puzzled. Neither man understood that the *Sydney* was making a coded challenge in accordance with Admiralty recognition procedure – of which the genuine *Straat Malakka* would have been aware.

Unable to answer the *Sydney*'s signal, Detmers had little alternative but to continue his game of bluff Veering sharply away from the cruiser, he increased speed and ordered his wireless operator to transmit the 'RRRR' signal in the name of the *Straat Malakka*. This was, Detmers hoped, typical of the action which would be taken by a panic-stricken merchant ship in a similar predicament.

Burnett must by now have been to some extent taken in by the *Kormoran*'s show of bumbling innocence, for instead of firing a shot across the German's bows he continued to overhaul her When the *Sydney* was abeam of the *Kormoran*, with only a mile of water between the two ships, Burnett slowed down to keep pace with her and flashed a message in plain language demanding that she answer with her secret call-sign

Detmers, who had no idea of the *Straat Malakka*'s secret call-sign, realized that he had now exhausted all means of deception and that the time had come to play his hand He still had the advantage over the Australian cruiser, for although the latter's forward turrets were trained on him her secondary armament did not appear to be manned In fact, there were a number of men idling on the cruiser's deck, some leaning over the rails, some even waving to the *Kormoran* Quite obviously the *Sydney* was not in a full state of readiness for action The *Kormoran* was

The drill was well practised, and at Detmer's command the bogus Dutch flag fluttered to the deck and the German ensign was run up in its place. At the same time the shutters concealing the *Kormoran*'s 5.9s were raised and she opened fire. At such close range the *Kormoran*'s gunners could hardly miss The first salvo, strategically aimed, demolished the *Sydney*'s bridge, knocked out her fire control and started a serious fire The cruiser replied at once with her 8-inch guns, but the shells whistled harmlessly over the *Kormoran* to explode in the sea beyond.

It was inexcusable that the Australian cruiser should have miscalculated so badly with her first salvo, which at a range of one mile should have crippled her adversary. Detmers took full advantage of his unexpected reprieve and all six of the *Kormoran*'s 5.9s opened up with rapid fire; her 33mm and 20mm cannon joined in, raking the cruiser's decks. The effect was devastating, the *Sydney* suffering a severe mauling as she staggered under the hail of fire Men were cut down with their mouths gaping open in surprise The Walrus aircraft, only then being warmed up on its catapult, exploded in a ball of flame. Severed steam pipes added their high-pitched scream to the tumult.

The *Kormoran* did not have it all her way. The *Sydney*'s gunners recovered from the initial shock and, operating under local control, began to hit back. For the next forty minutes the two ships steamed neck and neck, hammering away at each other with every weapon they possessed. They were so close – some witnesses put the range at 1,000 yards – that it was difficult for either ship to miss The *Sydney*, heavily on fire amidships and with much of her upperworks a tangled mess of jagged steel, put a four-shell salvo from her 'A' and 'B' turrets into the *Kormoran*'s engine room with terrible effect The German ship replied with two torpedoes, one of which exploded under the *Sydney*'s forward turrets,

putting them both out of action. The Australian cruiser's after turrets continued to fire, but she was hard hit, taking in water forward and losing way.

The *Kormoran*'s bridge was by now also in a shambles, with her wireless
room completely destroyed. But by far the worst damage she had sustained was
in her engine room. One of the enemy's shells had ruptured a fuel line and diesel
oil spilling on to the hot engines had resulted in a serious fire. This might have
been containable, but a second shell smashed the fire main and hoses reeled out
produced only a trickle of water. The conflagration spread unchecked

In the heat of the battle the sun had dropped below the horizon unnoticed,
and with night closing in around them the two ships fought on. All six of the
*Kormoran*'s 5.9s were still in action, but the *Sydney* was down to her two after
turrets and the fire of these was erratic. In the midst of the mêlée both ships
launched torpedoes but missed wildly Then, at 1740, the *Sydney* hauled
around to port and headed straight for the *Kormoran* Burnett had decided to
ram. At that crucial moment the fire in the *Kormoran*'s engine room reached
her generators, there was a sharp explosion and the German vessel lost all
power, including her steering gear. Now, with the *Sydney* bearing down on him,
Detmers was unable to get out of the way.

The German guns continued to hammer away at the *Sydney*, but still she
came on, her sharp bows cutting through the water with dreadful intent. Then,
when she was almost on the *Kormoran*, she suddenly veered to port and slid
past the raider's stern with only feet to spare. One good broadside from her
would have blown the *Kormoran* clean out of the water. But the *Sydney*'s guns
were all silent, their turrets smashed, their crews dead or dying She was
noticeably down by the head, and fires raged unchecked in a dozen places. The
*Kormoran* was now stopped, her engine room and all those below consumed by
fire. Detmers tried to bring his guns to bear, but without success. The
Australian cruiser, making no more than 5 knots and pouring out dense black
smoke, headed off into the night on a south-easterly course

Detmers stood down his guns' crews, who in the short, fierce action had fired
450 shells and registered at least 50 hits on the enemy. The men were now
exhausted, but if they wished to live they must join in the fight against the fire
eating away at the heart of their ship. What efforts they made were in vain, and
Detmer's only hope of subduing the blaze now lay in flooding the engine room.
Had they been in friendly waters and able to call for a tug, then this would have
been normal procedure. But there would be no help coming in this hostile place:
on the contrary, other enemy warships might already be racing in to finish the
*Kormoran* off. Detmers decided to abandon ship.

A number of the *Kormoran*'s lifeboats had been destroyed by gunfire and,
with no power for the winches, spare boats stowed in the holds were hoisted out
by hand – a long, laborious process It was 8 p.m. before four boats and three
inflatable rafts were in the water and provisioned ready to cast off All non-
essential men then left the ship, leaving one boat for Detmers and the few men
who stayed behind to lay scuttling charges. One of the inflatables sprang a leak
and sank soon after leaving the ship's side and eighty men died in the water
The fire in the *Kormoran*'s engine-room had taken twenty lives, and this
additional loss was a hard blow The German raider had paid a high price for
a chance meeting with the enemy.

The glow from the fires on the *Sydney* could still be seen when the boats left the *Kormoran*'s side  The cruiser was some six miles off and either stopped or moving very slowly in a south-easterly direction. She remained visible until around 11 p m , when Detmers, having set scuttling charges in the *Kormoran*'s bottom, finally abandoned ship. The charges proved to be unnecessary, for, 35 minutes later, the flames reached the mines in the raider's after hold and she blew apart with a thunderous detonation followed by a fireball soaring hundreds of feet into the night sky  When the last scraps of burning wreckage had fallen hissing into the water and a stunned silence had descended on the sea, both the *Kormoran* and the *Sydney* had gone

A total of 318 men, including Fregattenkapitän Theodor Detmers and all his officers, survived the loss of the *Kormoran*. Some were picked up by passing ships, other sailed their boats to Australia. The only trace ever found of HMAS *Sydney* and her crew of 645 was a battered Carley float, a few empty lifejackets and a dog kennel. It seems likely that she too blew up when flames reached her main magazine  Any men who were still alive when her shattered remains sank would have had little chance of survival in those shark-infested waters

HMAS *Sydney* is recorded in history as the only warship to be sunk by an armed merchant ship in the Second World War. The loss of this valuable cruiser and the lives of so many brave men appears to have been totally unnecessary  The question that must forever remain unanswered is, why did an experienced commander like Captain Joseph Burnett approach to within less than a mile of a ship that was so obviously suspect? The *Sydney* was vastly superior in speed and arms and could easily have stood well off when challenging the *Kormoran*  If in doubt, she could easily have crippled the German raider with a few well-placed salvos, as she had done with the *Bartolomeo Colleoni* in the Mediterranean  But no one will ever know what really happened on that late afternoon and evening of 19 November 1941 off the coast of Western Australia  Was Burnett guilty of incompetence, or were other, unknown factors involved? Those survivors of the *Kormoran* still alive today keep strangely silent.

# 13

# Java Sea

*27 February 1942*

When 1941 drew to a close Japan had acquired a fighting navy that had no equal anywhere in the world. The Imperial Japanese Navy, conceived seventy-eight years earlier in the ruins of Kagoshima, now had no fewer than 260 front-line vessels, including eleven battleships and eleven aircraft carriers, the majority of which were new or had been recently modernized. The men who crewed these ships had been trained along traditional Royal Navy lines.

Strangely enough, this enormous concentration of naval power poised on the edge of the Pacific Ocean did not unduly disturb the British or the Americans. Winston Churchill, a man of usually impeccable perception, said at the time, 'Should Japan enter the war on one side and the United States on ours, ample naval forces will be available to contain Japan by long range controls in the Pacific' He added, 'The Japanese Fleet is not likely to venture far from its home bases so long as a superior battle fleet is maintained at Singapore and Honolulu.'

There were indeed substantial Allied naval forces in the area at that time. The Americans had 100 ships on hand, including eight battleships and two aircraft carriers at Pearl Harbor and three cruisers, thirteen destroyers and 29 submarines in Manila Bay. In Singapore the British kept a battleship, a battlecruiser and four destroyers, while the Royal Netherlands Navy had three cruisers, seven destroyers and thirteen submarines based in Java. Numerically the odds were heavily in favour of the Japanese, but most agreed with Churchill that they would never have the capability, or the audacity, to mount a full-scale attack anywhere in the Pacific. The consensus of opinion was that the Allies need only adopt a purely defensive policy

As for Japan's substantial naval air force, this was again treated with contempt It was the opinion of the British Joint Planning Staff that '. . . the Japanese have never fought against a first class power in the air and we have no reason to believe that their operations would be any more effective than those of the Italians against the Royal Navy in the Mediterranean.' It was even genuinely believed by people who should have known better that Japanese pilots, because of their peculiarly shaped eyes, could not see properly to fly.

Such was the authoritative opinion of Japan's naval capability – or lack of it – on Sunday 7 December 1941 as the American garrison at Pearl Harbor went to breakfast. Alongside the wharves, and off-shore in the anchorage, the ships of the United States Pacific Fleet lay with white awnings stretched, anticipating a lazy day disturbed only by the routine of Divisions. When an Army radar operator reported a large group of aircraft approaching the island from the north he was told to forget about it until breakfast was over.

This was a breakfast that for many in Pearl Harbor would be their last. Before dawn a fleet of six Japanese aircraft carriers had reached a point 230 miles north of Pearl Harbor, having, contrary to the predictions of Churchill and others, ventured more than 3,000 miles from their home base Between 0800 and 0900 on that fine Sabbath morning a total of 353 Japanese aircraft hit Pearl Harbor, inflicting on the totally unprepared Americans the worst military defeat in their history. When the last Japanese bomber had flown away, a pall of black smoke hung over the harbour hiding the mangled wreckage of eight proud battleships, three cruisers, three destroyers and five auxiliary naval craft. Nearly 200 American aircraft had been destroyed – most of them on the ground – 2,403 army and naval personnel lay dead and another 1,178 were injured. The Japanese lost 29 aircraft, one submarine, five midget submarines and fewer than 100 men.

While Pearl Harbor suffered its mauling at the hands of an enemy hitherto not considered to be a serious threat, Japanese troops were landing in Thailand and Malaya in force. They moved quickly inland without meeting serious opposition. A few hours later bombs rained down on Hong Kong and Manila And still the message of Japanese air superiority had not got through to the British. That evening the battleship *Prince of Wales* and the battlecruiser *Repulse*, escorted by four destroyers but totally without air cover, sailed from Singapore and steamed northwards at full speed to deal with Japanese forces landing on the east coast of Malaya. Some forty-eight hours later the 36,727-ton *Prince of Wales*, only eight months old, and the veteran 33,250-ton *Repulse* were sent to the bottom by Japanese torpedo bombers, taking over 1,000 men with them. In the space of three days the Japanese had ruthlessly and efficiently wiped out the bulk of British and American naval power in the Far East. And that was only the beginning: Japanese troops landed in Borneo and the Philippines on the 10th, Hong Kong surrendered on a Christmas Day filled with bestiality and slaughter and Manila fell on the last day of the year.

With the opening of 1942 the unstoppable Japanese war machine gathered pace. On 15 February, in one of the most shameful defeats in recent history, 85,000 British and Australian troops laid down their arms and that impregnable bastion of the British Empire, Singapore, was delivered into Japanese hands The remainder of the Malaysian peninsula followed quickly. Bali surrendered on the 18th and Timor a few days later It would soon be the turn of Java, whence lay the oil riches Japan so coveted

A two-pronged attack was planned on Java, with simultaneous landings at Rembang in the north-east of the island and at Bantam Bay near Batavia The Western Attack Group, commanded by Vice-Admiral Jisaburo Ozawa and comprising 56 troop transports escorted by an aircraft carrier, seven cruisers and two flotillas of destroyers, left Cam Ranh Bay in French Indo-China on the 18th A day later the Eastern Attack Group, made up of 41 transports escorted by a light cruiser, eight destroyers and four minesweepers, sailed from Jolo Island in the Sulu Sea under the command of Rear-Admiral Shoji Nishimura

The two attack groups came together in the Java Sea on the 26th, where Admiral Tokagi Sokichi assumed overall command The combined force of 97 troop transports had by then amassed an escort of forty warships, among them the 11,200-ton heavy cruisers *Mogami*, *Mikuma*, *Suzuya* and *Kumano*, 35-knot ships armed with ten 8-inch and eight 5-inch guns, the light cruisers *Jintsu*, *Naka*, *Natori* and *Yura*, the light aircraft carrier *Ryujo*, the seaplane tenders *Chitose* and *Mizuho* and nineteen destroyers. The 13,000-ton cruisers *Nachi* and *Haguro*, armed with ten 8-inch and eight 5-inch guns, with two destroyers in company, followed astern of the invasion fleet, while four more carriers, two battleships and their escorting cruisers and destroyers were south of Java, on hand if required. All the Japanese cruisers and destroyers carried 24-inch 'Long Lance' torpedoes, deadly weapons with a speed of 50 knots and a range of 25 miles.

In the event the Japanese were being over-cautious. Vice-Admiral Conrad Helfrich, the Dutch admiral commanding Allied naval forces in the Netherlands East Indies, had at his disposal only two heavy cruisers, six light cruisers and eleven destroyers. Of these, the British light cruisers *Danae* and *Dragon* and the destroyers *Scout* and *Tenedos* were of 1918 vintage, three of the American heavy cruiser *Houston*'s 8-inch guns were out of action after bomb damage and the Dutch destroyer *Kortenaer* was restricted to 25 knots by a leaking boiler. All the ships were short of ammunition and the destroyers were also short of torpedoes Crucially, this motley, multi-national force had no experience of working together and, in the face of the staggering Japanese successes of the previous months, morale was low.

Alerted by one of his few land-based reconnaissance aircraft that the invasion force was approaching Java, Vice-Admiral Helfrich decided to split his meagre forces, concentrating the majority of his ships at Sourabaya, in the north-east of the island, under the command of Rear-Admiral Karel Doorman The heavy ships of Doorman's squadron, the 8,300-ton heavy cruiser HMS *Exeter* and the 9,050-ton USS *Houston*, mounted six and nine 8-inch guns respectively. His light cruisers, HMAS *Perth* and the Dutch *De Ruyter* (flag) and *Java*, were all under 7,000 tons and armed with 6-inch, or in the case of the Dutch ships 5.9-inch, guns. Additionally, *Doorman* had nine destroyers, four American, three British and two Dutch, mounting 4 7-inch guns, while all his ships carried the inferior 21-inch torpedo, which was ineffective at ranges of more than nine miles.

In Batavia were the Australian light cruiser *Hobart* and the *Danae*, *Dragon*, *Scout* and *Tenedos*. All these ships had been under constant air attack and were critically short of fuel and ammunition They had put to sea twice and failed to find the Japanese invasion fleet, after which Helfrich decided to send them to Ceylon for their own safety. That left Karel Doorman's squadron of fourteen ships to face the whole might of Admiral Sokichi's approaching armada

Doorman took his squadron out of Sourabaya on the evening of the 26th, the *De Ruyter* ramming and sinking a tug and a water barge as she left the port This was not an auspicious start to the venture; nor did things improve It soon became clear that communications between the various ships were to be a major problem. Doorman spoke no English, and even with a Dutch-speaking American officer translating on the flagship's bridge the relaying of orders was slow and confused. This aggravated the ships' lack of experience in working together to the extent that at times chaos reigned in the squadron

At dawn on the 27th the British destroyer *Jupiter*, scouting on the flank, was attacked by Japanese aircraft but suffered no damage. This was the only indication that the enemy was in the vicinity, but no ships were seen and, as fuel was running short in the destroyers, Doorman decided to return to Sourabaya. On entering the approach channel to the port at 1430 that day, word was received that a reconnaissance aircraft had sighted the Japanese invasion force eighty miles north of the island. Although he and his men had been continuously at action stations for 37 hours, Doorman turned his ships around and headed back out to sea.

The day was warm and humid, with a haze low down on the sea as Doorman put the coast astern again and steamed north at full speed. The *De Ruyter* was in the lead, followed by the heavy cruisers *Exeter* (Captain Oliver Gordon) and *Houston* (Captain A H. Rooks), with the light cruisers astern of them The starboard wing of the column was covered by the British destroyers *Electra*, *Jupiter* and *Encounter* while the American destroyers *John D. Edwards*, *Alden*, *Paul Jones* and *John D Ford* kept guard to port, supported by the Dutch destroyers *Kortenaer* and *Witte de With* The *Houston* was still without the use of three of her 8-inch guns

Doorman had requested spotter aircraft but none materialized. The truth was that the only aircraft available on Java, nine ancient torpedo bombers and a handful of RAF fighters, were then on their way to attack the Japanese troopships. As a compromise, Doorman sent HMS *Exeter*, the only ship equipped with radar, on ahead to attempt an early sighting of the enemy The Japanese, on the other hand, did not lack aerial reconnaissance Their seaplanes had been in the air since early morning, tracking Doorman's ships When it became obvious to Admiral Sokichi that the Allied ships were bent on attacking, he ordered the troop transports to reverse course and retire to the north, accompanied by a small force of destroyers. He then mustered his ships, now reinforced by the heavy cruisers *Nachi* and *Haguro*, to meet the enemy

HMS *Exeter*'s radar proved less than efficient, the first contact with the enemy being visual, made by one of the cruiser's masthead lookouts, who reported ships approaching from the north-west. These were Shoji Nishimura's Eastern Attack Group, the light cruiser *Jintsu* and eight destroyers, scouting ahead of the Japanese fleet. On the face of it, with four cruisers and nine destroyers, Doorman seemed to have the advantage, but the Dutch admiral was not aware that this was only the enemy's advance guard. Out of sight seven miles to the west were the light cruiser *Naka* and six destroyers and to the north-west the heavy cruisers *Nachi* and *Haguro* with four.

The Japanese heavy cruisers *Nachi* and *Haguro* were formidable ships Built in the late 1920s, they had been completely modernized and uprated to 15,000 tons displacement and a top speed of 34 knots in 1941 In comparison, the two Allied heavy cruisers *Exeter* and *Houston* were half their size and a good two knots slower Furthermore, the Japanese had the additional advantage of three spotter planes in the air at all times.

The action began just after 1600, and at the extreme range of the opposing cruisers' 8-inch guns Nishimura was quick to gain the upper hand. He approached to within seven or eight miles and then executed the classic 'crossing the T' manoeuvre, swinging his ships round through ninety degrees to starboard to run across the bows of the Allied column. The *Nachi* and *Haguro* were thus able to fire their full broadsides of twenty 8-inch guns while Doorman's cruisers could use only their forward turrets.

In order to make full use of his own big guns, Doorman was forced to alter course to the west to run parallel to the Japanese ships, thus moving away from his main objective, the troop transports, which were visible retiring to the north But to reach his quarry Doorman had first to fight Nishimura. He settled for a slightly converging course, hoping gradually to decrease the range to allow the 6-inch guns of his smaller ships to join the fray.

The Japanese gunnery was superior from the outset. In the first few minutes of the action the *De Ruyter*'s hull was pierced in way of her engine room by an 8-inch shell, which fortunately did not explode. The *Exeter* sustained minor damage from a near miss and the *Jintsu* straddled the *Electra* with a salvo of 5 5s which shook her severely. The Australian cruiser *Perth* narrowly missed complete annihilation when she was straddled eight times in succession by 8-inch salvos from Nishimura's heavy cruisers. No hits or near misses were registered on the Japanese

At 1630 the destroyers *Asagumo*, *Minegumo*, *Murasame*, *Harusame*, *Samidare* and *Yudachi* suddenly dashed in and ran down the line of Allied ships, loosing off a total of 43 torpedoes There was confusion as Doorman's cruisers made frantic alterations of course to avoid the shoals of torpedoes while the destroyers rushed to challenge the attackers. Fortunately for the Allied ships, the Japanese had launched their torpedoes prematurely, and at too great a range to be effective

Throughout the pandemonium created by the torpedo attack, Doorman's cruisers continued to exchange broadsides with the Japanese cruisers, but a smoke screen laid down by the retreating destroyers ruined their aim. The Japanese, on the other hand, had their spotter planes in the air and their guns lost none of their accuracy.

The gap between the lines of opposing ships was narrowing and at 1700 the Japanese launched another torpedo attack. The second group of destroyers, comprising the *Yukikaze*, *Tokitsukaze*, *Amatsukaze*, *Hatsukaze*, *Kawakaze*, *Yamakaze*, *Sazanami* and *Ushio*, came in at 30 knots and, under heavy fire from Doorman's guns, launched 52 torpedoes at a range of 7,000 yards before retiring under the cover of smoke Once again the Japanese torpedoes were wasted, but it was during the confusion of this attack that a salvo of 8-inch shells from the *Nachi* slammed into the *Exeter*'s boiler room. Six of the British cruiser's eight boilers were holed, and the thunder of escaping high-pressure steam drowned out the screams of scalded men. The cruiser lost way, her main armament out of action, and in order to avoid being run down by the *Houston*, the next ship astern, Captain Gordon made a bold alteration to port, out of the line As the *Exeter*, stationed astern of the *De Ruyter*, had until then been relaying Rear-Admiral Doorman's orders to the other ships, the *Houston* assumed that a general alteration of course had been called for and followed the *Exeter* round. The *Java* and *Perth* did likewise, leaving the flagship to continue on a westerly course alone. For the other cruisers the mistaken manoeuvre turned out to be a blessing Shortly before they turned away, the *Nachi* and *Haguro* had each fired a spread of eight torpedoes, all of which missed thanks

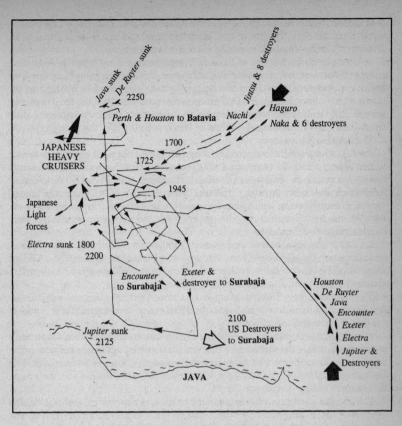

Battle of the Java Sea, 27 February 1942

to the sudden turn. The Dutch destroyer *Kortenaer* was not so fortunate A
Japanese torpedo struck her amidships and blew her into two halves.

Seeing the Allied ships in apparent confusion, the Japanese closed in to
complete their work *Exeter*'s damage control parties had by now restored
power to her main armament, but she was crawling along at 15 knots and it
seemed certain that she would now be finished off. But at that point Commander Cecil May, Senior British Destroyer Officer, in HMS *Electra*, came to
her rescue With the other British destroyers *Jupiter* and *Encounter* following,
May burst through the covering smoke screen then being laid by HMAS *Perth*
and charged at the advancing Japanese. On the other side of the smoke *Electra*
met the destroyers *Asagumo* and *Minegumo* preparing to launch torpedoes at
the *Perth*. A furious gunfight followed in which the *Electra* scored a hit on the
*Asagumo*, killing five of her crew and causing major damage that put the
Japanese destroyer out of the action. In turn *Electra* was hit in her after boiler
room and came to a standstill. *Encounter* and *Jupiter* rushed to her rescue but

were beaten back by a barrage of fire concentrated on them by the other Japanese ships. May fought to the finish, using guns and torpedoes to defend his ship. But the Japanese hauled off out of range, and their cruisers then pounded away at the *Electra* with their 8-inch guns until, at 1800, holed below the waterline and burning fiercely, she went down, leaving only a cloud of smoke and steam to mark her last resting place. Commander Cecil May and all his men were drowned with her. The *Electra*'s sacrifice was not to be entirely in vain. Her bold intervention allowed the damaged *Exeter* to retreat out of range. Then, with the destroyer *Witte de With* escorting her, the British cruiser limped back to Sourabaya.

Darkness was now closing in, and Rear-Admiral Doorman decided to break off the action while he regrouped his forces. But first he sent the American destroyers *John D. Edwards*, *Paul Jones*, *Alden* and *John D. Ford* in to discourage the Japanese with torpedoes. They scored no hits, but in the face of their aggressive action the Japanese cruisers pulled back. Doorman was now left with one heavy cruiser, three light cruisers and six destroyers, most with some damage and casualties and all running short of fuel and ammunition and with their crews in an advanced state of exhaustion. But they were all that stood between the Japanese invasion fleet and the island of Java. At 1840, at the start of the short tropical twilight, the Dutch admiral mustered his depleted squadron and went after the Japanese again.

Fifty minutes later Doorman regained contact with the enemy, surprising the *Nachi* and *Haguro*, which had both stopped to retrieve their spotter aircraft. There was a brief exchange of fire, then the Japanese destroyers launched a torpedo attack in defence of the heavy cruisers. Doorman was beaten back, while the *Nachi* and *Haguro* got away under the cover of smoke

The troop transports had completely disappeared from view, and, fearing that they may have slipped past him while he was fighting it out with Nishimura's ships, Doorman turned about and hurried back towards Java. When the coast of the island was in sight he steamed westwards, looking for any sign of a landing. He found nothing, and at 2130 was about to move out to sea again when the destroyer *Jupiter* struck a mine and began to sink; ironically, the *Jupiter* had hit one of the mines laid earlier in the day by the Dutch in the hope of keeping the Japanese at bay. Fortunately the British destroyer took some time to go down, allowing her crew to take to the boats, saved only to become prisoners of the Japanese later.

At this point it became evident that the four American destroyers had to return to Sourabaya. They had used up all their torpedoes and most of their ammunition and their fuel was dangerously low. They departed, leaving Doorman with the 8-inch gun cruiser *Houston*, the light cruisers *Perth*, *De Ruyter* and *Java* and one destroyer, HMS *Encounter*. The last was detached when the squadron came across survivors from the *Kortenaer* in the water. The *Encounter* picked up 113 men and returned with them to Sourabaya. That left Doorman's four cruisers to carry on alone, without even the comfort of a fast destroyer to protect them from torpedo attack.

After an hour's steaming at full speed Doorman again came up with the enemy. Nishimura had rounded up the troop transports and, with the heavy cruisers *Nachi* and *Haguro* in the lead, was making another bid to reach the coast. As soon as Doorman's ships were sighted, the *Jintsu* and eight destroyers closed around the transports while the *Nachi* and *Haguro* challenged the Allied cruisers. The opposing ships took up parallel courses at about eight miles and began a broadside-to-broadside battle that turned the warm, sultry night into an inferno of flame and smoke, the constant thunder of guns blotting out all human sound.

The Japanese guns far outweighed those of Doorman's ships, and the battle should have been short and with only one conclusion – annihilation for the Allies. But Nishimura's gunners were also suffering from fatigue, and although the shells flew thick and fast few damaging hits were scored by either side. The outcome of the confrontation was only decided when, at about 2320, at a range of five miles, the big Japanese cruisers launched torpedoes, the *Nachi* firing eight and the *Haguro* four Doorman's flagship *De Ruyter* was hit first, a 'Long Lance' blowing off her stern She caught fire and began to sink The *Houston* and *Perth*, following astern of the flagship, turned under full helm to avoid the sinking ship and in so doing saved themselves from a similar fate. The *Java* was slower to turn, and she rolled over within a few seconds of her hull being torn apart by a 'Long Lance'. Doorman went down with his ship, but not before signalling the *Houston* and *Perth* to withdraw without picking up survivors. The supreme sacrifice made by Rear-Admiral Karel Doorman and those who died in his multi-national force was largely in vain. They delayed the Japanese invasion of Java by only twenty-four hours.

The *Houston* and *Perth* reached Tandjong Priok, the port of Batavia, early on the 28th and refuelled. In Sourabaya the *Exeter* was burying her dead while her engineers worked feverishly to patch up her boiler damage. Nearby, the four American destroyers and HMS *Encounter* were also preparing for sea. No one on the island now entertained any false illusions as to the outcome of the impending invasion. Vice-Admiral Helfrich advised individual ship commanders to make their own plans for escape.

Captain Rooks of the USS *Houston* and Captain Waller of the *Perth* decided to join forces and left Tandjong Priok that evening with the intention of breaking out through the Sunda Strait into the Indian Ocean that night. They might well have done so had they resisted the temptation to strike one last blow against the enemy.

The Sunda Strait was only an hour's steaming away when, at 2300, the two cruisers ran into the Japanese Western Attack Group landing troops in Bantam Bay. The sight of fifty enemy merchant ships anchored in the bay, guarded by only three destroyers, was for Rooks and Waller too good a chance to pass up HMAS *Perth* led the way in with her guns blazing, while the startled guard ships *Harukaze* and *Hatakaze* struggled to lay smoke over the helpless transports. The third Japanese destroyer, the *Fubuki*, rather unwisely in the confined waters, launched nine torpedoes at the attacking cruisers: the *Perth* and *Houston* were unharmed but the unfortunate transport *Sakura Maru* was hit by two torpedoes and sank.

Rooks and Waller now turned their guns on the transports, causing such heavy damage to three of them that they ran ashore to avoid foundering. But that was as far as the cruisers' luck went. The guard destroyers had called for reinforcements, and when Rooks and Waller decided it was time to go they found their escape blocked by a wall of Japanese warships. In addition to the destroyers they were confronted by the heavy cruisers *Mogami* and *Mikuma*, the light cruiser *Natori* and seven more destroyers

It was a hopeless situation to be faced with, but the *Houston* and *Perth* fought a good fight, twisting and turning in the shallow waters of the bay to avoid the shoals of Japanese torpedoes coming at them from seaward. Their guns inflicted some damage on the *Mikuma* and the destroyers *Shirakumo* and *Harukaze*, but it was two against thirteen and the outcome was predictable The Japanese heavy cruisers stood off and shelled the *Houston* and *Perth* from 12,000 yards with their 8-inch guns, reducing the Allied cruisers to burning wrecks while their guns fired back in vain. It took four torpedoes to sink the *Perth,* and she went down five minutes after midnight, taking Captain Waller and more than half his crew with her

The *Houston*, stronger and more heavily armoured, fought on with the toll of her casualties mounting relentlessly. Her guns hit back until they ran out of ammunition, but Rooks still stubbornly refused to surrender – not that such a gesture would have been to any avail. The end came at 0045 on the 29th, when the *Houston* was hit by several salvos of shells and three torpedoes simultaneously She was finished and began to founder, and only then did Rooks give the order to abandon ship As his men fought to launch boats and rafts the Japanese destroyers closed in like slavering hyenas, raking the burning ship with cannon and machine guns Few of the Americans lived to face the horrors of a Japanese prisoner-of-war camp.

While the *Perth* and *Houston* were fighting their last fight against such overwhelming odds, the American destroyers *John D Edwards*, *Paul Jones*, *Alden* and *John D. Ford* had slipped out of Sourabaya and escaped through the narrow Bali Strait into the Indian Ocean. HMS *Exeter* was too big to use this passage, and Captain Gordon feared that if he attempted the Lombok Strait, to the east of Bali, his ship would be sunk by Japanese bombers now based on the island. He therefore choose the longer and less obvious escape route ≈ first to steam north-west towards Borneo, and when 150 miles or so out into the Java Sea make a full-speed dash for the Sunda Strait Gordon was unaware that the strait was already blocked by the Japanese.

The *Exeter* left Sourabaya in the evening of the 28th accompanied by HMS *Encounter*, commanded by Lieutenant-Commander E. V St John Morgan, and the American destroyer *Pope*, which, owing to engine problems, had not yet been in action against the Japanese. She was also the only destroyer still having torpedoes on board.

All went well at first, and at daybreak on 1 March the three ships were 270 miles north-west of the Sunda Strait and making 23 knots. Gordon was aiming to reach the strait at dusk and make a fast night passage. This was not to be Full daylight brought a Japanese reconnaissance aircraft overhead, and the fate of the Allied ships was sealed.

At 0930 the *Exeter*'s lookouts reported ships to the south. Gordon sent his men to their action stations with the bitter taste of disappointment in his mouth. Through his binoculars he had recognized the ships as the heavy cruisers *Nachi* and *Haguro*, enemies from whom he had so recently escaped. With the Japanese cruisers were the destroyers *Yamakaze* and *Kawakaze*. A few minutes later Gordon was appalled to see four more ships coming over the horizon ahead of the *Exeter* The new arrivals were the heavy cruisers *Ashigara* and *Myoko*, accompanied by the destroyers *Ikazuchi* and *Akebono*, all fresh and eager to play a part in the Battle of the Java Sea.

Gordon immediately turned his ships about and laid down smoke in an attempt to escape But the *Exeter*'s engines were still unable to give of their best and the enemy gained steadily By 1100 the three Allied ships were caught in a deadly sandwich, the cruisers *Ashigara* and *Myoko* to port and the *Nachi* and *Haguro* with the four destroyers to starboard Seaplanes from the Japanese cruisers flew overhead For more than half an hour the three separate groups of ships steamed neck and neck, the *Exeter*, *Encounter* and *Pope* in the middle and the target of Japanese salvos fired with the aid of the spotter planes circling overhead.

The *Exeter* hit back with her 8-inch guns and also fired her six remaining torpedoes at the *Nachi* and *Haguro* – all of which missed. She was constantly straddled from both sides, and then the Japanese, guided by their spotter planes, began the systematic destruction of the British cruiser. Her fire control went first, smashed by a direct hit, then a shell in her boiler room started a serious fire and her speed dropped away to a mere 4 knots. Her guns were knocked out one by one and then, as her engines ceased to turn, she lay dead in the water and engulfed in flames. Gordon ordered those of his men still alive to abandon ship, but even as they did so the destroyers *Akebono* and *Ikazuchi* raced in and launched eighteen torpedoes at the dying ship Several found their mark, adding carnage to the destruction already caused by the Japanese guns At 1140 the *Exeter*, gallant victor over the German pocket battleship *Admiral Graf Spee* two years earlier off Montevideo, rolled over and sank.

The *Encounter* was next to go, blasted to a halt by the combined firepower of the *Ashigara* and *Myoko*. A double salvo finished her off and she followed the *Exeter* down. The *Pope* postponed her end for a while by hiding in a rain squall, but, when the rain passed, aircraft from the Japanese carrier *Ryujo*, which had joined the chase, smothered her with bombs The American destroyer's engine room was flooded and she was an easy target for the guns of the Japanese cruisers, who shelled her at their leisure until she too sank

The joint British/Australian/American/Dutch effort to save Java from invasion by sea had ended in complete disaster, with eleven out of the fifteen Allied ships involved being sunk with fearful loss of life The Japanese lost only one ship, the transport *Sakura Maru*, and the invasion was an unqualified success. Allied troops fought magnificently to hold the island, contesting every yard with their blood as they retreated, but in six days it was all over.

Throughout the bitter struggle for Java and the Dutch oilfields, the only branch of the Allied forces to be found seriously wanting was the US Navy's submarine force There were 26 American submarines in the area when the Japanese invasion fleet was known to be on the way Vice-Admiral Helfrich called on these submarines to help in the defence of the island, but they refused to travel on the surface during daylight and so arrived too late For more than a week the Java Sea was thick with Japanese ships, yet the American submarines failed to sink one of them Their only contribution to the battle was to pick up 118 survivors from sunken Allied ships

# 14

# Savo Island

*9 August 1942*

On 8 March 1942, while the hopelessly outgunned Allied garrison on Java surrendered to the Japanese, British troops were fighting a rearguard action on the outskirts of Rangoon 1,500 miles to the north. By nightfall the ships evacuating the tattered remnants of the defeated army had gone from the port and Burma, under British rule since 1885, fell to the victorious Japanese. A month later, after stubborn but unavailing resistance, Bataan, the only remaining American stronghold in the Philippines, was also forced to raise the white flag of surrender. On the same day that Bataan fell, an infamous Easter Sunday, the Royal Navy tasted bitter defeat in the Indian Ocean for the first time in its long and glorious history In a few hideous hours Japanese carrier-borne aircraft devastated the naval base of Colombo and sank the British heavy cruisers *Dorsetshire* and *Cornwall*, the light aircraft carrier *Hermes* and the destroyer *Vampire.* The next day Japanese cruisers turned their guns on an unescorted convoy off Colombo and blew 23 British merchant-men out of the water, thus confirming their complete ascendancy over the Indian Ocean Admiral Sir James Somerville, C-in-C Eastern Fleet, had little option but to gather up his few remaining ships and retire to the comparative safety of East African waters.

Japanese eyes now turned away from the Indian Ocean, to New Guinea and the myriad islands to the east and south-east known as Melanesia, the occupation of which would cut off Australia and New Zealand from America. The dispatch of an expeditionary force on 4 May to capture Tulagi, in the Solomon Islands, resulted in a clash in the Coral Sea between Japanese and American carrier fleets which ended in substantial defeat for the Japanese A turning point in the naval war in the Pacific was reached a month later when the carrier fleets again met, this time off Midway Island in the Hawaiian group The Japanese lost four carriers, 250 aircraft and over 2,000 men, among them many irreplaceable, highly trained carrier pilots. The Americans' losses were small by comparison, and the next day their planes went on to sink the heavy cruisers *Mogami* and *Mikuma*, so avenging the loss of the USS *Houston* and HMAS *Perth* in the Java Sea three months earlier.

The Coral Sea and Midway battles were significant in that they were actions fought mainly by naval aircraft – long-range battles with blows delivered on both sides by carrier-borne aircraft rather than guns. Midway in particular was a historical milestone as it was the first sea action at which on no occasion did opposing ships sight each other After Midway the heavyweights of naval warfare, the battleship and battlecruiser, became obsolete.

Despite all American efforts, the Japanese gained a foothold in the Solomons and began building an airfield on Guadalcanal, posing a serious threat to Allied forces in the South Pacific. Japanese aircraft flying from Guadalcanal would dominate the shipping lanes between US ports and Australia, and even be within reach of American bases in New Caledonia and the New Hebrides. At the beginning of July aerial reconnaissance showed the airfield to be nearing completion. Swift intervention was needed, but it was a month later, on 7 August, when American Marines waded ashore at Guadalcanal.

The Solomon Islands, first discovered by the Spanish explorer Alvaro de Mendana in 1568, are a 700-mile long archipelago lying 1,000 miles off Australia's Queensland coast. The double line of volcanic islands and islets runs north-west/south-east, separated by the New Georgia Sound, a 50-mile wide deep-water channel. The climate is hot and humid, blighted by frequent and heavy rainfall all year round, with sudden, destructive hurricanes sweeping across the region in the summer months. Guadalcanal, the principal island, is rocky and densely forested, and it was here, on the northern coast, that the Japanese were building their airfield. They had also established a small base on Florida Island on the other side of the sound.

The Allied invasion force assembled 400 miles south of Fiji on 26 July. It consisted of 22 transports carrying 19,000 US Marines, escorted by the battleship USS *South Carolina*, the aircraft carriers USS *Saratoga*, *Wasp* and *Enterprise*, five heavy cruisers, an anti-aircraft cruiser and a flotilla of destroyers Also in support were the Australian cruisers *Canberra*, *Australia* and *Hobart*. Six American submarines were acting as scouts. In overall command was Rear-Admiral R. K Turner USN, while the close escort to the transports was under the command of Rear-Admiral Sir Victor Crutchley VC RN

Rehearsals for the landings were carried out on a remote island in the Fijis, and on the 31st the expedition sailed northwards, arriving off the Solomons during the night of 6 August. Next morning the US Marines landed on the northern coast of Guadalcanal and at Tulagi on Florida Island. The resistance at Tulagi, where 1,500 Japanese troops were dug in, was fierce. The garrison, although outnumbered ten to one, fought to the bitter end, inflicting heavy casualties on the Americans. On Guadalcanal Japanese troops consisted largely of labour corps engaged in building the airfield and offered only token resistance before retreating inland. In both landings the Japanese appeared to have been taken completely by surprise. As the American Marines settled down to consolidate their positions in the steamy, mosquito-plagued jungles of the island, out in New Georgia Sound – quickly renamed 'The Slot' by the straight-talking Americans – ships of the escort force began a monotonous patrol with the feeling of a job well done.

When news of the American invasion reached the Japanese C-in-C, Vice-Admiral Shigeyoshi Inouye, 700 miles away in Rabaul, he reacted swiftly, dispatching land-based bombers to attack the American beach-heads and ships. This put a rude end to all the complacency pervading the Allied camp in the Solomons US positions on Guadalcanal and Tulagi were subjected to continuous air attack, despite desperate battles fought overhead between Japanese planes and aircraft scrambled from the American carriers The ships of the escort force also came under heavy attack by enemy bombers, and they were constantly on the move, dodging and weaving, their guns running hot as they hammered away at their airborne attackers. One troop transport was set on fire and the destroyer USS *Jarvis* was damaged. The American Marines succeeded in occupying the airfield on Guadalcanal, but the landing of their supplies on the beaches was seriously interrupted by the air attacks and it was feared that the vulnerable carriers would have to be withdrawn.

In Rabaul Vice-Admiral Inouye had little news of the fate of his troops in the Solomons, but his instinctive reaction was to reinforce the beleaguered garrison on Guadalcanal as quickly as possible This would prove difficult, for now that the Americans were on the offensive Inouye's resources were sorely stretched. He could spare only 500 marines, who were hurriedly embarked on six transports and dispatched to Guadalcanal escorted by a single destroyer.

At around midnight on 7 August the American submarine *S38* lay stopped on the surface in St George's Channel off Bougainville. It was fine, dark night, with good visibility, and *S38*'s lookouts sighted the approaching ships at five miles. Lieutenant-Commander Henry Munson, called to the conning tower, identified the small convoy as six merchantman escorted by one destroyer, all heading in the direction of Guadalcanal and obviously Japanese. Munson dived quickly, ran in under the unsuspecting destroyer and fired two torpedoes at what he judged to be the largest ship. Luck was with the American commander that night, for both torpedoes hit the 5,600-ton *Meiyo Maru*, which was carrying the bulk of the Japanese marines She went to the bottom, taking her human cargo with her When word of the disaster reached Inouye in Rabaul he immediately recalled the remaining transports With a chance meeting, *S38* had saved many American lives on Guadalcanal.

Vice-Admiral Inouye was unhappy, but he had no intention of allowing the Allies to take the Solomons without paying a heavy price. Earlier that day he had assembled a cruiser force, which he directed to sail from Rabaul that evening. In command was Rear-Admiral Gunichi Mikawa, flying his flag in the 13,400-ton heavy cruiser *Chokai* Mikawa had with him four other heavy cruisers, the *Aoba*, *Furutaka*, *Kinugasa* and *Kako*, all of 9,000 tons, the light cruisers *Tenryu* and *Yubari*, and the *Kamikaze* class destroyer *Yunagi* The top speed of the squadron, governed by the elderly *Furutaka* class cruisers, was 33 knots

Mikawa's orders were to mount a massive attack on the Allied invasion force on Guadalcanal while it was still in an exposed position He planned to approach the island during the night of 8/9 August, in darkness, when there would be little risk of US carrier-borne aircraft being in the air His own men were highly trained in the art of night fighting, whereas the Americans at least were not, and, still holding the Japanese ships in some contempt, were likely to be off their guard.

Mikawa was not aware that the Allies were anticipating a surface attack, or that shore-based and carrier aircraft were out searching for him, before he left Rabaul. The first American sighting of the Japanese ships was off New Ireland that evening. Later, around midnight, Henry Munson's *S38* again found herself in close proximity to the enemy Patrolling on the surface, she was almost run down by Mikawa's ships as they raced south at 24 knots. Munson crash-dived only minutes before the enemy ran over him, and in the confusion mistakenly reported the ships as a force of destroyers.

Arriving off Bougainville before dawn on the 8th, Mikawa lay close in to the east coast of the island, hidden from the enemy's eyes, and called his commanders aboard the *Chokai* He explained his plan, which was to make a high-speed dash down The Slot, passing south of Savo Island on the way in, and swoop on the American transports unloading off Lunga Point. Having caused havoc amongst the anchored ships, he then proposed to swing across the intervening twenty-mile wide stretch of water to Florida Island and make a similar attack on ships discharging off Tulagi. Escape to the north-west would be made by passing north of Savo Island It was a bold, imaginative plan, if highly risky, but Mikawa was leading a powerful force, mounting in all thirty-four 8-inch, eleven 5.5-inch, eight 5-inch, nineteen 4.7-inch and two 3-inch guns, as well as 62 torpedo tubes and a variety of smaller armament His crews were alert, determined and well-practised in the art of night fighting

Rear-Admiral Turner's force, on the other hand, was seventeen days out from its base in New Zealand and had suffered almost continuous air attack during the daylight hours since arriving off Guadalcanal. Its commanders, perhaps with some excuse, appeared not to be fully awake to the danger threatening. Munson's report had been treated with suspicion, as had other reports from patrolling B-17 bombers of enemy warships seen at sea The most definite sighting of Mikawa's ships was made at 1026 on the 8th by a Hudson of the RAAF, but this aircraft did not report the sighting until it arrived back at its base in the afternoon. It was not until late in the evening that the Hudson's report reached Turner, and then the information it contained was misleading. However, it should have by now been clear to the American admiral that something was afoot But Turner, again underestimating the capability of the Japanese, concluded that there would be no threat to his ships before the daylight hours of the 9th, if then. They would rest easy

Before settling down for the night, Turner and General Vandegrift, in command of the Marines, joined Rear-Admiral Crutchley on board his flagship, HMAS *Australia*, anchored off Guadalcanal Over nightcaps the three men discussed the progress of the expedition so far They had good cause to congratulate themselves, for the landings had gone well and, despite determined Japanese air attacks, casualties were comparatively light. Only another twenty-four hours was required to complete the off-loading of the transports, and meanwhile Turner and Crutchley were satisfied that the outer perimeter of their operation was well guarded in the highly unlikely event of a Japanese night attack It was assumed that any threat would come from the north-east, against which the 8-inch gun cruisers HMAS *Canberra* and USS *Chicago* and two destroyers were on station in the seven-mile wide channel between Savo Island and Cape Esperance The waters between Savo and Florida Island were guarded by three more heavy cruisers, the USS *Astoria*, *Quincy* and *Vincennes*, and three destroyers As early warning lookouts, the American destroyers *Blue* and *Patterson* patrolled The Slot north-west of Savo Island; HMAS *Australia*, when she had finished playing host to Turner and Vandegrift, would join the *Canberra* and *Chicago* off Savo Island. The American carriers were some distance east of the Solomons with the 16-inch gun battleship *South Carolina*

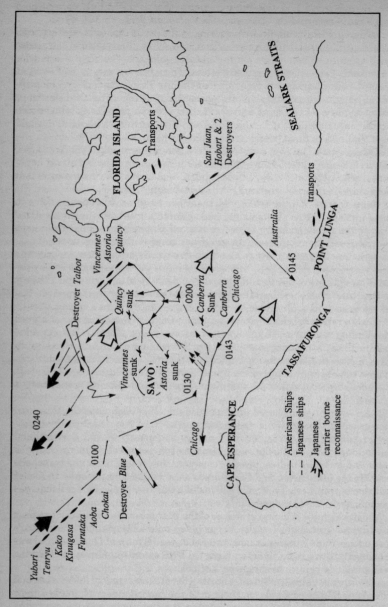

Battle of Savo Island, 9 August 1942

As a further precaution, the southern approaches to the islands were covered by the cruisers USS *San Juan* and HMAS *Hobart* and two destroyers.

It was a hot, sultry night, with passing rain squalls that did nothing to cool the air. Lightning flashed on the horizon, and the ominous rumble of thunder rolled around the brooding mountains of Guadalcanal. The night was one for the lookouts to be uneasy and on their toes, which to some extent they were. At around 2220 two seaplanes were sighted circling Savo Island, clearly identifiable as scout planes from a Japanese cruiser, but no report reached Turner or Crutchley. The Allied ships continued their tedious patrolling, relaxed and sure in the knowledge that no Japanese would dare to attack at night. It would seem that nothing had been learned from the fiasco of Pearl Harbor

Midnight came and went, and aboard the Allied guard ships eyelids drooped – understandable after a long and stress-filled day. Dawn was still six hours away, and what the new day would bring no one knew. It was rumoured that the aircraft carriers were being withdrawn altogether, in which case the Japanese 'Zeros' and 'Bettys' would be over in swarms. It would be down to ships' guns against dive bombers, and, bearing in mind the Japanese pilots' total disregard for their own lives, no quarter would be given on either side. Few gave any thought to what might happen before the sun came up.

Twenty miles to the north-east, cloaked in darkness, Mikawa's squadron was coming down The Slot at full speed, the *Chokai* leading, followed by the heavy cruisers *Aoba*, *Kako*, *Kinugasa* and *Furutaka* and the light cruisers *Tenryu* and *Yubari*, with the destroyer *Yunagi* acting as rearguard. The Japanese had no radar, but Mikawa had supreme confidence in his lookouts, all of whom were hand-picked for their exceptional night vision and equipped with high-power, high-definition night glasses. Under a black velvet sky filled with brilliant, twinkling stars, the long line of Japanese ships swept on in silence, each ship steering by the phosphorescent wake of the one ahead. In complete contrast, the Americans could be heard chattering on their TBS (Talk Between Ships) radio sets, whiling away the night and oblivious to the enemy's listening ears.

At 0054, when twelve miles from Savo Island, the *Chokai*'s lookouts sighted the destroyer USS *Blue* fine to starboard  The *Blue* was guarding the north-western approaches to Savo, and then on the westerly leg of her patrol and steaming away from the Japanese column. She was, however, equipped with radar and presumably had lookouts covering all points of the compass, yet she failed to see or hear the Japanese ships as they slipped past her stern, boiler fans roaring and propellers noisily thrashing the calm water. No challenge was flashed; her radio remained silent.

At 0105 Mikawa's column was clear of the guard destroyer and six miles from Savo Island. The island was already visible as a dark hump fine on the *Chokai*'s port bow, while Cape Esperance, the north-western tip of Guadalcanal, was showing up to starboard. Mikawa adjusted course to pass mid-way between the two, unable to believe his amazing luck

The Japanese ships raced on, and at 0130, still apparently undetected and with Savo island abeam to port, three of the heavy cruisers launched their spotter aircraft. The tiny Aichi seaplanes, their exhausts glowing red in the darkness, roared into the air and began to circle ahead of the squadron. The sound of their engines was heard aboard several of the American guard ships, but it was assumed that the planes, one of which switched on its navigation lights, were friendly. Captain Frederick Riefkohl, commanding the USS *Vincennes*, was called to the bridge but decided that there was no cause for alarm. It must have been that Riefkohl was lulled by the soporific mood of the warm equatorial night, for he went back to his bed.

Soon after 0130 a ship suddenly appeared out of the shadows and crossed ahead of the *Chokai* from port to starboard as the leading cruiser approached Cape Esperance  Mikawa ordered his guns to hold their fire and launched four torpedoes at the enemy ship  She was the American destroyer *Jarvis*. The torpedoes missed their target, but their phosphorescent tracks should have been clearly visible to the *Jarvis*'s bridge and lookouts. But she gave no indication of being aware of the enemy: as with the USS *Blue*, the *Jarvis* made no challenge and did not raise the alarm.

Mikawa's run of luck finally came to an end at 0142 when the squadron, then two miles south of Savo Island, ran into the destroyer USS *Patterson*  The *Patterson*'s lookouts were awake and her radio telephone burst into life with the urgent call, 'Warning – warning. Strange ships entering harbour'. A few minutes later another destroyer, the USS *Ralph Talbot*, on patrol north of Savo, heard the sound of aircraft engines and used her R/T to broadcast 'Warning – warning. Plane over Savo Island headed east'.

The warnings came too late for the Allied ships, the night being abruptly turned into day as the circling Japanese planes dropped parachute flares  The brilliant light revealed to Mikawa on the bridge of the *Chokai* a scene of unbelievable unpreparedness  To starboard were the American transports huddled around Lunga Point, their derricks still swung out and barges alongside. Ahead and to port, no more than three miles off, were the heavy cruisers *Canberra* and *Chicago*, idling along at 12 knots with all guns trained fore and aft. Over towards Tulagi, but still clearly visible in the harsh light of the flares, were the cruisers *Astoria*, *Quincy* and *Vincennes*, also dawdling and with guns unprepared for action. Mikawa had caught them all unawares, but he knew that he had to act swiftly and decisively while he still had the upper hand  For the first time that night the Japanese admiral broke radio silence, ordering the other ships of his squadron to follow him as he swung to port to 'cross the T' of the unsuspecting *Canberra* and *Chicago*

Captain Getting had been on the *Canberra*'s bridge for some time, worried by the presence overhead of unidentified aircraft. The *Canberra*, built in 1927, had little defence against air attack – just two 42-pounder guns, cumbersome weapons with a slow rate of fire and designed for use against high-flying aircraft  This was in stark contrast to American cruisers, all liberally armed with batteries of 40mm and 20mm quick-firers.

Getting was jerked rudely awake when the *Chokai* snapped on her searchlights, bathing the *Canberra*'s bridge in a blinding white light. Alarm bells shrilled and men tumbled out on deck and ran to their action stations  Most of them would never reach their posts. Before a single gun could be manned the gentle tropical night became a horrific nightmare as the *Chokai*'s broadside of 8-inch shells crashed into the Australian cruiser at point blank range  Each Japanese ship fired in turn when she crossed the *Canberra*'s bows  The

Australian ship was systematically destroyed by at least 24 heavy shells ripping through her thin armour like shotgun pellets through paper  Her upperworks were smashed, her engine and boiler rooms were turned into scalding death-traps and fire swept through the decks  As she slewed around to port, already sinking, two 'Long Lance' torpedoes completed her destruction. Captain Getting died without really knowing what had hit his ship, as did 83 of his men

Captain Howard Bode, commanding the USS *Chicago*, had been asleep in his sea cabin when the Japanese struck  He was still drowsy when he reached the cruiser's bridge seconds later, but alert enough to wrench the ship around to starboard to comb the tracks of the torpedoes racing towards her at 50 knots  The *Chicago* almost succeeded, but as the helmsman spun the wheel to steady her on course, one of the torpedoes slammed into her bows

It was as though the *Chicago* had hit a brick wall  She stopped dead in her tracks and a huge wave of water and debris came over her shattered bow, drenching the ship as far back as her bridge and beyond. Complete confusion followed. Guns fired blindly at non-existent targets; searchlights were switched on but could find no enemy, for Mikawa's squadron had already moved on  Then Bode caught a glimpse of one of his own destroyers crossing the *Chicago*'s bow  He went after her, thinking she was the enemy  The crippled *Canberra* was left to her fate, and Bode made no attempt to warn other ships of the danger.

The confusion among the Allied ships deepened. The attack on the *Canberra* and *Chicago* had been hidden from the others by a heavy rain squall, and the situation was not clear to anyone except the Japanese  Captain Frederick Riefkohl, on the bridge of the *Vincennes*, leading the *Quincy* and *Astoria* on the north-western leg of their patrol, saw flashes and heard gunfire. As a precaution against the unknown, he ordered an increase of speed. The other cruisers followed suit, and as they did so they found themselves caught in a battery of searchlight beams directed at them from astern.

After rounding the bottom of Savo Island, and dealing so decisively with the *Canberra* and *Chicago*, Mikawa was then confronted with the *Vincennes*, *Quincy* and *Astoria* steaming in line ahead, seemingly oblivious to his presence. He split his force and, with the *Yubari*, *Tenryu* and *Furutaka* going to port and the *Chokai*, *Aoba*, *Kako* and *Kinugasa* to starboard, swept up on the unsuspecting American ships from both quarters  When the Japanese switched on their searchlights and opened fire, the Americans were completely at their mercy

The *Astoria*'s gunnery officer was one of the first to recover and react to the situation  Using his initiative, he fired a salvo from cruiser's after turret, and was about to continue when the order came from the bridge to cease fire  The *Astoria*'s captain, having been roused from his bed by the outbreak of bedlam, refused to believe that the Japanese were attacking and thought his guns were firing on friendly ships  When the realization dawned that the enemy was at hand, Japanese 8-inch shells were coming at the *Astoria* from both sides and blowing her apart  A lucky shell from the American cruiser's after turret hit the *Chokai*'s bridge, killing 30 men, but that was the full extent of the *Astoria*'s retaliation  She ended up drifting out of control, on fire and with many of her men killed or wounded.

Mikawa now switched his fire to the *Vincennes*. A shell ploughed into the American ship's two spotter aircraft, which were on deck, fully fuelled up and ready for launching. Both planes burst into flames, providing a beacon for every Japanese gun in the vicinity to home in on. This they did with their usual efficiency and accuracy.

It seems that even then Captain Riefkohl did not grasp the situation. He came to the conclusion, as had the *Astoria*'s commander before him, that he was being fired on by his own ships and could think of no better defence than to hoist an extra large Stars and Stripes at the masthead. The net result of Riefkohl's action was to bring down a hail of Japanese shells on the *Vincennes*. Repeatedly hit below the waterline, and with her superstructure reduced to a burnt-out shell, she capsized an hour later, taking 332 men down with her and leaving another 250 struggling in the water.

If anything, the commander of the *Quincy*, also suffering the delusion of friendly fire, acted even more foolishly by switching on his coloured recognition lights. The Japanese cruisers needed no further invitation. They opened up on the conveniently illuminated ship with every weapon they had, including anti-aircraft guns depressed to minimum elevation. At almost point blank range hardly a shell missed, and the *Quincy* was shot to pieces in the crossfire. The American gunners hit back, gaining, in the time left to them, the distinction of firing more shells than all the other Allied ships present on that night of humiliation. Their brave effort was to no avail. Heavily on fire, and with her captain and most of his officers lying dead on her bridge, the *Quincy* drifted away into the night, finally sinking at 0235 in the morning of the 9th.

Rear-Admiral Mikawa, having summarily dispatched the Allied ships guarding Guadalcanal, now considered the task that had been his primary object, the destruction of the American transports and supply ships. However, his cruisers were by this time scattered, and he feared to delay his departure further lest his ships still be within range of American carrier-borne aircraft when daylight came. He was not aware that the carriers had been withdrawn during the night. At 0240 Mikawa regrouped his ships to the north of Savo Island and set course for Rabaul, leaving behind him four Allied heavy cruisers lying on the floor of what the Americans would thereafter call Ironbottom Sound. The Japanese guns and torpedoes had claimed the lives of 1,270 Allied seamen and left 709 others wounded. The only ship capable of any rational action against Mikawa, Rear-Admiral Crutchley's HMAS *Australia*, had gone south before the battle and arrived on the scene long after the Japanese had gone. Hers was the unenviable task of pulling survivors from the water, some of them horribly mutilated by sharks.

The Battle of Savo Island was another humiliating defeat for the Allies, and for the United States Navy in particular The ships on station off Guadalcanal, seven heavy cruisers and eight destroyers, outnumbered and outclassed Rear-Admiral Gunichi Mikawa's squadron, but their state of readiness was appalling This, above all, led to their annihilation

The Japanese ships had no radar; the Allied ships did, although it was of an early type and often difficult to interpret. The evidence is that the two US destroyers on forward sentry duty to the north-west of Guadalcanal placed too much reliance on their radars, forgetting that the 'Mark I Eyeball' as it is known in the Royal Navy, is indispensable at sea. If the lookouts on the *Blue* and *Patterson* had been at all vigilant, then it is highly unlikely that Mikawa's squadron of eight ships, thundering along at full speed, would have slipped past unseen. Then there is the question of 'careless talk'. The Japanese kept complete radio silence throughout their approach, communicating with each other only when absolutely necessary, and then only by shaded lamp. The Americans, on the other hand, blatantly advertised their presence off Guadalcanal. They used their TBS to help pass away the long hours of the watch, chattering constantly and jamming the air waves which should have been kept clear for urgent messages only to be passed. As for the Morse lamp, they appeared to have lost the will, or the ability, to use this silent communicator.

That the Allied ships were caught napping on that infamous night shows complacency bordering on downright slackness. Even when unidentified aircraft were seen and heard overhead, and the possibility of enemy ships being in the area was very strong, nothing was done  It must be said, however, that the Allied ships did the job entrusted to them, which was the protection of the transports anchored off Lunga Point. But the price they paid was an extortionate one, and it was not paid in full that night. During the afternoon of the 9th the destroyer USS *Jarvis,* damaged in an air attack on the 7th, was torpedoed by a Japanese aircraft when south of Guadalcanal and sank with the loss of 247 men. At the conclusion of this sorry episode the Allied ships had lost nearly 1,500 officers and men. There were two later casualties: Captain Howard Bode of the *Chicago* committed suicide, and Captain Frederick Riefkohl of the *Vincennes*, although rescued after his ship went down, was said to be 'broken in spirit'.

Some small consolation for the Allied losses came during the morning of the 10th when the US submarine *S44*, commanded by Lieutenant-Commander John Moore, sighted four of Mikawa's cruisers off New Ireland as they returned to their base at Rabaul. Moore closed in and fired a salvo of four torpedoes, one of which hit the 8,800-ton cruiser *Kako*. She sank with heavy loss of life

# 15

# Stephen Hopkins and Stier

*27 September 1942*

I n the spring of 1941, when the Battle of the Atlantic was moving towards its awesome climax, German U-boats were sinking Allied merchant ships faster than they could be built in the hard-pressed British yards. Unless replacement ships could be found in large numbers, then Britain's vital Atlantic sea links would be cut and she must surely fall. And when she went, crushed under the heel of an invading German army, then with her would go the last hope of the Western world. It was a grave situation requiring an urgent solution.

Some four years before the outbreak of war the J. L. Thompson shipyard in Sunderland produced plans for a cheap, 'off the peg' tramp steamer The ship was to be of 7,000 tons gross, with a speed of 11 knots, designed to carry maximum cargo at minimum cost – the ultimate aim of every British shipowner in those depression-hit days. An upturn in the freight market condemned Thompson's plans to gather dust on the shelf, and this ideal ship was never built – that is, until war gave the proposal a new meaning In that momentous spring of 1941 the shelved plans were taken down, dusted off and dispatched across the Atlantic to the United States, where all things impossible in the Old World were made to come true. The American Government, as yet uncommitted to war but aware of the consequences should Britain go under, called in Henry J Kaiser, a builder of dams with no experience of shipbuilding but with the will to work miracles. This Kaiser did, using a revolutionary new process involving all-welded hulls and extensive prefabrication that horrified the traditional shipbuilders. Within a few months Kaiser's yards all over America were turning out the new 'Liberty' ships at the unprecedented rate of one every 42 days. These ships were not handsome, and they were underpowered and difficult to handle in bad weather, but they could lift 9,000 tons of cargo at a time It was felt that if a Liberty made just one crossing of the Atlantic with supplies for a beleaguered Britain, then she would have fulfilled her destiny The majority of them did a great deal more: in fact, of the 2,710 Liberty ships built, only 200 were sunk in the course of the war. Many were still afloat and trading twenty years after – which says a great deal for Henry Kaiser's ridiculed, but brilliant, approach to shipbuilding.

Liberty Hull No 247 was launched in Richmond, California, on 14 April 1942 She was a ship of 7,181 tons gross, 423 feet long and 57 feet in the beam Her triple-expansion steam engine developed 2,500 indicated horse power, giving her a sea speed of 11 knots. On completion she was handed over to the United States War Shipping Administration, which in turn passed her on to the

Luckenbach Steamship Company of New York to manage on its behalf On 12 May 1942, in a simple ceremony, Hull No 247 became the SS *Stephen Hopkins*.

On the same day that the *Stephen Hopkins* ceased to be just another number on Henry Kaiser's books, 4,000 miles away on the other side of the world the German armed commerce raider *Stier* left the port of Rotterdam and made her way down the River Maas to the sea. The *Stier*, like the *Stephen Hopkins*, had acquired a new name, but there the resemblance ended. The *Stier* boasted a distinguished pedigree. Built in 1936 at the Krupp Germania yard in Kiel for the Deutsche Levant Linie, who named her *Cairo*, she was a motor vessel of 4,788 tons, having a speed of 18 knots. In the years before the war her sleek, white-painted hull, with its elegant clipper bow and cruiser stern, was a familiar sight in the Mediterranean fruit trade.

After the outbreak of war the *Cairo* was laid up, but it was inevitable that a vessel of her calibre should attract the attention of the German Navy She was requisitioned and taken into Stettin, appearing again in December 1941 as *Hilfskreuzer 23* To the casual observer, apart from her coat of wartime grey paint she seemed little changed, but behind her innocent façade lurked all the trappings of war. Hidden by counterbalanced steel shutters that swung open at the touch of a lever were six 5.9-inch, 42-calibre guns and under canvas covers two 37mm and four 20mm anti-aircraft cannon Equally carefully concealed on her main deck were two 21-inch torpedo tubes, and in hangars on the upper deck were two small Arado 231 reconnaissance aircraft Her crew, commanded by Kapitän zur See Gerlach, were all highly trained and experienced naval personnel The *Cairo*, now *Stier*, had emerged as a heavily armed commerce raider, self-sustaining up to a range of 60,000 miles – a deadly threat to the Allied shipping lanes.

But first the *Stier* had to run the gauntlet of the Royal Navy in order to reach her appointed hunting grounds German warships breaking out into the Atlantic usually took the longer but safer route via the Norwegian Sea, north of Iceland and through the Denmark Strait; in the case of the *Stier* it was decided to send her out through the English Channel under heavy escort – a calculated risk that some said might end in disaster

The *Stier* sailed from Rotterdam during the night of 12 May 1942, escorted by the sea-going torpedo boats *Kondor*, *Falke*, *Iltis* and *Seeadler* and sixteen minesweepers. Keeping as close in to the Belgian and French coasts as the depth of water would allow, with the minesweepers sweeping in a double line ahead and the torpedo boats forming a screen around the *Stier*, the convoy escaped detection until it entered the narrows of the Dover Strait at about 0230 on the 13th. Inevitably the cluster of ships was picked up by radar on the English shore, and the 14-inch guns at Dover opened fire However, it was a dark night, with rain showers, and the guns, being on their maximum range, did no more than urge the German ships on their way.

With Gerlach and all those who realized the tremendous risks they were taking heaving a collective sigh of relief, the convoy raced on down-Channel But the Germans' euphoria was short-lived At about 0330, when abeam of Cap Gris Nez, Gerlach became aware of a number of unidentified small craft, which appeared out of the shadow of the land and crossed his bows. He at first dismissed the strangers as fishermen sailing out of Boulogne, but he changed his mind and reached for the alarm button when the throaty roar of Rolls-Royce engines was borne on the wind. The *Stier* and her escort had run into an ambush.

The innocent 'fishermen', now recognizable as a flotilla of British motor torpedo boats and motor gunboats, suddenly accelerated, their flared bows throwing aside the choppy Channel seas in arcs of tumbling white foam. They divided and raced down on either side of the convoy, tracer spitting from their 2-pounder guns.

The *Stier*'s escorting torpedo boats at once revved up and moved out to meet the challenge. This they should have been able to do with ease. The *Kondor*, *Falke*, *Iltis* and *Seeadler*, each of around 900 tons displacement and armed with three 4.1-inch and four 37mm guns, were the equivalent of British 'Hunt' class destroyers, while not one of the attackers was much over 35 tons nor, torpedoes apart, armed with anything bigger than a quick-firing 2-pounder cannon. But the British boats had the advantages of speed, high manoeuvrability and sheer, unbridled aggression In the ensuing dog-fight the *Stier* escaped unharmed, but torpedoes sank the *Iltis* and *Seeadler* while the British lost only one MTB.

When the attack was over and the British boats had gone roaring back into the night whence they had come, the *Stier*, escorted by the *Kondor* and *Falke*, took shelter in Boulogne. Having seen their charge safely behind the breakwaters of the French port, the two escorts then returned to sea to search for survivors, eventually picking up 88 German and three British. It had been a bad night for the Germans, for although the *Stier* was safe they had lost two vessels and almost 200 men. Thereafter Gerlach took care not to be caught again, making short dashes from port to port under cover of darkness until he reached the Gironde estuary deep in the Bay of Biscay.

It was the end of May before the *Stier*, having topped up with fuel and stores, set off for her operational area in the South Atlantic. Her orders were to seek out and destroy Allied merchant shipping sailing between the Cape of Good Hope and the Americas, which since the entry of the United States into the war was plentiful. The beginning of June found the raider mid-way between Sierra Leone and Brazil, in the vicinity of St Paul's Rocks, an area little frequented since the demise of the sailing ship.

Penedo de San Pedro, or St Paul's Rocks, are a small cluster of barren, guano-covered islets lying 520 miles east of the coast of Brazil and 60 miles north of the Equator. Of volcanic origin, they rise steeply from 2,000 fathoms to 70 feet above sea level and are home only to boobies and bosun birds. They offer no anchorage to a ship and, because of the unceasing rise and fall of the swell, landing is extremely hazardous One early visitor, Captain Amnasa Delano of the American ship *Perseverance*, said in 1799, 'On shore the aspect was most dreary, the sea roaring and surging on all sides.' Having no fresh water or vegetation, it is little wonder that St Paul's Rocks have been shunned by seamen down through the ages, occasionally sighted but always given a wide berth Their only real claim to usefulness was as a convenient point of reference for the windjammers of the last century running their northing before the North-East Trades.

Taking a leaf out of the book of the old sailing ship men, Gerlach did not linger at St Paul's Rocks and, after verifying his position on 4 June, continued south  Later that day he found his first victim, the British *Gemstone*. The 4,986-ton cargo ship was completely taken in by the *Stier*'s disguise and had little chance to defend herself when the raider's shutters swung open to reveal her loaded 5.9s. The British ship went to the bottom, an easy first conquest for the *Stier*. It was a different story when, 300 miles south of St Paul's Rocks, the *Stier* fell in with the 10,169-ton, American-owned, Panama-flag tanker *Stanvac Calcutta*. The tanker put up a stiff resistance, and it was only with great difficulty and the expenditure of a large amount of ammunition that the *Stier*'s gunners finally subdued and sank her.

After transferring survivors from the two sunken ships to the supply tanker *Charlotte Schliemann* at a prearranged rendezvous, Gerlach continued to sweep back and forth across the shipping lanes, but many frustrating weeks passed before another victim was found. She was again American, the 7,983-ton *William Humphrey*, sighted on 15 July some 600 miles off the West African coast and sunk without resistance. There followed another fruitless interval, during which time the *Stier* moved steadily southwards. She had reached 22°S, 285 miles east-north-east of Trinidade island in the South Atlantic, on 9 August when she came across the 7,250-ton British ship *Dalhousie*, bound from Cape Town to the West Indies. The merchantman, again taken in by the *Stier*'s outwardly innocent appearance, made the mistake of closing the raider to exchange pleasantries. Gerlach showed his guns as soon as he was within range, and the startled *Dalhousie* presented her stern and made off at her best speed. Her action was in vain. The *Stier* had the advantage of speed and her guns soon halted the fleeing ship, though not before the *Dalhousie* had used her wireless to good effect.

Worried that the *Dalhousie*'s calls for help might bring Allied warships into the area, Gerlach lost no time in striking south. When in the vicinity of Tristan da Cunha he began to sweep back and forth across the Cape Town to Buenos Aires and Rio de Janeiro routes  It was winter in these latitudes, and the weeks that followed were bleak and filled with grey monotony. On 27 August a second rendezvous was kept with the *Charlotte Schliemann* to replenish fuel and stores before the tanker left for Japan. Eight days later, on 4 September, a large passenger liner was sighted and the *Stier* gave chase but was unable to close the range sufficiently for her guns to be effective. This may have been just as well, for the liner sighted was the 29,253-ton troopship *Pasteur*, fast and very heavily armed. She might easily have brought the *Stier*'s piratical activities to a sudden and disastrous end.

Disappointed with the dearth of enemy shipping in the south, Gerlach returned north and on the 24th met up with the ex-Hansa Line ship *Tannenfels* 500 miles south-east of Trinidade  The *Tannenfels*, which normally ran the blockade between Japan and the south of France, was acting as supply ship while the *Charlotte Schliemann* was in the Far East. Following a transfer of stores in this lonely spot midway between South Africa and South America, the two ships agreed to keep each other company for a few days while both carried out routine repairs and maintenance  Hove-to, they drifted together at the whim of wind and current.

The maiden voyage of the *Stephen Hopkins*, commenced at the end of May, had taken her to New Zealand, Australia, the Middle East and South Africa and by and large had been pleasant and uneventful. There had been time and opportunity for Captain Paul Buck and his crew of 46 to become a functioning team and to get to know their ship. After four months the *Stephen Hopkins* was no longer a carbon copy of one of the dozens of her type coming out of Henry Kaiser's shipyards: her chief mate, 38-year-old Richard Mocskowski, with the help of boatswain Allyn Philip and his men, had cleared away the last vestiges of shipyard clutter on deck, while her Swiss-born chief engineer, Rudolph Rudtz, had at last tuned his engine and its auxiliaries to his satisfaction. Ensign Kenneth Willett and his fourteen Armed Guard gunners, a wartime addition to the *Stephen Hopkins'* crew, had also spent their time well, stripping, cleaning and endlessly drilling with their armament. The Liberty carried a stern-mounted 4-inch, two 37mm quick-firers and six machine guns, four of 50 calibre and two of 30 calibre  If and when the time came, Willett was confident that his guns would speak with some authority.

When the *Stephen Hopkins* sailed from Cape Town on 14 September after taking on bunkers, water and fresh provisions, she was a tightly run, well-maintained ship, manned by a well-disciplined, contented crew. She was bound in ballast to Paramaribo, Dutch Guiana, to pick up a cargo of bauxite for an as yet unspecified United States port. The *Stephen Hopkins* was going home

During the morning of the 27th, thirteen days out of Cape Town, the *Stephen Hopkins* was approaching the Tropic of Capricorn. The weather was fair, and with the last of the South-East Trades behind her she was making a steady 10½ knots on a north-westerly course. It was a Sunday, a day of rest for those not on watches, and, with the promise of roast turkey with cranberry sauce and fresh South African vegetables for lunch, an air of contentment dominated the ship. When the sky clouded over and the rain began to fall, it did little to dampen the spirits of men looking forward to a return to home and family within three weeks. Third Mate Walter Nyberg, keeping watch on the bridge, grumbled at the falling visibility, but the possibility of meeting another ship in this empty area was so remote that he gave no thought to posting extra lookouts.

The *Stier* and the *Tannenfels* were in position 24°44'S 21°50'W and still in close company on the morning of the 27th. Aboard the raider her first lieutenant, Kapitänleutnant Petersen, was making good use of the idle time to repair some of the ravages of wind and sea on the ship's paintwork. Stages were rigged overside, and men had been busy wire-brushing and painting over the patches of red rust since sun-up  At about 0800, when dark clouds moved in from the south-west and the wind backed sharply and began to keen, Petersen brought his men back inboard. The signs were that a pampero was in the offing. He sent word below to warn the Captain.

By the time the painters were back on board and their pots and brushes stowed away, it was blowing a gale and raining heavily, and the visibility was down to two miles. Gerlach came to the bridge, but, having satisfied himself there was no danger of the *Stier* drifting down on the *Tannenfels*, he took no action. Soon after 0900 he was about to leave the bridge to continue his breakfast when there was a cry from the masthead lookout. Gerlach spun on his heel in time to see a large, grey-painted merchant ship bearing down on the *Stier* out of the rain.

It was fortunate that Walter Nyberg was alert, otherwise the *Stephen Hopkins* might well have run down one of the two stationary ships that suddenly emerged from the rain under her bows Acting instinctively, Nyberg ordered the helm hard over to port and lunged for the bridge telephone.

Captain Buck took in the situation at a glance when he reached the wheelhouse. One of the strangers, a ship of about 4,000 tons, had distinctive clipper bows and a cruiser stern, her silhouette suspiciously like those he had seen of Axis commerce raiders. The other, of about 7,000 tons, had a tall funnel and three masts and could be Japanese. Both ships were painted a dirty grey and had patches of red lead on their hulls.

Buck sounded the general alarm and, as he did so, the *Stier* hoisted the German ensign and opened up with her 37mm guns Following recommended procedure, Buck altered course hard to port, swinging the *Stephen Hopkins* in a tight circle to present her stern to the enemy. His radio officer, Hudson Hewey, needing no prompting, began transmitting the raider attack signal The *Tannenfels* responded by jamming Hewey's transmission.

Gerlach was puzzled by the American's 'RRRR' call He later said, 'It was immediately clear that this was not an ordinary merchantman. She was either an auxiliary, [or] possibly even an AMC, whose armament was estimated as one 5 9 on the stern, two 4-inch or 5-inch on the bow, two of the same forward of the funnel and two more behind it, plus some 40mm and 20mm.' It is difficult to imagine how Kapitän Gerlach mistook a slow, awkward Liberty ship in ballast for an armed merchant cruiser, and even harder to understand how he credited her with being armed with seven heavy guns – although, in the light of what followed, his seemingly deliberate exaggeration of the odds he faced is perhaps not surprising

The *Stephen Hopkins'* chief steward, Ford S. Stilson, was in his cabin composing the menu for the next day when the *Stier*'s guns opened fire:

> My first knowledge was the sound of a shot, 37mm or the like, striking into the superstructure amidships above the waterline There was no mistaking this sound for a shot fired from the ship I knew we were under attack and grabbed my lifejacket and papers I went to my station amidships The general alarm rang as I was on my way and I assured my men that this was not a drill, and those who had no station to go to should not go onto the boat deck until the abandon ship signal I also rallied such men as I saw amidships to their stations After a minute or two word was passed to me that the First Mate was wounded I went back to my room, secured bandages and I proceeded to the bridge deck, where I found the Chief Mate reclining on the deck in the thwartships passage adjacent to the bridge, and very active shouting orders and advising the Captain to keep her with her stern bearing on the enemy He was shot high in the chest and in the left forearm The chest wound did not bleed or froth very much, but the arm wound had touched an artery and he had lost considerable blood He was too active and excited to keep the artery compressed I applied a tourniquet and bandaged both wounds I started below to get more materials ready for the next casualty and returned at the sound of severe groans He had gotten to his feet with the aid of one of the ordinary seamen, Piercy, and had turned the opposite passage, where he was again struck in the leg by a fragment All this time shells had been riddling the superstructure and our own 4-inch had started a rapid rate about the time I was bandaging the Mate

Chief Mate Mocskowski's wounds had been caused by shrapnel from the *Stier*'s 5.9-inch guns, which had gone into action six minutes after the ships had come in sight of each other. She registered a hit with her third salvo. From then on, at a range of about only 1,000 yards, the *Stephen Hopkins* was subjected to broadside after broadside from the *Stier*'s six 5.9s, while her 37mm and 20mm guns kept up rapid fire. The *Tannenfels* joined in with her machine guns, sweeping the decks of the American freighter with a murderous hail of bullets.

Ensign Kenneth Willett, commander of the Armed Guard, raced out on deck at the first sound of the alarm bells straight into a storm of bursting shells and ricocheting bullets. The young Californian was immediately seriously wounded in the stomach, probably by flying shrapnel, but he staggered aft to the poop, collecting a second wound on the way. Although grievously hurt – some observers claimed that his entrails were spilling out of his stomach wound – Willett took charge of the 4-inch and opened fire on the *Stier*. At the same time Second Mate Joseph Layman was directing the fire of the twin 37mm guns forward and other gunners had gone to the six machine guns and were in action

Firing over open sights, Willett, assisted by Cadet Edwin O'Hara, fought a hopelessly one-sided duel with the *Stier*, his single 4-inch against the raider's centrally controlled battery of 5.9s. The ensign concentrated his fire on the *Stier*'s waterline, scoring a series of hits  In retrospect, it might have been better if he had aimed to knock out the other ship's guns, for their six-shell broadsides were wreaking havoc in his own ship.

The end seemed near when a shell exploded in the *Stephen Hopkins'* boiler-room, smashed the main steam line and killed a number of men. The Liberty slowed to a crawl and, when another enemy shell wrecked her steering gear, began to circle aimlessly. She was then an even easier target for the *Stier*'s guns, and they did their work well, hitting the American below the waterline and demolishing her unarmoured superstructure. Men rushing to fight the fires were cut down by shrapnel and machine-gun bullets, their screams drowned by the crash of the guns and the roar of escaping steam.

The *Stephen Hopkins* was beam-on to the rough seas heaped up by the line squall and rolling awkwardly, driving rain seriously reducing visibility. Kenneth Willett was by now barely conscious, but some kindly Providence must have been guiding his aim on that grim September morning in the South Atlantic. He put two shells into the enemy's vitals, smashing her generators, and, being a motor ship, she was then completely immobilized: her engine would not run, her steering gear was inoperative, her torpedo tubes were unable to train and her fire pumps were useless.

The two ships, merchantman and ex-merchantman, fought it out at close range for another twenty minutes in the midst of a howling gale. The outcome of the fight should never have been in doubt, for the German's guns were heavier, were precisely aimed and outnumbered the American's six to one. But, although the *Stephen Hopkins* was steadily being reduced to a burning wreck by the *Stier*'s 5.9s and many of her crew were dead or wounded, there was no sign of her yielding. Willett and his Armed Guard crew handled the single 4-inch superbly, putting 35 shells into the *Stier*, fifteen of them below the waterline. Fuel lines were cut in the raider's engine room and hot oil spewed out and ignited, filling all spaces below decks with choking black smoke. Men escaping on to the decks found fires raging all around them, with no pressure on the hoses to fight them.

The plight of the *Stephen Hopkins* was no better. In all, she had been on the receiving end of sixty salvos of 5.9-inch shells, around 900 rounds of 37mm and 20mm ammunition and untold numbers of machine-gun bullets. She was well alight on deck and in the accommodation, and the sea poured into her empty holds through a dozen holes in her hull. Yet she fought on. Then, at about 0950, a German shell hit her after magazine, and the resulting explosion killed most of the 4-inch gun's crew. The gun was intact, and five rounds remained in the ready-use box. These Cadet O'Hara loaded and fired single-handed in a last magnificent gesture of defiance. The forward-mounted 37mm guns had by then been destroyed, leaving the *Stephen Hopkins* without any real means of defence.

At 1000, with all hope gone, Captain Buck sounded the 'Abandon ship' signal on the ship's whistle. Second Assistant Engineer George Cronk described the end:

> The *Stephen Hopkins* was hit repeatedly from stem to stern by four salvos at a time, until she was a complete wreck and on fire all over When the abandon ship signal was given, the raider was using shrapnel and incendiary shells I lowered the after fall of the only remaining lifeboat, which was about five feet from a roaring inferno of flame A shell burst among the boat on the way down, killing two and wounding four men The remaining crew was putting over the rafts when I jumped overboard I was later picked up by this boat, and with all the able men in it we got out the oars, and among the dying and wounded we got several men from the water and from the rafts. The wind started rising and the sea running high, the visibility becoming very bad All sighted the Third Mate in the smashed lifeboat that had been blown off the *Stephen Hopkins* by shell fire He had it bolstered up at one end by a doughnut raft, but, pull as hard as we would, we could not get to him on account of the wind and sea A doughnut raft went by with at least five men on it, one of whom I think was the Captain We rowed for two hours until our hands were blistered and still could not pick up the men The wind and sea were getting higher and higher all the time and poor visibility blotted out everything

The nineteen occupants of the lifeboat, five of them wounded, saw the *Stephen Hopkins* go down by the stern as they rowed away George Cronk, being the senior man in the boat, took command, while Ford Stilson, also among the survivors, tended the wounded, using the limited contents of his first aid kit. A sea anchor was streamed, and they hove-to for the rest of that day and the night, hoping to pick up more survivors. When morning came the weather was, if anything, worse, and although they rowed around for a while they found no one else At noon Cronk called off the search and made sail, steering a course due west.

The voyage was long and harrowing, but, carried by the prevailing north-easterly winds, the lifeboat eventually fetched up on the coast of Brazil near Barro de Itabopoana thirty-one days later, having sailed 1,860 miles Despite dedicated nursing by Stilson, four of the injured died on the way, but that fifteen men stepped ashore in Brazil, weak and emaciated but in good spirits, was largely due to Second Assistant Engineer George Cronk, who under the most difficult circumstances had led by example and maintained order and discipline in the boat. Cronk was no navigator, and he had no charts or navigational instruments, but he did have with him Able Seaman August Reese, a 59-year-old Dane who had passed through these waters many times before in sailing ships. It was Reese who kept the boat heading in the right direction

Those who landed in Brazil were the only survivors of the *Stephen Hopkins'* complement of 56, which included a passenger taken on board in Durban. It was later established that Captain Paul Buck was last seen on the bridge and that his second in command, Chief Mate Richard Mocskowski, was left lying wounded on the boat deck when the only lifeboat got away. Radio Officer Hudson Hewey undoubtedly died when a shell demolished the radio room, and Second Mate Joseph Layman appears to have met his end when the 37mm guns were destroyed. Ensign Kenneth Willett, mortally wounded from the outset, was last seen cutting away liferafts for the surviving members of his Armed Guard. Willett's behaviour throughout had been in the highest realms of gallantry, and he richly deserved the Navy Cross awarded to him posthumously His memory lived on for many years in a destroyer and a Merchant Marine Academy building named after him Captain Buck and Cadet O'Hara also received posthumous recognition, each being awarded the Mercantile Marine Distinguished Service Medal A Liberty ship was named in honour of Richard Mocskowski

There is no doubt that luck was on the side of the *Stephen Hopkins* in her battle with a vastly superior enemy, but it must be said that Sunday 27 September 1942 was a day for American heroes to be made The *Stephen Hopkins* was a civilian ship, manned mainly by civilians, and if having made her protest with a few shots she had then surrendered, then no one would have thought any the worse of Captain Paul Buck and his men. As it was, they chose to fight on, and did so very effectively The *Stier*, listing heavily and with her fires raging out of control, was abandoned four hours after the action. She blew up and sank, taking three men with her Her survivors, 33 of them wounded, were taken off by the *Tannenfels* Thus ended the not particularly spectacular career of *Hilfskreuzer 23*.

# 16

# Guadalcanal

## *13 November 1942*

T he crushing defeat suffered by Allied ships at the Battle of Savo Island in August 1942 was to some extent avenged two months later, when Japanese and American surface forces clashed off Cape Esperance By this time the Americans had 16,000 of their best fighting troops ashore on Guadalcanal and Tulagi, and Henderson Field, the half-finished airfield earlier wrested from Japanese hands, was complete and fully operational The Japanese Army, meanwhile, had retreated into the dense jungle in the east of Guadalcanal, and it was the determined efforts to supply and reinforce these troops that led to the nightly run by destroyers of Rear-Admiral Raizo Tanaka's squadron. On most evenings, when American aircraft were safely grounded by darkness, it was the routine for four or five of Tanaka's destroyers to race down The Slot crammed with troops, stores and equipment Running flat out at 33 knots, they found it comparatively easy to slip unseen between Savo Island and Cape Esperance and land their men and supplies at Taivu, twenty-five miles east of Henderson On their way back up The Slot the destroyers took the opportunity to bombard American positions on Tulagi with their 4 7s The US Navy found itself constantly occupied, usually unsuccessfully, in trying to thwart the nightly excursions of aptly named 'Tokyo Express'.

During the night of 11 October Rear-Admiral Norman Scott was at sea off the north coast of Guadalcanal, determined once and for all to put an end to this audacious Japanese supply run Flying his flag in the heavy cruiser *San Francisco*, Scott had with him another heavy cruiser, the *Salt Lake City*, the light cruisers *Boise* and *Helena* and the destroyers *Duncan*, *Buchanan*, *Farenholt*, *Laffey* and *McCalla* The *Helena* was equipped with the latest radar, while the heavy cruisers, both heavy ships, mounted between them nineteen 8-inch guns, the light cruisers fifteen 6-inch and the destroyers twenty 5-inch guns, plus torpedoes Scott had ample means to make short work of any lightly armed Japanese destroyers that came his way

It was a typical Guadalcanal night, hot and dripping humidity, with the stench of rotting vegetation wafting off the shore and lightning flickering around the mountains forming the spine of the island. Scott was steaming at easy speed up The Slot, with three destroyers in the van, the *San Francisco* leading the cruisers in line ahead and two destroyers covering the flanks. Lookouts were doubled and all guns' crews stood-to

In these sheltered waters, the land being close on both sides, there was a great deal of clutter of the *Helena*'s radar screen, severely restricting its performance, so much so that, at about 2330, Scott ordered the four Kingfisher scout planes carried by the heavy cruisers to be launched. Two of these aircraft crashed on take off – not a good omen for the coming night. Twenty minutes later the two Kingfishers that did successfully take to the air radioed back a report of enemy cruisers sighted ahead. By some incredible coincidence, the Japanese had also chosen this night to be out in force.

No one was more surprised than Rear-Admiral Aritomo Goto when the American planes appeared out of the darkness and flew low over his ships. Goto's squadron, made up of the heavy cruisers *Aoba*, *Kinugasa* and *Furutaka* and the destroyers *Fubuki* and *Hatsuyuki*, was on its way down The Slot with the troop-carrying destroyers of the Tokyo Express following some miles behind. Goto's object, apart from providing a heavy escort for the destroyers, was to carry out a bombardment of Henderson Field with the cruisers' guns. It was an assignment he had expected to carry out without undue interference

At 0230 the *Helena*'s radar picked up the approaching Japanese cruisers at fourteen miles. For some reason this was not reported to the flagship until 0245, by which time Scott had embarked on a manoeuvre to 'cross the T' of the Japanese, unaware that the enemy was then only four miles off and closing rapidly. When Goto's cruisers came in sight with the Americans in the midst of their manoeuvre there was confusion in their ranks. Fortunately the radar-less Japanese were also taken by surprise, all their guns still being trained fore and aft

The Americans were quick to recover, Scott's cruisers opening up with massed broadsides as they crossed ahead of the Japanese at point blank range. Salvo after salvo of well-aimed shells crashed into Goto's ships, inflicting tremendous damage and casualties. Rear-Admiral Goto was himself one of the first to die. A shell demolished the *Aoba*'s bridge before he had time to give a single order. As Goto died, his leading destroyer, the *Fubuki*, was blown apart by the guns of the *San Francisco* and *Salt Lake City*.

The lightning American attack appeared to have knocked the fight out of the Japanese, and, uncharacteristically, they turned and ran back up The Slot, with the *Kinugasa* in the lead. Scott now had the advantage, but, once again, American indiscipline spoiled the day and what should have been a victorious stern chase ended up in chaos. In the confusion the American ships turned their guns on one another, resulting in serious damage to the destroyers *Duncan* and *Farenholt*, the *Duncan* being so badly hit that she was later beached and abandoned. Only the Japanese cruiser *Furutaka* was sunk, but not before she had severely mauled the *Boise*, leaving her with 107 men dead.

Despite the incompetence of the Americans, the night had ended in defeat for the Japanese They lost a heavy cruiser and a destroyer, and their proud flagship limped home with Rear-Admiral Arimoto Goto lying dead on her shattered bridge. The hurt went deep, for this was the Imperial Navy's first defeat in a night action – a defeat that, had it not been for the Americans' tendency to turn their guns on themselves, might have been of catastrophic proportions. But the Japanese did not fail completely on that night. While Scott was preoccupied with Goto's squadron, the destroyers of the Tokyo Express slipped past Savo Island to Taivu, landed their troops and some heavy guns and retired unscathed. But, from then on, the opportunities for the Japanese to supply and reinforce their 32,000 troops on Guadalcanal via the Tokyo Express became fewer and fewer. By the end of October the predicament of these men was serious Ammunition was short and they were reduced to living on berries and roots from the jungle as their food ran out.

Early in November the Japanese High Command decided that they must make a major effort to resolve the worsening situation on Guadalcanal To this end they assembled a force of 13,000 troops on board eleven transports off the Shortland Islands, near Bougainville. It was planned to land the troops near Cape Tassafaronga, at the north-western end of Guadalcanal, during the night of 12/13 November, and it was hoped at the same time to divert the Americans' attention from the landing by a simultaneous bombardment of Henderson Field from the sea

The 27,613-ton sister battleships *Hiei* and *Kirishima*, each mounting eight 14-inch, fourteen 6-inch and eight 5-inch guns, left Truk in the morning of the 11th, accompanied by the light cruiser *Nagara* and fourteen destroyers. In command was Vice-Admiral Hiroaki Abe, flying his flag in the *Hiei*. It was Abe's intention to enter The Slot between Santa Isabel and Malaita during the night of the 12th, pass north of Savo Island and then swing hard around to run down on Henderson. All went well on the 1,000-mile passage from Truk, with only a few high-flying American aircraft seen, none of which made any move to attack the Japanese ships Abe began to assume that he would arrive off Guadalcanal unannounced. His optimism was, however, grossly misplaced: US intelligence sources had obtained advance information of Japanese intentions and a trap was being laid.

When word of the approach of Abe's battle squadron first came through, the Americans had no heavy ships on hand to meet the attack. Vice-Admiral Thomas Kinkaid, with the aircraft carrier *Enterprise* and the two new battleships *Washington* and *South Dakota*, was 750 miles to the south in New Caledonia. Kinkaid put to sea immediately he received news of the Japanese plans, but it would take him some time to reach Guadalcanal. In the meantime the seaward defences of the island were in the hands of Rear-Admiral Daniel Callaghan, who was on the spot with the heavy cruisers *San Francisco* and *Portland*, the light cruiser *Helena*, the anti-aircraft cruisers *Atlanta* and *Juneau* and eight destroyers. The *Helena*'s modern radar would be invaluable in any action, but the 5-inch dual-purpose guns of the AA cruisers would not amount to much against Japanese battleships.

Abe's battle squadron entered The Slot late on the 13th, passing south of Santa Isabel in line ahead With the end of the island abeam they ran into an intense tropical downpour, which reduced visibility to no more than a dozen yards. They completely missed Savo Island, where they should have turned sharply to port, and were entering the Coral Sea on the other side of Guadalcanal before the rain eased and the mistake was realized. With some difficulty – for the rain was still heavy and radio reception poor – Abe led the squadron through a 180-degree turn and headed back towards Savo. It was now after midnight and the proposed bombardment of Henderson Field was well behind schedule, but, after some discussion with his senior officers, Abe decided to continue the operation.

The Japanese ships rounded Cape Esperance soon after 0100 and, leaving Savo Island to port, took up formation for the bombardment, with two

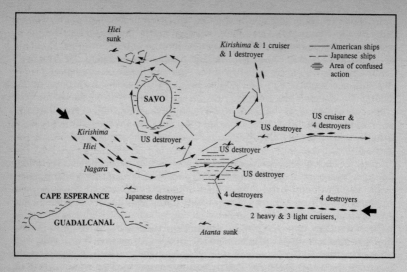

Battle of Guadalcanal, 13 November 1942

destroyers scouting ahead and the light cruiser *Nagara* leading the *Hiei* and *Kirishima*, which were flanked by six destroyers to port and three to starboard. The three remaining destroyers were somewhere astern, having become detached from the others in the rainstorm. Once the formation was complete Abe ordered full speed and the 14-inch guns of the battleships were loaded with high-explosive shells and their barrels raised in anticipation  Henderson Field lay twenty miles away on the starboard bow

Rear-Admiral Callaghan's squadron was then a similar distance to the east of Henderson, just south of Florida Island. Callaghan was steaming in line ahead with four destroyers in the van, followed by the AA cruiser *Atlanta*, in which the second in command of the squadron, Rear-Admiral Norman Scott, flew his flag. Then came the 8-inch gun cruisers *San Francisco* and *Portland*, with the *Juneau* leading four more destroyers in the rear  The night was moonless and the darkness intense, and although there had been rain it had done little to ease the suffocating heat.

As was usual, the American ships were using their TBS with complete abandon. Consequently, when the *Helena*'s radar picked up Vice-Admiral Abe's squadron thundering down The Slot towards them, the Japanese were already aware of their approach. However, Abe was not able to judge the strength and location of the opposition, and when, twenty minutes later, the two destroyers running ahead of his squadron sighted the enemy he was not fully prepared for battle. The 14-inch guns of the *Hiei* and *Kirishima* being loaded with HE shell ready for the bombardment of Henderson, it was necessary to reload with armour-piercing. Even allowing for the brisk efficiency of the Japanese gunners, the change of ammunition for these big guns would take at least fifteen minutes

In those crucial fifteen minutes the 8-inch guns of Callaghan's heavy cruisers could have inflicted enough damage on the Japanese battleships to change the outcome of the night completely But the American admiral held his fire, and he was still debating whether to attempt 'crossing the T' of the Japanese ships when the gunners of the *Hiei* and *Kirishima* completed their change of shells. At 0151 a powerful searchlight lanced the darkness and the leading American cruiser, Scott's *Atlanta*, was held fast in its beam.

Scott reacted quickly enough, ordering his 5-inch guns to shoot along the beam of the searchlight. There was no time, for the ship behind the blinding light was Abe's 27,613-ton *Hiei* and she was only two miles off. When the battleship's 14-inch guns spoke, the first salvo of 1,500lb shells wiped out the *Atlanta*'s bridge, killing everyone on it, Rear-Admiral Norman Scott included The Japanese destroyers then passed either side of the *Atlanta* and launched torpedoes The 'Long Lances' went home and the 6,000-ton American cruiser drifted off into the darkness, listing heavily and burning fiercely. She had not fired a single shot in her defence.

The American ships were in complete disarray and being attacked by the Japanese from all sides. Callaghan's commanders, still hopelessly inadequate in the art of night fighting, used their primitive radar sets rather than their eyes, screamed into their radios and fired on everything in sight, including their own ships The chaos was unbelievable

When the *Kirishima* turned her searchlight on the *San Francisco*, the light revealed that the American cruiser was shelling the poor, crippled *Atlanta* Before she could turn her guns on the real enemy, the *San Francisco* was in receipt of a full broadside from the *Kirishima* The devastation wreaked by the huge 14-inch armour-piercing shells was appalling The cruiser's bridge received much of the blast and Daniel Callaghan was killed outright, the second United States Navy admiral to die in the space of a few terrible moments that night

The confused battle went on for another half an hour with the American ships getting the worst of it, being savaged from all sides by the big guns of Abe's battleships and the torpedoes of his destroyers. A 'Long Lance' blew off part of the *Portland*'s stern, sending the heavy cruiser circling out of control The destroyer *Cushing* charged in to torpedo the *Hiei*, but no sooner were her torpedoes launched than she was blown out of the water by the battleship's guns The *Hiei* was unharmed

As the burning wreckage of the *Cushing* fell back into the boiling sea, her fellow destroyer *Laffey* made a similar brave attack on the *Hiei* She was also hit by a 14-inch salvo and went the same way as the *Cushing* It was a bad night for the American destroyers. The *Barton* was next to go, torpedoed by one of her Japanese opposite numbers and sunk with a heavy loss of life The *Monssen* was badly knocked about by shellfire, caught fire and was abandoned at 0220 by those of her crew who still lived The *Helena*, which seemed to bear a charmed life, was only slightly damaged, but the *Atlanta*'s sister, the *Juneau*, was hit hard

The Japanese did not have it all their own way The destroyers *Yudachi* and *Akatsuki* went down under the American guns, while the *Hiei* was hit by over eighty shells. Most of these bounced off the battleship's heavy armour, but one exploded on her bridge, setting it on fire, while another hit her steering flat, jamming the rudder hard over. She went round in circles until checked with her engines, but from then on accurate steering was impossible. Abe transferred his flag to the destroyer *Yukikaze* and led his ships home with the *Hiei* zigzagging in the rear.

When the sun came up on Ironbottom Sound, the blue waters were covered by a film of black oil. On top floated a mass of charred wreckage – all that was left of the six destroyers, four American and two Japanese, which had joined the other ships on the bottom of the sound. Men were still alive in the water, dozens of them, kept afloat by lifejackets and clinging to planks and boxes. Few of them would live much longer, for the sharks were gathering. The crippled *Atlanta* was still afloat, her dead admiral still lying on his bridge among the bodies of his staff. In all, half the cruiser's men were dead, but, with the dawn, those who survived made a determined effort to save their ship. The fires were doused and at 0940 the *Atlanta* was taken in tow by a tug from Guadalcanal. It was a brave attempt but doomed from the start: the damage to the AA cruiser was too great, and she also found her grave in Ironbottom Sound.

The rest, all that remained of the late Rear-Admiral Daniel Callaghan's squadron, were heading south  Nursing their damage, the *San Francisco*, *Portland* and *Juneau* were making all possible speed for the safety of the US base at Espiritu Santo. And their ordeal was far from finished. At 1100, soon after clearing Indispensable Strait, the *Juneau* was hit by a torpedo fired by the Japanese submarine *I-26*. The torpedo tore the bottom out of the cruiser, and she was already sinking when her main magazine blew up  Miraculously, 140 of her crew of 700 survived the blast, but there was no early rescue for them. The other American ships, fearful of more torpedoes, did not stop to pick up survivors. Nine days later, when the rescue ships finally came, only ten of the *Juneau*'s men were still alive.

It has been said that the battle of the night of 12/13 November 1942 off Guadalcanal was one of the most furious sea actions ever fought. This may be so, but for the US Navy it was another inexcusable disaster. Through an incredibly naïve belief in the infallibility of radar, the blatant misuse of voice communications and general indiscipline they had lost two cruisers, four destroyers and nearly 1,000 men, including the two admirals commanding the action. It can only be said in their favour that their sacrifice, needless though much of it may have been, did result in the thwarting of Vice-Admiral Hiroaki Abe's planned bombardment of Henderson Field  The troop transports due to come in under the cover of the shelling were also forced to turn back  Ironically, the *coup de grâce* for the *Hiei* was administered by bombers flying from Henderson Field, who found the crippled battleship north of Savo Island during the morning of the 13th and pounded her until she was abandoned and scuttled.

The loss of the *Hiei* was a severe setback for the Japanese but they persevered with their main object, which was the reinforcement of their hard-pressed troops on Guadalcanal. That same night Vice-Admiral Gunichi Mikawa came back for another attempt on Henderson in his heavy cruiser *Chokai*, with two other heavy cruisers, the *Maya* and *Kinugasa*, and the light cruiser *Isuzu* in company. This time the only opposition encountered was a small force of PT boats based at Tulagi The light craft made courageous attempts to stop Mikawa's cruisers, but without success. During the course of the night the 8-inch guns of the heavy cruisers, supported by the Isuzu's 5.5s, lobbed over 1,000 shells at Henderson Field, destroying eighteen aircraft on the ground and severely damaging the runway. From the sea it looked like a good night's work, but the raid was really only of nuisance value. As soon as Mikawa withdrew on the approach of dawn, American Seebees began filing in the craters, and by sunrise planes were taking off again.

It was those same aircraft that, at around 1000 on the 14th, sighted Mikawa's squadron 150 miles to the north-west, off New Georgia, and heading down The Slot again. Ten miles astern of the cruisers came Rear-Admiral Tanaka's troop transports, returning for a second attempt at landing on Guadalcanal. The eleven ships, carrying 13,000 men, were escorted by eleven destroyers The Henderson aircraft, joined by dive bombers from the carrier *Enterprise*, swooped first on Mikawa's cruisers and within minutes the *Kinugasa* had been crippled by a torpedo. The dive bombers finished her off and she sank at 1020. The *Chokai*, *Maya* and *Isuzu* all received major damage but escaped back to Rabaul.

The American aircraft now turned their attention to Tanaka's troop convoy. An angry fight developed, with the Japanese escort destroyers throwing up an accurate hail of anti-aircraft fire as they made smoke to hide their charges The dive bombers were held at bay for some time, but when waves of high-flying B-17s arrived from Bougainville the overwhelming advantage held by aircraft over surface ships began to tell and by mid-afternoon the sea was littered with burning and sinking vessels. The Japanese fought with grim determination, but by sunset, when the last of the American planes were forced to return to their bases, only four transports and a handful of destroyers were still afloat At this point Tanaka was ready to admit defeat and return to the Shortlands. This he would have done had he not then received orders from Admiral Yamamoto himself. Help was on the way, Yamamoto pledged, but meanwhile the landing must go ahead. Tanaka regrouped his tattered forces and continued on towards Guadalcanal.

Yamamoto was as good as his word. At that moment Vice-Admiral Nobutake Kondo, the Japanese Second Fleet Commander, was on his way south with the battleship *Kirishima*, entering the Battle of Guadalcanal for the second time, the heavy cruisers *Atago* (flag) and *Takao*, the light cruisers *Nagara* and *Sendai* and nine destroyers The strategy was as before: Kondo's cruisers were to create a diversion by shelling Henderson while Tanaka put his troops ashore on Cape Tassafaronga, thirteen miles to the west of the airfield.

Kondo's squadron was sighted off New Georgia at 1600 by an American submarine on patrol, by which time Rear-Admiral Willis Lee was on the way with the battleships *Washington* and *South Dakota*, escorted by the destroyers *Preston*, *Walke*, *Benham* and *Gwin*. This was a powerful force, the 35,000-ton battleships each mounting nine 16-inch guns and being equipped with the latest radar. Willis Lee was an acknowledged radar expert, capable of using the new technology to its best effect. He sped north with his ships at 28 knots, his intention being to meet Kondo in the more open waters off Cape Esperance, where interference from the land on his radars would be minimal.

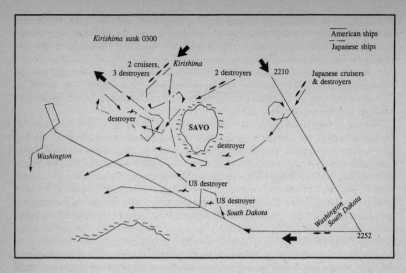

Within the map:

*Kirishima* sunk 0300

American ships
Japanese ships

2 cruisers, *Kirishima*
3 destroyers    2 destroyers    2210    Japanese cruisers
& destroyers

destroyer

SAVO

destroyer

*Washington*

US destroyer

US destroyer
*South Dakota*

*Washington*
*South Dakota*

2252

*Savo Island, 14–15 November 1942*

Lee's objective was unfortunately not achieved. The American battleships were still crossing Ironbottom Sound when, at 2300, the *Washington*'s radar picked up echoes of ships moving down between Savo Island and Cape Esperance. Lee sent his destroyers in to investigate, and they were soon engaged with Kondo's destroyers running ahead of his main force. A spirited battle ensued, with the opposing escort ships challenging each other with gun and torpedo in the harsh light of starshell and flares

The light cruiser *Nagara* joined in the fight on the Japanese side, and it was her 5.5-inch guns that sent the destroyer *Preston* to the bottom with 116 of her crew  The *Walke* was hit by a torpedo fifteen minutes later, but took longer to go down, losing only 75 men. The *Benham* was also torpedoed, caught unawares when a Japanese destroyer raced down her side at close range in the confusion of the fight  With her bows blown off, the *Benham* retired from the action and made for Espiritu Santo  She lost her fight for survival some fifteen hours later when she began to break up  Her crew was forced to abandon ship and were picked up by the *Gwin*, the only American destroyer to come out of action unscathed.

Lee's battleships came into the fray, zigzagging through the wreckage of their escorting destroyers and throwing out liferafts as they passed. They dared not stop, for the *Kirishima* and her cruisers, led by the *Sendai*, were coming through the channel between Savo and Cape Esperance.

The *Washington*'s first 16-inch salvo was squandered on the destroyer *Ayanami*, already damaged in the fighting. The enemy ship sank immediately. Captain Thomas Gatch, commanding the *South Dakota*, gave the order to open fire, at which precise moment an electrical fault shut down the battleship's generators, leaving her without power – and without power her gun turrets would not function. The two great ships raced on side by side, the *South Dakota*'s guns mute, the *Washington*'s hurling salvos ahead of her. The enemy destroyers scattered, leaving the light cruisers *Nagara* and *Sendai* in the line of fire

It was only when they shot clear of Savo Island that the Americans saw the real strength of the opposition The heavy cruisers *Atago* and *Takao* were an unwelcome surprise, but when the *Kirishima* loomed up out of the shadows, her 14-inch guns blazing, the action was joined in earnest.

Lee was afraid that the odds were heavily against him, but, fortunately, at this point the *South Dakota* regained electrical power Gatch lost no further time and opened up with his big guns. In reply he found his ship suddenly caught in the beams of searchlights from the Japanese cruisers The *South Dakota* was bathed in light, and with the range at five miles she was a target the *Kirishima*'s gunners could not miss. A squarely placed salvo of 14-inch shells crashed into the US battleship, bringing down her masts, wrecking her gun control systems and communications and killing and maiming. Fires broke out on deck

The *South Dakota*, a new ship never before tested in battle, lay helpless under the enemy's guns a matter of minutes after firing her first shots in anger. She was saved only by the skill of the *Washington*'s radar operators, who enabled Lee's gunners to find their target with complete accuracy Their 16-inch guns, guided by radar, fired nine salvos in rapid succession, every one of which struck home on the *Kirishima*. The Japanese battleship was hit above and below the waterline and soon on fire, her steering gear smashed and losing the pressure in her boilers

With his heaviest ship out of action, Vice-Admiral Kondo concluded that it was time to withdraw. He turned the *Atago* about and led the squadron back up The Slot, the disabled *Kirishima* protected on all sides by cruisers and destroyers, making her best speed and steering an uncertain course with her engines Lee gave chase in the *Washington* for some miles but, in the face of determined torpedo attacks by Kondo's destroyers, decided it was not prudent to risk his unescorted battleship any further He fired a last salvo after the retreating enemy and turned back to rejoin the *South Dakota*, still heavily on fire but making her way home at good speed

By the early hours of the 15th the *Kirishima* had reached the end of her endeavours She lay stopped off Santa Isabel, most of her watertight compartments flooded and with her fires still burning As a fighting unit she was finished and at 0300 Kondo ordered her to be abandoned. She was torpedoed by one of her own destroyers and went down, taking with her the bodies of 120 men killed in the night action

The Japanese may have lost one battle, but while Lee and Kondo were confronting each other the tenacious Rear-Admiral Tanaka had used the opportunity to slip unseen into Ironbottom Sound with his remaining ships The four transports were run aground on Cape Tassafaronga, then Tanaka, knowing full well that daylight would bring swarms of enemy aircraft from Henderson Field, withdrew up The Slot with his destroyers. Tanaka's deduction was correct. At first light US Avengers swooped in over the beached transports, showering them with high explosive and incendiaries. In all, only

2,000 Japanese soldiers and ten tons of supplies were finally put ashore at Tassafaronga – this at the cost of two battleships, one heavy cruiser, three destroyers, seven transports, 11,000 troops and several hundred seamen.

The price paid by the Japanese had been too high, and the naval battles off Guadalcanal proved to be the turning point in the struggle for the island. The Japanese still had 32,000 men ashore and the Tokyo Express still ran, but with dwindling enthusiasm and regularity for the US Navy now had control of the sea  In early February 1943 Tanaka brought his destroyers in for the last time and the half-starved remnants of the Japanese force that had hoped to make this steamy, disease-ridden island their own were evacuated. For both sides the cost of Guadalcanal had been higher than even the most pessimistic had imagined.

# 17

# Barents Sea

*31 December 1942*

I n August 1939, when the threat of war in Europe lay heavily in the air,
Soviet Russia signed a pact of non-aggression with Germany The Soviet
Premier, Josef Stalin, knew full well what was in Adolf Hitler's mind
regarding Russia and in signing the treaty he was only buying time to gather
his country's resources for war.

On Sunday 22 June 1941 – ironically 129 years to the day after Napoleon
Bonaparte crossed the River Niemen with an army of over half a million men
and marched on Moscow – German tanks rolled into Russia. In three months
they advanced 300 miles eastwards, smashing, pillaging and killing  Britain,
herself hard-pressed and fighting alone for more than a year, offered Russia
what help she could in the way of war materials  The United States of America,
not yet in the war but conscious that her days of isolation were numbered,
promised to meet every Soviet need short of fighting men.

There were two obvious gateways into Russia from the West, through
Vladivostok and via the Persian Gulf and Iran  The difficulty was that both
routes involved long hauls overland, and Russia's few good roads and her
railways could not cope. The only feasible alternative was by ship, through the
Arctic Sea to the northern ports of Murmansk and Archangel – a voyage of
2,500 miles fraught with the most terrible dangers

The first convoy, consisting of six ships, left Liverpool for Archangel on 12
August 1941. From then, convoys to Russia ran regularly, one or two a month,
with only one short interruption, until the end of July 1944  During that time
British and American merchant ships, escorted mainly by the Royal Navy,
poured into the Russian Front 3,480 tanks, 3,200 aircraft, 7,800 vehicles and
over half a million tons of stores  The route followed by the ships was from the
west coast of Scotland to Iceland, where the escorts refuelled, through the
Denmark Strait into the Norwegian Sea, south of Jan Mayen and Bear Island
and into the Barents Sea  The hazards faced by the ships were twofold. Heavy
units of the German Navy were stationed in the fjords of northern Norway, and
up to 350 Luftwaffe long-range bombers were at airfields on this northern
coast. This necessitated the convoys' keeping as far north as possible, skirting
the Arctic pack ice and battling against some of the worst weather known in the
northern hemisphere  A winter voyage was abject misery, a long nightmare
that alternated only between storm-force winds and freezing fog. Ice floes
worried at the ship's side, bergs like small islands glided ominously past,
rolling in the heavy seas, and icy spray stung the face like a whiplash and froze
solid on the decks and rigging, threatening to capsize a ship if not cleared

regularly  There was snow, hail and sleet, and all this in near constant darkness, for in these high latitudes the winter day runs to no more than three short hours of grey twilight in mid-morning. In summer the storms were less frequent, but twenty-four hours of continuous daylight left the ships wide open to enemy attack as they crawled along the top of the world.

When the convoys to North Russia first began they were heavily escorted, and apart from the odd circling Focke-Wulf and occasional hit-and-run attacks by lone U-boats the enemy left them well alone. But as the months went by it became apparent to the Germans that the steady stream of war materials flowing into Russia by sea was contributing heavily to the defeat of their armies on land. The attacks on the convoys then began in deadly earnest. As the Germans became more proficient in Arctic fighting, then so the Allied losses mounted, until ships were being sunk at eight times the rate of the North Atlantic convoys. The toll in men was even higher, for this was a battle fought under the most extreme weather conditions, and any man unfortunate enough to end up in the icy water had only a few minutes left to live.

The breaking point was reached in the summer of 1942 with the débâcle of Convoy PQ.17. Made up of 34 merchantmen – 24 American, nine British and one Dutch – this convoy sailed from Iceland for Archangel on 27 June 1942 PQ.17 was a vital convoy, carrying 200,000 tons of sorely needed military supplies for the Russian Front, and its escort was commensurate to the need. Immediate cover was provided by an all-British force of six destroyers, two anti-aircraft ships, two submarines and eleven assorted small craft, corvettes, trawlers and minesweepers. Close at hand were two British and two American cruisers and three more British destroyers, while some way to the west were the battleships HMS *Duke of York* and USS *Washington*, the aircraft carrier HMS *Victorious*, three cruisers and a flotilla of destroyers. The presence of the Allied capital ships was prompted by the possibility that the battleship *Tirpitz* and other heavy units of the German Navy might sail to attack the convoy

The Admiralty's precautions were well founded. The Germans were aware of the passage of PQ.17 and had initiated Operation 'Rösselsprung', a plan to decimate the convoy. Already at Altenfjord, the German Navy's base near the North Cape, was the 15-inch gun battleship *Tirpitz*, the pocket battleship *Admiral Scheer*, the heavy cruiser *Admiral Hipper* and nine destroyers. At Trondheim, ready to move north, was another pocket battleship, the ex-*Deutschland*, now renamed *Lützow*, and three more destroyers  Ten U-boats were on station in the Barents Sea while 300-plus aircraft stood by at airfields in the north

PQ 17 passed close to the north of Bear Island during the night of 3 July, the pack ice holding it to within 300 miles of the enemy's airfields  It had been spotted by a German long-range reconnaissance aircraft two days earlier and was being constantly shadowed by similar aircraft. The *Lützow* and her three destroyers had left Trondheim on the 2nd, but all four ships ran aground in fog on their way north to Altenfjord, putting them temporarily out of service. Meanwhile the *Tirpitz*, *Scheer* and *Hipper* and their destroyer escort were making preparations to put to sea.

The movement of the German capital ships, reported to London by the Norwegian Resistance, caused panic at the Admiralty, resulting  first in the withdrawal of PQ.17's cruisers, then in the recalling of her destroyer escort and finally in orders for the convoy to scatter. The merchant ships ended up in small groups, some unescorted, others in company with armed trawlers. German U-boats and aircraft had a free rein, and a massacre followed. Of the 34 merchantmen that sailed from Iceland, 23 were sunk, their crews perishing in the freezing waters. There had been no call for the German Navy to use its big ships – these had in fact been hastily recalled to port when it became known that the *Duke of York* and *Washington* were at sea

After PQ 17 there was a great reluctance to risk more ships on the run to North Russia in the continuous daylight of summer and it was not until mid-September that the next convoy, PQ 18, sailed from Iceland. This also ended in disaster, thirteen out of 39 ships going down. Although the German Army was then mounting a determined offensive in the East, it was decided to suspend all convoys to North Russia until the protection of the winter darkness came. In the meantime the Malta convoys and the Anglo-US landings in North Africa drew many ships of the Home Fleet into the Mediterranean. Attempts were made to get through to Archangel with fast merchantmen sailing independently, but the losses proved too heavy to bear. (This was at a time when Allied shipping losses were running at the highest level of the war.) It was late December before thought was given to clearing supplies for Russia that had been piling up in British ports.

The Admiralty at first considered attempting to push through a large, heavily escorted convoy on the lines of PQ 18, but as the darkness was now almost continuous and would frustrate German air reconnaissance it was decided that smaller convoys might succeed. The first JW convoy – the PQs had been redesignated – was therefore split into two parts. JW 51A, consisting of fifteen merchant ships and a Royal Fleet Auxiliary tanker, sailed on 15 December with an escort of seven destroyers and five corvettes and trawlers. The light cruisers HMS *Sheffield* and *Jamaica* with two destroyers were providing distant cover. After a fast passage in relatively fair weather, and apparently unsighted by the enemy, JW 51A arrived in the Kola Inlet on Christmas Day. The Admiralty congratulated themselves on the success of their new policy. Their elation was to be short-lived.

Loch Ewe, a deep, fjord-like gash on the north-west coast of Scotland, is about as bleak a spot as to be found anywhere in the British Isles in December. Even though it is shielded from the worst excesses of the North Atlantic by the Outer Hebridean island of Lewis, a bitter, keening wind haunts the loch, scouring its snow-covered hillsides and whipping up angry white horses on the black, cold water. Overhead, beneath a sombre canopy of winter stratus, scraps of scud race past at mast-top height, harbingers of a storm to come or reminders of one just past. It was from here that Convoy JW 51B, the other half of JW 51, assembled in the late morning of 22 December.

JW.51B was made up of nine American, one Panamanian and four British merchant ships, carrying between them 2,046 vehicles, 202 tanks, 120 aircraft, 11,500 tons of fuel oil, 12,650 tons of aviation spirit and 54,321 tons of general cargo. The ships were all overloaded, their decks piled high with vehicles and crated aircraft; the Americans and the Panamanian, having already made the Atlantic crossing, were salt-stained and running red rust. The British ships, two of which carried the high-octane aviation fuel, were no strangers to the Arctic run and had about them an air of tired resignation.

The short winter day was turning to night when at about 1530 the ships of JW 51B cleared the entrance to Loch Ewe and turned into the North Minch on the first leg of their long voyage to Archangel. In the lead was the 7,000-ton British ship *Empire Archer*, which carried the convoy commodore, Captain R A. Melhuish, an ex-Royal Indian Navy officer, who would organize and control the progress of the merchantmen As the ships formed up in two columns, the escort for the first leg, led by Commander H T. Rust in the minesweeper HMS *Bramble*, with the small 'Hunt' class destroyers *Blankney*, *Ledbury* and *Chiddingfold*, the corvettes *Hyderabad*, *Rhododendron* and *Circe* and the armed trawlers *Northern Gem* and *Vizalma*, positioned themselves ahead, astern and on the flanks. The wind was strengthening, the barometer was falling and the thermometer, already hovering around freezing, would go lower as they steamed northwards Christmas was just three days away, and, as the Highland hills faded into the gloaming, there was many an envious glance to starboard. For the men of JW.51B, Christmas 1942 would hold no comforts

The falling barometer did not lie, and for the next forty-eight hours the convoy clawed its way north-north-westwards in the teeth of hurricane force winds, the little ships of the escort taking cruel punishment from the wind and sea But it was that time of the year when even the elements must call a truce, and Christmas morning dawned fine and clear. The convoy was then just inside the Arctic Circle and 150 miles east of Iceland. Later in the day six destroyers of the 17th Flotilla arrived to reinforce the escort, and the 'Hunt' class destroyers, on the limit of their endurance, then detached to return to Iceland

The reinforced escort, now under the command of Captain Robert St Vincent Sherbrooke in the destroyer *Onslow*, positioned itself around the merchantmen for the ocean passage Well in the van were the minesweeper *Bramble* and the corvette *Hyderabad*, *Onslow* was at the head of the convoy, the destroyers *Orwell*, *Oribi*, *Achates*, *Obedient* and *Obdurate* covered the outside columns and the *Northern Gem* and *Vizalma* brought up the rear. Much further astern, almost out of sight, was the *Rhododendron*, appointed by Sherbrooke as rescue ship, ready to pick up survivors if required The convoy's speed was set at 8 knots, the speed of the slowest ship, and the course was north-easterly, using a zigzag pattern. That night a few half-remembered carols were sung and the odd cigar was smoked, but otherwise the feast of Christmas passed unnoticed.

The latest Admiralty intelligence reports indicated that the pocket battle-ship *Lützow*, the heavy cruiser *Hipper*, the light cruiser *Köln* and five destroy-ers were in Altenfjord; further south, at Narvik, were the light cruiser *Nürnberg* and one destroyer, while the battleship *Tirpitz* and three more destroyers were at Trondheim The ships at Altenfjord posed the greatest threat to JW 51B, being less than 200 miles – a few hours' steaming – from the convoy's proposed track. The *Lützow* alone, with her six 11-inch guns, had the capacity to stand off out of range of Sherbrooke's 4 7s and blow the Allied ships out of the water one by one. The same might be said for the 14,000-ton *Hipper* with her eight 8-inch guns Even the light cruiser *Köln*, mounting nine 5.9-inch, and the German destroyers, all with 5-inch guns, had the edge on the British destroyers. The almost continuous darkness might hide the convoy from the Focke-Wulfs, but it must inevitably be sighted by a patrolling U-boat The danger to JW.51B was very great, and to meet it Rear-Admiral Burnett, with his light cruisers *Sheffield* and *Jamaica* and the destroyers *Musketeer* and *Matchless*, was returning west at all speed, having delivered JW 51A to Archangel Furthermore, the battleship *Anson*, the 8-inch gun cruiser *Cumberland* and three destroyers had sailed from Iceland They would give cover to JW.51B while it passed south of Bear Island, one of the crucial points of the voyage

For two days after Christmas the weather remained fair, although as the convoy neared the Polar ice pack the temperature fell steadily and remorselessly The visibility was never above three miles, and, with the darkness broken over by a brief hour or so of twilight near noon, it seemed that JW 51B might just slip through to Russia unseen by the enemy Then, in the evening of the 27th, the radio officer on watch in the British tanker *Empire Emerald* heard what appeared to be homing signals transmitted on 434kc A report was passed to Captain Sherbrooke, but for some reason he took no action – a mistake he would live to regret The radio transmissions almost certainly came from a U-boat shadowing the convoy

But first the other enemy waiting in the wings would mount an assault on JW 51B That night the barometer fell steeply, and by midnight it was blowing a gale from the north-west The water in this area is comparatively shallow, and it did not take long for a short, rough sea to build up The waves came in square on the beam of the deep-laden merchant ships and, being top-heavy through their high deck cargoes, they were soon rolling their gunwales under. Flying spray freezing on all exposed surfaces above decks added to the topweight and the length of the roll Driving squalls of sleet and snow wiped out the visibility, and station-keeping became an impossibility The trawlers and corvettes suffered worst, not one of them really big enough to be challenging such malevolent weather. They were like half-tide rocks, rolling and pitching in a welter of foam and spray.

No one saw the destroyer *Oribi* go Her gyro compass failed, and with the card of her magnetic compass swinging crazily from side to side she wandered away from the convoy and never found it again. She arrived in the Kola Inlet on the 31st, weather-beaten and completely alone.

During the night, as the weather worsened, ship after ship was forced to heave-to as their deck cargoes threatened to break adrift. By noon on the 29th, when the weather at last moderated, four ships were missing The *Bramble*, which had the most efficient radar, dropped back to search for the stragglers The minesweeper was not seen again by British eyes

Three of the missing merchantmen rejoined the convoy of their own volition in the morning of the 30th The American ship *Chester Valley* was unaccounted for; so, too, it was then discovered, was the trawler *Vizalma*. Unknown to the convoy commodore, the *Vizalma* had dropped back to look after the American when she fell astern on the night of the 29th The two ships, in trying to catch up when the weather improved, had overshot the convoy. They were now ahead of JW 51B, making 11 knots and steadily increasing their lead

The gale had blown itself out and fine, calm weather took its place The relief from the constant jerking roll of the ships was a welcome blessing, and there

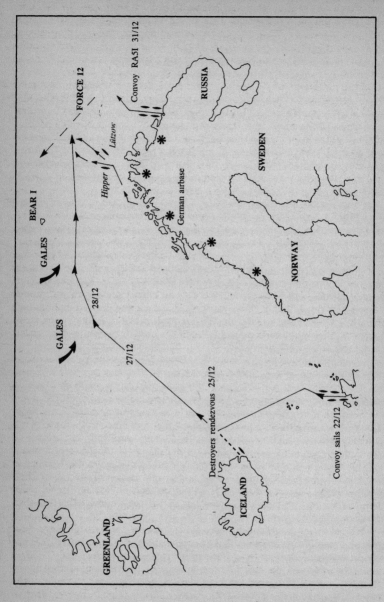

The Course of Convoy JW.51B and the Battle of the Barents Sea, December 1942

was the chance to clear away the ice on deck. But there was a price to pay for the deliverance As the wind dropped so the air cleared, and the visibility improved to ten miles and more This was good for navigation, but Captain Sherbrooke, leading a depleted escort force, would have preferred it otherwise.

Sherbrooke's concern was justified. At 1240, when the convoy was fifty miles due south of Bear Island and less than two and a half days' steaming from the Kola Inlet, it inadvertently crossed the path of a patrolling U-boat

*U354*, commanded by Kapitänleutnant Karl-Heinz Herbschleb, was lying stopped on the surface when the eastbound convoy came in sight. Herbschleb immediately signalled the sighting to Narvik and then submerged to attack. Three times the German commander manoeuvred into a favourable position and fired his torpedoes. Each time he missed the target. On the third occasion the U-boat was picked up by the asdics of the destroyers *Obedient* and *Obdurate* and narrowly escaped destruction by a flurry of depth charges. Herbschleb dived deep, resurfaced when the danger was past and then settled down to shadow the convoy, sending regular reports to Narvik.

News of the Allied convoy was passed to Altenfjord, and that night the *Lützow*, the *Admiral Hipper* (with Vizeadmiral Kummetz on board) and six destroyers put to sea and raced northwards to rendezvous with the enemy. Kummetz commanded a force to be reckoned with. The *Lützow*, ex-*Deutschland*, mounted six 11-inch, eight 5 9-inch and six 4.1-inch guns while the *Hipper* had eight 8-inch and twelve 4.1-inch. Both ships were capable of speeds in excess of 26 knots. Their escorting destroyers, the *Z29*, *Z30*, *Z31*, *Richard Beitzen*, *Theodor Riedel* and *Friedrich Eckholdt*, all outweighed and outgunned Sherbrooke's ships. The 'Z' class were of 2,603 tons and carried five 5.9-inch guns while the others, slightly smaller at 2,270 tons, had five 5-inch guns. Sherbrooke's biggest barely topped 1,500 tons, and only two ships, the *Onslow* and *Achates*, had modern 4.7s.

Early on New Year's Eve Convoy JW.51B was 130 miles north-north-east of the North Cape and steering due east at 9 knots The weather was fair, with the wind north-north-westerly force 2, the sea smooth, and a long, low swell running. It was a crisp, clear morning, the thermometer reading 25°F. In any other circumstances the duffle-coated men standing watch in the Allied ships might have been forgiven if they had relaxed their vigilance while contemplating the imminent dawn of a new year. But there were hidden dangers all around, and they had no truck with such indulgence. In the merchant ships men tightened lashings on the deck cargoes with half an eye on the horizon; in the escorts lookouts were doubled up and guns' crews loitered near their weapons It was expected that they would be met by Russian naval ships around midnight, and the thought was that, if they could survive this day, then the worst would be over

Sherbrooke had reorganized his reduced escort force to give the best protection possible to the convoy. The corvettes *Rhododendron* and *Hyderabad* and the trawler *Northern Gem* were scouting ahead *Onslow* and *Obedient* guarded the port and starboard bows respectively *Orwell* kept station on the port beam and *Obdurate* was to starboard. *Achates* covered the rear of the convoy. There had been no word of the three missing ships *Bramble*, *Vizalma* and *Chester Valley* The *Bramble* was in fact very close, fifteen miles to the north and only just out of sight. She was still diligently searching for lost merchantmen. The *Vizalma,* in company with the *Chester Valley,* was forty miles to the north, both ships still steaming determinedly to the east at 11 knots and drawing ever further ahead.

Help was nearer at hand than Sherbrooke imagined. The cruisers *Sheffield* and *Jamaica* with their attendant destroyers, which had sailed from the Kola Inlet on the 27th, were only thirty miles north of JW.51B However, the convoy's heavy covering force, HMS *Anson* and *Cumberland,* having ventured as far east as their orders allowed, had turned for home.

Captain Sherbrooke was also not aware that his ships were being shadowed by the enemy. *U354* had now been joined by *U626,* and the two boats were reporting the convoy's position every two hours. Vizeadmiral Kummetz, on the receiving end of the U-boats' reports, had no knowledge of the presence of Burnett's cruisers – not that the 6-inch guns of the *Sheffield* and *Jamaica* were likely to make much impression on the heavily armoured *Lützow* and *Hipper* But the German admiral was under orders from Berlin not to risk his ships in any engagement where the enemy might have the slightest advantage.

It was Kummetz's intention to come up on the enemy convoy from astern, guided in by the U-boats. His flagship, the *Hipper,* and the destroyers *Friedrich Eckholdt, Richard Beitzen* and *Z29,* would go in first, approaching from the north-west to draw off the escorts. The *Lützow, Theodor Riedel, Z30* and *Z31* would then pounce on the undefended merchant ships from the south and destroy them in their own time. It was a sound, if unimaginative, plan.

Meanwhile, JW.51B, ignorant of the danger threatening, maintained course and speed With the exception of a few passing snow squalls, the weather was clear and fine, the visibility being between seven and ten miles. The sea was a flat calm, but the temperature had dropped to 16°F, cold enough to make watchkeeping in the open a miserable trial of endurance. At 0800 there was a perceptible lightening of the sky in the east, indicating the approach of the short twilight. On the bridge of the destroyer *Onslow,* keeping station slightly ahead and to the north of the convoy, Robert Sherbrooke was uneasy as he scanned the horizon to the south through his binoculars. He had a strong premonition that if the enemy was to make a bid for the convoy, then it would come this day. At 0805 he passed the word for all hands to go to breakfast and to change into clean underwear. There could be no more obvious way of telling his men to prepare for battle.

Sherbrooke's premonition soon became hard reality. At 0820 the tanker *Empire Emerald* hoisted two red lights, indicating that she had engine trouble, and began to drop astern A few minutes later the corvette *Hyderabad* reported three unidentified destroyers to the south-west It was at first thought that these were the Russians arriving early, and the *Obdurate* was sent to investigate The ships were difficult to identify in the poor light, but *Obdurate*'s challenge by lamp solved the problem The straggling tanker was occupying Sherbrooke's attention when the strangers – they were the German destroyers *Friedrich Eckholdt, Richard Beitzen* and *Z29* – opened fire He immediately called for *Orwell, Obdurate* and *Obedient* to join him and peeled off to starboard, heading straight for the enemy at 20 knots, at the same time sending out an enemy sighting report on the Fleet wavelength

Only *Orwell* had joined *Onslow*, and the two ships were racing side by side to intercept the attacking destroyers when the *Hipper* suddenly appeared out of a snow squall on the port quarter of the convoy: the 14,000-ton, 8-inch gun cruiser was bow-on and coming in at full speed. It occurred to Sherbrooke that his puny 4.7s, and the *Orwell*'s even smaller, 1918-vintage 4-inch guns, would have little effect on this heavily armoured giant, but he was not deterred Signalling the *Orwell* to follow, he turned towards the new enemy.

As the two destroyers hurled themselves at the German cruiser, the *Hipper* suddenly turned to port under full helm away from the convoy. She then opened fire with a full broadside of her eight 8-inch guns The unfortunate target of the broadside was the destroyer *Achates*, commanded by Lieutenant-Commander A H T. Johns. The *Achates*, on Johns' own initiative, was laying down smoke astern of the convoy and failed to see the *Hipper*. She was holed below the waterline and suffered heavy casualties when the German's 8-inch shells slammed into her, but Johns carried on with his work

By this time the *Onslow* was within range of the *Hipper* and she opened fire, followed seconds later by the *Orwell* The firing of both ships was spasmodic, for the spray thrown up by their bow waves was freezing up their forward guns. Flurries of snow were also spoiling the visibility, and no hits were observed. But the *Hipper*, wary of a torpedo attack, sheered away to the north

Despite the size of his enemy, Sherbrooke had the bit between his teeth, and, signalling the *Obedient* and *Obdurate* to assist the *Achates*, he went after the *Hipper* It was a hopelessly gallant action that almost cost the destroyer captain his life The *Hipper* turned like a lion at bay and defended herself with her full arsenal, the blast of the massed guns, eight 8-inch and twelve 4.1-inch, surrounding the cruiser in a cloud of black smoke speared by gouts of flame The German destroyers joined in with their 5-inch guns, and so began a savage, one-sided action that could have only one ending The *Onslow* and *Orwell* fought back as best they could, zigzagging wildly to avoid the shells raining down on them.

At 1020 Sherbrooke, who was using the age-old tactic of steering for the splash of the shot, tempted Fate once too often and ran straight into a salvo from the *Hipper*'s 8-inch guns. One shell struck the *Onslow*'s funnel, sending a shower of jagged steel splinters scything across her bridge Sherbrooke was hit and seriously wounded Another shell blasted a huge a hole in the destroyer's hull forward and erupted upwards, shattered the barrel of 'A' gun and killed most of its crew and members of a damage control party standing by on deck. A third shell landed alongside 'B' gun, wiping out its entire crew and jamming the mechanism of the weapon Fires broke out on deck, threatening ammunition stocks Sherbrooke, although blinded in one eye, stayed with the bridge and, making smoke to cover his escape, took the *Onslow* out of range

The *Orwell*, meanwhile, stood her ground, returning the *Hipper*'s fire and blocking her way to the convoy Fortunately for the *Orwell* Vizeadmiral Kummetz, no doubt due to the tenacious efforts of the British destroyers, lost his enthusiasm for the fight and turned away to the north-east. But one man's good fortune can be another man's disaster, and it was so on this occasion Twenty minutes later, when emerging from a snow squall, the *Hipper* ran into HMS *Bramble*, still steaming in isolation to the north of the convoy Commander Rust put up a spirited fight with his single 4-inch, and escaped the *Hipper*, only to be sunk by the guns of the destroyer *Friedrich Eckholdt*. There were no survivors from the 875-ton minesweeper

While Kummetz was occupied chasing the *Bramble*, the *Lützow* and her destroyers moved in on JW.51B from the south. When the pocket battleship came in sight, all the convoy's escorts were to the north or west, fending off the *Hipper* – except HMS *Rhododendron*. Against the *Lützow*'s six 11-inch, eight 5-inch and six 4.1-inch guns, plus those of her destroyers, the little corvette's 4-inch pop-gun could offer only a futile gesture of defence, but she turned resolutely to face the enemy.

It was fortunate for the *Rhododendron* that although the *Lützow* and her escort crossed the ahead of the convoy only three miles from the leading ships, she either did not see the corvette or chose to ignore her Neither did the German ships, to the utter astonishment and great relief of all watching, open fire on the defenceless merchantmen In his report, the *Lützow*'s commander, Kapitän zur See Stange, blamed the onset of complete darkness and the lack of visibility due to smoke and snow squalls for his failure to attack and destroy the convoy

At 1100 the snow squalls cleared away and the *Hipper* returned from the north with two of her destroyers. Lieutenant-Commander David Kinloch, in HMS *Obedient*, who had taken command of the escort when the injured Sherbrooke was no longer able to stay on his bridge, at once took his three undamaged destroyers towards the enemy, making smoke as he went. The *Hipper*'s primary target, however, was the *Achates*, then striving to re-join the convoy. When the first shells straddled the crippled destroyer, Lieutenant-Commander Johns commenced zigzagging violently and hit back resolutely with his 4.7s. The *Achates* survived unscathed for only a few minutes, then an 8-inch salvo wrecked her bridge. Johns, two of his officers, his signalmen, lookouts and asdic operators all died in the tangle of smoking wreckage left by the enemy shells; only the helmsman, in the wheelhouse below the bridge, survived

The *Achates*, her compasses smashed and all communications cut, ran out of control, steaming in circles at 28 knots. Her decks were littered with the dead and fires raged around the remains of her bridge. It was thus when the command of the ship passed to 24-year-old Lieutenant Loftus Peyton-Jones, her first lieutenant. Peyton-Jones did the only thing he could do in the circumstances: he ordered the engine room to make smoke and, with the emergency steering gear in, attempted to run to the south-east But there was no escape for the *Achates*. The *Hipper*'s gunners had her range, and their salvos queued up to reduce the destroyer to a smoking wreck. Three minutes later, with all her guns' crews lying dead at their posts, the *Achates* rolled over to port and slipped into her Arctic grave The *Northern Gem*, which was close by when the destroyer sank, raced in and picked up 81 survivors, including Lieutenant Peyton-Jones, before they died in the freezing water.

Surprisingly, the *Hipper* again ignored the merchant ships and now turned her guns on the remaining destroyers, *Orwell*, *Obdurate* and *Obedient* The British ships seized the initiative and charged at the German cruiser, returning her fire as they went This was not at all the response Kummetz expected, and again the spectre of a torpedo crippling his ship raised its head. The German admiral turned the *Hipper* away from the danger, but as he did so a double salvo of 6-inch shells came screaming out of the sky to bracket her.

Kummetz was taken completely off guard, and, as his gunners were not using flashless ammunition, he and those around him on the bridge were temporarily blinded by their own guns. It was several minutes before Kummetz realized that the attack was coming from the north, by which time the *Hipper* had received several direct hits. One shell burst in her starboard boiler, which lost its pressure, and so the starboard turbine stopped. On one engine, and with a number of fires burning on board, the *Hipper* made smoke and limped away to the west, still unaware of the identity of her attacker.

When the British cruisers *Sheffield* and *Jamaica* burst through the smoke, the *Hipper* was nowhere to be seen, but the destroyers *Friedrich Eckholdt* and *Richard Beitzen* were caught unawares. The *Eckholdt*, mistaking the *Sheffield* for the *Hipper*, held her fire and approached the British cruiser. As a reward for her imprudence, the destroyer felt the full force of the *Sheffield*'s broadside. The *Friedrich Eckholdt* blew apart and sank: the brave little *Bramble* was avenged. *Jamaica* had meanwhile engaged the *Richard Beitzen*, but the latter escaped into the smoke with only minor damage.

Rear-Admiral Burnett pursued the *Hipper* and *Lützow* as they fled westwards, but although there was a brief running fight no damage was done to either side. At 1400 Burnett lost touch with the German ships and returned to watch over JW.51B. The convoy arrived intact in the Kola Inlet on 3 January 1943.

Admiral Sir John Tovey, Commander-in-Chief Home Fleet, said of the Battle of the Barents Sea:

> That an enemy force of at least one pocket battleship, one heavy cruiser and six destroyers, with all the advantages of surprise and concentration, should be held off for four hours by five destroyers and driven from the area by two 6-inch cruisers is most creditable and satisfactory.

Seen in retrospect, the real wonder is that the Allied convoys to North Russia got through at all. At that time, the German surface fleet was still a very powerful force. Hiding in the Norwegian fjords and North German ports were the 56,000-ton battleship *Tirpitz*, the battlecruisers *Scharnhorst* and *Gneisenau*, the pocket battleships *Admiral Scheer* and *Lützow*, the heavy cruisers *Prinz Eugen*, *Admiral Hipper* and *Nürnberg* and the light cruiser *Köln*. If these ships had been prepared to go to sea in force and with some determination, they could easily have cut the Allied supply line to Russia – and it would have remained cut. As it was, the convoys went through right to the end, although at a frightful cost in ships and men – and to what avail? The conclusions of Field Marshal Lord Alanbrooke were:

> We kept on supplying tanks and aeroplanes that could be ill spared and in doing so suffered the heaviest of losses in shipping conveying this equipment to Arctic Russia. We received nothing in return except abuse for handling the convoys inefficiently. We had absolutely no information as to what the Russian situation was as regards equipment. Russia even refused to keep us informed as to the distribution of her forces.

# 18

# Surigao Strait

## *25 October 1944*

The rugged island of Corregidor stands guard at the entrance to Manila Bay in the Philippines. The Spaniards first fortified the island in the eighteenth century, and in the early 1900s the Americans built extensive defences, including deep tunnels under the island As they sweated to burrow deep into 'The Rock', it would have been of considerable satisfaction to the American engineers had they known how much their efforts would be appreciated forty years later

In March 1942, when the Bataan peninsula fell to the advancing Japanese, 2,000 American and Filipino troops, under the command of General Douglas MacArthur, took refuge on Corregidor to make their last stand. The Japanese then laid siege to the island with their usual ruthless efficiency, assaulting it day and night with a continuous hail of shells and bombs. Thanks to the foresight of those early engineers who had planned and built its defences, Corregidor held out for almost two months, only surrendering when its defenders were starving. The flamboyant Douglas MacArthur fought with his men until he was ordered to leave by President Roosevelt. The General's words as he stepped from the PT boat that had taken him to Australia to carry on the fight were, 'I came through and I shall return.'

Corregidor, America's last foothold in the Philippines, fell to the Japanese on 5 May 1942, and the pathetic remnants of its defenders went to the barbaric Japanese prisoner-of-war camps, from which few would emerge alive. But Corregidor was only a tiny ripple in the surging tide of Japanese victories spreading across the Pacific. At the beginning of 1943 they held everything from Sumatra in the west to the Gilbert Islands in the east and from Timor in the south to the Aleutians in the north. It seemed inevitable that they must soon follow MacArthur to Australia. Then, thanks largely to the growing dominance of the US Navy in the Pacific, the tide slowed and began to turn. Gradually, and at a terrible cost in men and equipment, the Japanese were blasted out of their positions island by island and pushed into the sea

On 16 April 1943 Admiral Isoroku Yamamoto, Commander-in-Chief of the Combined Fleet and revered hero of the Japanese nation, boarded an aircraft on a morale-boosting tour of the Pacific islands. The aircraft was shot down over the jungles of Bougainville by an American P-38 from Guadalcanal's Henderson Field The admiral died in the crash, but it was felt that news of his death would be such a blow to the Japanese people that it was kept secret until his ashes were brought home to Tokyo a month later Japan was grief-stricken, but the Imperial Navy was hardest hit by Yamamoto's untimely death, for it had lost a seaman and leader considered to be without equal. The dead hero's successor, Admiral Koga Mineichi, was a competent professional, but unlike Yamamoto he was a cautious man, conservative in his thinking and lacking in the charisma that marks a great leader Without Yamamoto the Imperial Japanese Navy lost much of the dash and efficiency that had enabled it to best the numerically more powerful American Fleet time and time again.

American troops landed on Attu Island in the Aleutians on 11 May 1943 and on New Georgia on 2 July that year, each time without interference from the Japanese Navy. On 11 November an American invasion fleet of sixteen transports carrying 18,000 Marines, escorted by three battleships, five aircraft carriers, five cruisers and 21 destroyers, set out from the New Hebrides. The destination of the force was Tarawa Atoll, 1,000 miles away across open ocean in the Gilbert Islands. Although the ships were at sea for nine days, they reached their destination unchallenged by the Japanese Navy In June the following year a huge armada of 535 ships landed 127,517 American troops in the Marianas unopposed from the sea. Guam fell on 10 August, and Tokyo was then within range of American B-29 Superfortress bombers taking off from the island's airstrip. For the first time the Japanese civilian population began to experience some of the horrors meted out in their name for more than two years to the innocents of the Pacific

On the other side of the world, in Europe, the tide had long turned against the other Axis powers Allied troops, who had landed on the beaches of Normandy on 6 June, were well inland. Paris, Brussels and Antwerp had been liberated and the Rhine was about to be crossed In the east, the invincible Red Army had swept through the Balkan states and was on the borders of East Prussia. At sea the Battle of the Atlantic was drawing to its inevitable close, the U-boats finally routed and skulking in their concrete pens. German backs were to the wall. It would be the turn of the Japanese next.

On 17 September 1944 men of the US 31st Infantry Division landed on Morotai Island and soon afterwards gained control of the northern entrance to the Molucca Sea. The Philippine island of Mindanao lay less than 250 miles to the north-west, and it became obvious to Tokyo that General Douglas MacArthur's long-promised return to the islands would not be much delayed. The fears were confirmed by diplomatic sources in Moscow, and orders went out to reinforce the garrison on Mindanao by moving south some of the 250,000 troops already in the main islands of the Philippines. With typical arrogance, Field Marshal Terauchi, commanding the Southern Army Group, said, 'The best opportunity to destroy the conceited enemy has come.' The Japanese naval staff also welcomed an American attack on the Philippines, firmly believing that it would give them a long-awaited opportunity to smash the US Navy once and for all. The reality was that a successful defence of the Philippines was Tokyo's last chance to stave off complete and utter defeat If the Philippines fell to the Americans, then Japan's supply of oil from the East Indies would be cut off If this happened, the Imperial Japanese Navy, already savagely depleted by American naval air power, would be the first to suffer.

As the Japanese suspected, General MacArthur, then at his forward HQ at Hollandia in the north of New Guinea, was indeed about to make good his promise to return to the Philippines. That being done, it was planned to make

Luzon the base for the invasion of the Japanese islands, commencing with Okinawa. But MacArthur had no intention of storming ashore on the heavily defended Mindanao as had been predicted: his plan was to bypass Mindanao and use the shelter of the Leyte Gulf to land on the smaller island of Leyte, progressing north from there to Luzon. Nor was MacArthur exhibiting any signs of the conceit Field Marshal Terauchi had spoken of: on the contrary, the American general was leaving nothing to chance

It was not until 17 October that the Japanese in the Philippines knew where the Americans would land, and by then it was too late On the morning of the 18th Rear-Admiral Jesse Oldendorf entered the Gulf of Leyte with six battleships, four heavy cruisers, four light cruisers and 21 destroyers. For the next forty-eight hours the battleships, mounting between them sixteen 16-inch and forty-six 14-inch guns, supported by the cruisers, kept up a continuous bombardment of Japanese defensive positions on Leyte. At the same time American carrier-borne aircraft bombed and strafed all enemy airfields in the vicinity.

D-Day Leyte was fixed for the 20th, and late during the night of the 19th a huge armada of Liberty ships, landing craft and amphibious craft, some 800 vessels in all, crowded into the gulf. Guided by the gun flashes of Oldendorf's bombarding ships, they anchored and settled down to await the dawn. To the east, in the Philippine Sea, Admiral William Halsey's Third Fleet, consisting of eight fleet carriers and eight light carriers, escorted by six battleships and various cruisers and destroyers, stood by to give support if required Many other ships were on hand, the whole covering force amounting to thirteen battleships, 32 aircraft carriers, 23 cruisers and 100 destroyers. Further out to sea, 48 submarines kept watch on the approaches to the Philippines, ready to give warning of any enemy foolish enough to challenge this, the greatest assembly of warships ever seen.

At dawn on the 20th the first wave of General Walter Krueger's Sixth Army landed on the beaches of Leyte, to be followed by a ludicrous, stage-managed return to the Philippines of General Douglas MacArthur, who waded ashore for the benefit of the assembled photographers. Meanwhile the real business of the invasion went ahead, and in the next few days 170,000 troops and over a quarter of a million tons of supplies and equipment were landed. At first Japanese resistance was not unduly stiff, but Field Marshal Terauchi had ordered two divisions to be moved south from Luzon to reinforce the 50,000 men defending Leyte. He also called for urgent naval intervention.

Much of what was left of the heavy units of the Japanese Navy was then anchored off Singapore, handy to the first class naval repair yards bequeathed to them intact by the Royal Navy Force 'A', under Vice-Admiral Takeo Kurita, included the newly built battleships *Yamato* and *Musashi*, the world's biggest warships The two giants, 64,000 tons apiece, 862 feet long and 121 feet in the beam, were each armed with nine 18.1-inch and twelve 6.1-inch guns. In answer to the now accepted vulnerability of such ships to air attack, each carried twenty-four dual purpose 5-inch anti-aircraft guns and 98 heavy machine guns mounted in nests, and their decks were protected by 8-inch armour plate, said to be capable of resisting a 2,500lb bomb dropped from a height of 10,000 feet. The ships had a top speed of 30 knots and a cruising range of 7,200 miles at 16 knots. Statistically, the *Yamato* and *Musashi* had no equal afloat, but they had not yet been tried in action with the enemy

Also lying off Singapore under Kurita's command were the First World War battleships *Nagato*, *Kongo* and *Haruna*, ten heavy cruisers, two light cruisers and fifteen destroyers. Force 'C', likewise anchored off the base, and under the command of Vice-Admiral Shoji Nishimura, victor of the Battle of the Java Sea, comprised the 30-year-old 14-inch gun battleships *Yamashiro* and *Fuso*, the heavy cruiser *Mogami* and four destroyers

When news of the impending invasion of Leyte reached Tokyo, Kurita and Nishimura were ordered to sail at once for the Philippines, where they were to intervene with maximum effect It should then have been a simple matter of replenishing fuel tanks where required before setting off on the 1,300-mile passage to the Philippines. However, recent raids by American B-29s based in China had destroyed the refineries at Singapore and nearby Palembang, and not a drop of oil was available. As all the ships were low on fuel, it was decided that they must first call at Brunei, 800 miles away, where oil was available

The Japanese ships left Singapore in the early morning of 19 October and, working up to 22 knots, the maximum speed of Nishimura's ageing battleships *Yamashiro* and *Fuso*, steamed north-east into the South China Sea. They arrived off Brunei at noon on the 20th and bunkering began at once, the ships receiving oil direct from the storage tanks on shore without refining. Officials of the oil company gave assurances that the oil was of light enough grade to burn in boiler furnaces without being refined, but the Japanese engineers were not entirely convinced. They believed the oil to be highly volatile and to contain impurities certain to choke the fine orifices of their furnaces But there was no alternative.

The oil installation at Brunei was not equipped to bunker such a large fleet of ships at short notice and the operation was a lengthy one It was late in the evening of the 22nd before Vice-Admiral Kurita, flying his flag in the cruiser *Atago*, led his ships out to sea The Americans had already landed on Leyte and were moving inland, but Kurita reasoned that if the American fleet covering the landings could be brought to battle and defeated decisively, then the invasion might still fail. The Japanese admiral was obviously not aware of the strength of his enemy

The Japanese plan was for Kurita's Force 'A' to pass south of Mindoro and through the San Bernardino Strait to swoop down on Leyte from the north while Nishimura took his ships through the Surigao Strait to attack from the south. Reinforcements for Nishimura's squadron, three cruisers and four destroyers led by Vice-Admiral Kiyohide Shima in the heavy cruiser *Nachi*, would join off Mindanao It was also planned that a decoy force commanded by Vice-Admiral Jisaburo Ozawa would approach Luzon from the north-east to draw off Admiral Halsey's carriers operating in the Philippine Sea Ozawa's force was made up of the battleships *Hyuga* and *Ise*, which had been converted to seaplane carriers, and the carriers *Zuikaku*, *Chitose*, *Chiyoda* and *Zuiho*, with an escort of three light cruisers and eight destroyers It must be assumed that Ozawa had no intention of locking horns with Halsey, for the Japanese carriers had between them only 116 serviceable aircraft, and these were flown by pilots without proper training or experience in combat

Any element of surprise the Japanese hoped to gain was lost when Kurita's force was sighted by two American submarines during the morning of the 23rd. The USS *Dace* (Commander Bladen Claggett) and *Darter* (Commander David McClintock) were on the surface in the Palawan Passage off North Borneo when the Japanese ships, steaming slowly in line astern and belching out great clouds of black smoke from their unrefined oil, came into view.

Claggett and McClintock found it hard to believe their eyes. The long line of Japanese warships appeared to be oblivious to any danger which might come from below the sea. They were not zigzagging, neither were the destroyers using their asdics. The two submarines needed only to submerge and wait for the slow-moving targets to line up with the cross wires of their periscopes At 0532, at a range of 1,000 yards, McClintock fired a salvo of six torpedoes at a heavy cruiser. Without waiting for a result he spun the *Darter* around and fired all four stern tubes at the next ship in line. Claggett, who was running short of torpedoes, had to be content with a salvo of six from his bow tubes at another cruiser

McClintock's first salvo hit Vice-Admiral Kurita's flagship, the 12,986-ton cruiser *Atago*; his stern shots struck her sister ship, the *Takao*. The *Atago* sank in less than twenty minutes, leaving Kurita and his staff floundering in the water. The *Takao* was severely damaged but stayed afloat. Claggett's torpedoes found the heavy cruiser *Maya*, which went down in four minutes This brilliant victory for American submarines was unfortunately marred by the subsequent loss of the *Darter*, which in pursuing the damaged *Takao* ran aground on the notorious Bombay Shoal and had to be abandoned

After being pulled from the water, Kurita hoisted his flag in the *Yamato*, reformed his ships and pressed on, but warning of his approach had been radioed to Leyte by the USS *Dace*. MacArthur responded by sending out reconnaissance aircraft, which reported not only the size of Kurita's squadron but also the approach of Nishimura and his two battleships. A combined force of this size – seven battleships and nine heavy cruisers, plus light cruisers and destroyers – was capable of causing havoc in the Gulf of Leyte, perhaps even turning the invasion into a hasty evacuation. MacArthur decided to act without delay.

An attack force of 250 aircraft from Admiral Halsey's carriers found Kurita's ships during the morning of the 24th, just as they entered the Sibuyan Sea to the east of Mindoro. The planes attacked immediately, their priority targets being the easily identifiable battleships *Yamato* and *Musashi*. The huge ships used their massed anti-aircraft weapons to put up a ferocious defence, but this did not deter the American bombers The *Musashi* took the brunt of the attack, being hit by eighteen torpedoes and sixteen heavy bombs that even her 8-inch armour plate could not withstand. The sea poured into her hull, her watertight bulkheads gave way and the 64,000-ton battleship sank with the loss of over 1,000 men. The *Yamato* fared better, being hit by only two bombs which caused but minor damage. Two cruisers and five destroyers were also sunk before the American planes, sighting Vice-Admiral Ozawa's carriers to the east of Luzon, flew off to deal with what they thought was a greater threat In this respect, Ozawa's decoy role worked, allowing Kurita to regroup his ships and continue towards his objective

Throughout that day Nishimura's squadron, which was in the Sulu Sea, was subjected to attacks by American planes, but only the battleship *Fuso* received minor damage  In view of the number of aircraft at Halsey's disposal, said to be 1,400, the failure to stop Nishimura's ships is difficult to understand

When darkness fell Nishimura, his force still intact, was in the channel between Mindanao and Negros and about 150 miles west of the Surigao Strait, which leads into the Gulf of Leyte. Vice-Admiral Shima's heavy cruisers were still fifty miles astern, but Nishimura, encouraged by having come so far without serious challenge, was anxious to push ahead. With his destroyers in the van and the battleships using their radars to probe ahead, Force 'C' hurried on through the night  Nishimura was aware that he was running a grave risk by steaming straight into the enemy's lair, but he was relying on the Americans' proven incompetence at night fighting to see him through.

On this occasion Nishimura was seriously underestimating his opponents Rear-Admiral Thomas Kinkaid, commanding the Seventh Fleet, was being kept well posted of the approach of Force 'C' by Halsey's reconnaissance planes and rightly assumed that it would try to force the Surigao Strait that night. With the help of Rear-Admiral Jesse Oldendorf he prepared a formidable welcome A screen of 39 PT boats was deployed sixty miles west of the approach to the strait, while behind them 28 destroyers, fourteen on each side, formed a deadly ambush at the entrance. At the eastern end of the strait waited Oldendorf's six battleships, their huge batteries of 16- and 14-inch guns levelled, and behind them four light and four heavy cruisers, among them two Australian ships, the cruiser *Shropshire* and the destroyer *Arunta*.

It was midnight when Force 'C' neared the western end of the Surigao Strait. The night was dark and moonless, relieved only by the distant flash of lightning over Mindanao  Nishimura's four destroyers, steaming in line abreast, were in the lead, followed by the two battleships *Yamashiro* and *Fuso* in line astern and the heavy cruiser *Mogami* bringing up the rear of the column  The Japanese radars, a recent gift from the German Navy but of an early design, lost much of their effectiveness as the ships neared the clusters of rocks and islets in the entrance to the strait  They failed completely to pick out the American PT boats hiding in the shadows, and the first attack came as an unwelcome shock. The PT boats raced in at 40 knots, launched their torpedoes and were gone before a single gun could be brought to bear on them  The torpedoes scored no hits but the PT boats achieved their primary object, which was to harry the Japanese and then radio back to Oldendorf's waiting battleships the progress of the enemy

The threat of the PT boats behind him, Nishimura moved deeper into the Surigao Strait at 20 knots, conscious of the dark, forbidding shores closing in around him. Now that he had lost the element of surprise, the Japanese admiral accepted that the enemy's big guns must be lying in wait for him up ahead  He dispensed with the unreliable radars and posted his hand-picked lookouts to use their powerful night glasses to search the darkness.

For the next two hours the Japanese ships raced on, their bow waves spreading ripples of blue-green phosphorescence across the narrow waters of the strait  It was quiet, deathly quiet, every small sound setting nerves jangling. Then, shortly after 0230, the American destroyers shot out of the darkness on both sides like packs of slavering hounds. The Japanese ships fired starshell and switched on their powerful searchlights, revealing the extent of the attack. The enemy destroyers were now so close that the guns could not be depressed low enough to beat them off. The *Fuso* was hit by a fan of torpedoes that brought her up short. She dropped out of the column, on fire and listing heavily.

The destroyers raced back into the night, chased by a hail of Japanese shells. So occupied were Nishimura and his commanders that no one noticed that the *Fuso* was no longer with them. Nor were they given time to recover, for the second wave of attackers was upon them, this time led by Commander H. J. Buchanan in the Australian destroyer *Arunta*. The Japanese 5-inch dual-purpose guns and 25mm anti-aircraft cannon laid down a devastating defensive barrage, but much of it went over or around the fast-moving destroyers. Two of the *Arunta*'s torpedoes slammed into the *Yamashiro*'s hull but she ploughed on. Three of the battleship's escorting destroyers, the *Michishio*, *Yamagumo* and *Asagumo*, were less fortunate, all being sunk in a few minutes by the US destroyers *Hutchings* and *McDermut*. The attackers retired unharmed, but the success of the action was spoiled by a 'friendly fire' incident, the destroyer *Albert W. Grant* being badly damaged and sustaining 120 casualties when one of Oldendorf's cruisers fired on her as she returned

When the last of the enemy destroyers had departed, comparative calm settled over the Japanese column and Nishimura gathered the remnants of his brutally savaged force together. There remained only his flagship, the *Yamashiro*, damaged and steaming at reduced speed, the *Mogami* and the destroyer *Shigure*, the latter two so far undamaged Knowing that an even more hostile reception must await him deeper in the Surigao Strait, it now would have been wise for Nishimura to withdraw, or at least wait for Shima, coming up astern with his three heavy cruisers and four destroyers But that was not the Japanese way. Nishimura steamed on.

At the eastern end of the strait Rear-Admiral Jesse Oldendorf had positioned his ships so that there could be no way out for Nishimura The exit into the Gulf of Leyte was completely blocked by five battleships, the *California*, *Tennessee*, *West Virginia*, *Maryland* and *Pennsylvania*, lying broadside-on, bow to stern, across the sixteen-mile wide channel Behind them, also broadside-on to make maximum use of their guns, were Oldendorf's seven cruisers. These double-banked ships mounted between them over 300 heavy guns, including sixteen 16-inch and thirty-six 14-inch – a massed array of weaponry never before seen in the history of naval warfare. For the five battleships, all survivors of the treachery of Pearl Harbor, the revenge they were about to exact would be sweet indeed With all guns loaded and trained, they lay across the waters of the strait like a gigantic firing squad waiting for Oldendorf's sword to give the signal There can be no doubt that, even before his keen-eyed lookouts reported the wall of steel barring his way into the Gulf of Leyte, Shoji Nishimura knew that he was on his last voyage. It may be that he regarded what was to come as the ultimate in *hara-kiri* – a glorious way for a Japanese admiral and his men to die in the service of the Emperor And die they did.

Some two hours remained to sunrise, and the first pale streaks of dawn were showing behind the American ships when the *Yamashiro* came in sight, closely

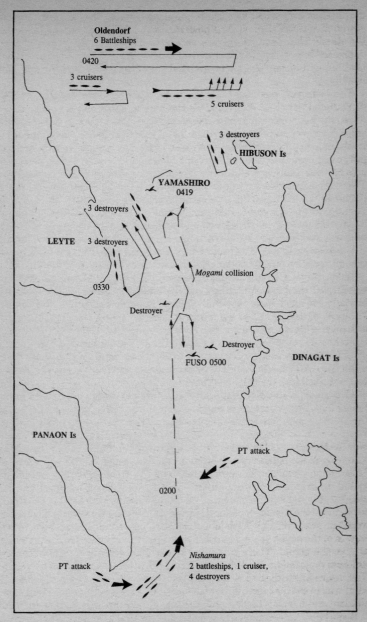

*Battle of Surigao Strait (1)*

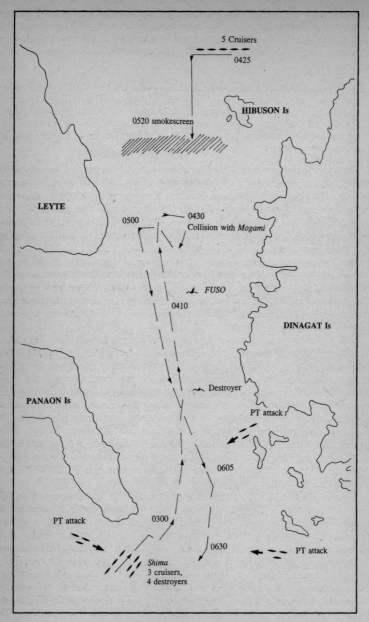

5 Cruisers

0425

**HIBUSON Is**

0520 smokescreen

**LEYTE**

0500          0430
Collision with *Mogami*

FUSO

0410

**DINAGAT Is**

Destroyer

PT attack

**PANAON Is**

0605

PT attack          0300

0630          PT attack

*Shima*
3 cruisers,
4 destroyers

*Battle of Surigao Strait (2)*

182    *Salvo!*

followed by the *Mogami* and *Shigure*. To Nishimura the overwhelming strength of the enemy he faced must by now have been quite clear, yet he made no move to turn back or take the least evasive action. At 0400 Rear-Admiral Oldendorf, who was aboard the cruiser *Louisville*, gave the order to open fire and, in his own words,

> it seemed as if every ship in the flank forces and the battle line opened up at once, and there was a semi-circle of fire which landed squarely on one point, which was the leading battleship  The semi-circle of fire so confused the Japanese that they did not know what target to shoot at  I remember seeing one or two salvos start towards my flagship but in the excitement of the occasion I forgot to look where they landed

The Japanese were undoubtedly confused, but they were also completely swamped by the storm of shot that came hurtling at them from the massed ranks of the American warships. Rushing through the still air at more than twice the speed of sound, swarms of 16-, 14-, 6- and 5-inch shells rained down on them, bent on a terrible retribution. The *Yamashiro* sought to defend herself, but within minutes three of her 14-inch turrets were smashed, the long barrels of their guns split and twisted.

The firestorm continued and the Japanese battleship's upperworks became a roaring holocaust  Admiral Shoji Nishimura died with his face to the enemy, as he would have wished; so did many of his men, who might not have welcomed this honour  Yet still the *Yamashiro* held her course, her surviving guns firing spasmodically. Nishimura's last command before he fell had been, 'You are to proceed and attack all ships'

In the twenty minutes following Oldendorf's order to open fire, the guns of the American ships loosed off over 3,250 shells. It was a tremendous, sustained bombardment that even the fanatical Japanese ships could not withstand  First the *Shigure*, then the *Mogami* and finally the *Yamashiro* turned under full helm and fled  For the *Yamashiro* the withdrawal came too late. The colossal firepower of Oldendorf's guns had blasted away most of her superstructure and a salvo of torpedoes launched by an American destroyer completed the night's work. The great ship capsized and sank at 0420, before the light of the new day broke through  And as the *Yamashiro* went down, taking most of her 1,200 men with her, many miles astern at the western entrance to the Surigao Strait her sister ship, the *Fuso*, gave up the unequal struggle against the fires consuming her and also slipped beneath the waves

The destroyer *Shigure*, using her full speed of 33 knots, escaped to fight another day, but the cruiser *Mogami*, on fire and making water, could only limp along in her wake, pursued by salvos of American shells  She might still have got away had it not been for the arrival of Vice-Admiral Shima and his three cruisers and four destroyers. Shima, unaware of the true state of affairs, came thundering up the strait at full speed, straight into the pathetic remains of Shoji Nishimura's squadron  In the confusion attending the sudden meeting of the Japanese ships, Shima's flagship, the heavy cruiser *Nachi*, rammed the *Mogami*, both ships being severely damaged. That was enough for Shima, and he turned his ships around and headed for the open sea without delay  The battered *Mogami*, assaulted by both friend and foe, trailed along behind them

Four hours later the *Nachi* and *Mogami* were surprised by American carrier-borne aircraft in the Sulu Sea and sunk

The Battle of the Surigao Strait was a defeat for the Japanese on a scale they had never thought possible  This misguided mission had cost them two 36,000-ton battleships, two heavy cruisers and three destroyers ≈ and all this for an objective not achieved  The Americans, on the other hand, lost only one PT boat, and one of their destroyers was damaged by their own fire.

Vice-Admiral Takeo Kurita, leading the northern arm of the intended pincer attack on the Leyte beach-heads, although suffering the loss of the giant battleship *Musashi* and two cruisers, came very near to victory. While Nishimura faced up to his nemesis in the Surigao Strait, Kurita slipped through the San Bernardino Strait unseen and emerged into the Philippine Sea. When daylight came, Force 'A' was racing down the coast of Samar towards Leyte when it steamed into a group of six American light aircraft carriers escorted by seven destroyers  Kurita's force, with four battleships, nine cruisers and fifteen destroyers, was too much for the Americans, who retired at maximum speed. The Japanese followed, and in a running fight one US carrier and three destroyers were sunk. Kurita in turn lost two of his heavy cruisers, a setback which persuaded him to call off the fight and turn his ships about. For the Japanese, the Surigao Strait, Leyte and eventually the war were lost.

The beginning of the end of an era had been signalled on 10 December 1941 when the mighty *Prince of Wales* succumbed to the overwhelming superiority of the bomber. Three and a half years later, on the other side of the Malaysian peninsula, the last gun action between surface ships of the Second World War – and perhaps of all time – was fought out on the night of 16 May 1945. Four British destroyers, the *Saumarez, Venus, Verulam, Vigilant* and *Virago*, under the command of Captain Manley Power, chased and brought to battle the 12,734-ton Japanese cruiser *Haguro,* another victor of the Battle of the Java Sea. The *Haguro* went down, hit by three torpedoes simultaneously in a triple explosion an eye witness described as sending up 'three gold-coloured splashes like a Prince of Wales feathers'. Hallucination or portent – who is to say? But so ended the day of the big gun at sea.

# Bibliography

Baldwin, Hanson, *Battles Won and Lost*, Hodder & Stoughton (1966)
Barnett, Correlli, *Engage the Enemy More Closely*, Hodder & Stoughton (1991)
Beesly, Patrick, *Room 40*, Hamish Hamilton (1982)
Bednall, Dundas, *Sun on My Wings*, Paterchurch Publications (1989)
Bennett, Geoffrey, *Naval Battles of the First World War*, B T Batsford (1968)
Blair, Clay, *Silent Victory*, Bantam Books (1975)
Brinnin, John Malcolm, *The Sway of the Grand Saloon*, Arlington Books (1986)
Brown, David, *Warship Losses of World War II*, Arms & Armour (1990)
Brown, Malcolm, *The Imperial War Museum Book of the First World War*, Sidgwick & Jackson (1991)
Costello, John, *The Pacific War*, Collins (1981)
Churchill, Winston, *The Second World War*, Vols 1–6, Cassell (1950)
Dupuy, Trevor Nevitt, *The Naval War in the Pacific*, Edmund Ward (1966)
Evans, Capt E R G R , *Keeping the Seas*, Sampson, Low, Marston (1919)
Fletcher, C R L , *The Great War 1914–1918*, John Murray (1921)
HMSO, *British Vessels Lost at Sea 1914–18 and 1939–45*, Patrick Stephens (1988)
Hough, Richard, *The Great War at Sea 1914–1918*, Oxford University Press (1983)
——, *The Longest Battle*, Weidenfeld & Nicolson (1986)
Howarth, Stephen, *Morning Glory*, Hamish Hamilton (1983)
Jellicoe, Viscount, *The Grand Fleet 1914–16*, Cassell (1919)
Kersaudy, François, *Norway 1940*, Collins (1990)
Liddell-Hart, B H , *History of the First World War*, Papermac (1992)
Liddle, Peter H , *The Sailor's War 1914–18*, Blandford Press (1985)
Lochner, R K , *The Last Gentleman of War*, Stanley Paul (1988)
Martienssen, Anthony, *Hitler and his Admirals*, Secker & Warburg (1948)
Mayer, S L , *History of World War I*, Black Cat (1988)
McKee, Alexander, *Against the Odds*, Souvenir Press (1991)
Montgomery, Michael, *Who Sank the Sydney?*, Leo Cooper (1983)
Muggenthaler, August-Karl, *German Raiders of World War II*, Robert Hale (1978)
Padfield, Peter, *The Great Naval Race*, Hart-Davis, MacGibbon (1974)
Palmer, Alan, *The Banner of the Battle*, Weidenfeld & Nicolson (1987)
Roskill, Captain S W , *The War at Sea*, HMSO (1954–61)
Stewart, Adrian, *The Underrated Enemy*, William Kimber (1987)
Van de Vat, Dan, *The Grand Scuttle*, Hodder & Stoughton (1982)
——, *The Last Corsair*, Hodder & Stoughton
——, *The Pacific Campaign*, Hodder & Stoughton (1992)
Young, George, *Ships That Pass*, J F Midgley (1976)

**Main sources of research**
*The Times*; *The Western Mail*; *The Daily Telegraph*; The Public Record Office, Kew;
Department of the Navy, Washington, DC; The Imperial War Museum

8
8
6
1
6
2
───
31

# Index

2

Cassell Military Classics are available from all good bookshops
or from:

        Cassell C. S.
        Book Service By Post
        PO Box 29. Douglas I-O-M
        IM99 1BQ
        telephone: 01624 675137, fax: 01624 670923